THE LANGUAGE
OF WINNICOTT

THE LANGUAGE OF WINNICOTT

A Dictionary and Guide to Understanding His Work

Jan Abram

Bibliography compiled by
Harry Karnac

JASON ARONSON INC.
Northvale, New Jersey
London

1996 Edition (London) — H. Karnac (Books) Ltd.
1997 Edition (U.S.) — Jason Aronson Inc.

Library of Congress Cataloging-in-Publication Data

Abram, Jan.
    The language of Winnicott : a dictionary and guide to understand
his work / Jan Abram ; bibliography compiled by Harry Karnac.
        p.   cm.
    Includes bibliographical references and index.
    ISBN 1-56821-700-5 (alk. paper)
    1. Winnicott, D. W. (Donald Woods), 1896-1971. 2. Psychoanalysis.
3. Winnicott, D. W. (Donald Woods), 1896-1971—Bibliography.
    I. Karnac, Harry.   II. Title.
    RC438.6.W56A27   1997
    616.89'17—dc21   96-50065

Printed in the United States of America on acid-free paper. For information and catalog write to Jason Aronson Inc., 230 Livingston Street, Northvale, New Jersey 07647-1731. Or visit our website: http://www.aronson.com

For John

For Tamsin, Zak, and Ben

with all my love

CONTENTS

PREFACE

My study of Winnicott's work began seriously when I joined The Squiggle Foundation's Saturday series, "The Original Themes of Winnicott". Over the years, this annually run series has enabled hundreds of students to share confusions, to struggle with paradox, to find, to create, and to use Winnicott for themselves.

The strong desire to make Winnicott's work more accessible resulted in my organization of his themes into this lexicon of 22 words and phrases, which represent the major theories in Winnicott's work—theories that are richly rooted in clinical work conveying the original thinking of a master clinician. Each entry is a journey through his papers, spanning almost forty years, to illuminate the breadth and depth of the concepts as well as the substance and clarity of the theories. My aim has been to guide impartially, so that the reader may personally discover the intricate aspects of Winnicott's celebration of human creativity.

ACKNOWLEDGEMENTS

I am very grateful to the publishers, Cesare Sacerdoti of Karnac Books and Michael Moskowitz of Jason Aronson, Inc. A warm thank-you to Cesare Sacerdoti, whose enthusiastic response to the synopsis urged me on.

By a fortunate coincidence, Harry Karnac, the founder of Karnac Books, had completed his chronological and alphabetical bibliography of Winnicott's papers just as I began my research in earnest, and I was very grateful to receive it at the time. My task would have been much more arduous without it. I am equally thankful and delighted that Harry agreed to its inclusion in this book. For any serious student of Winnicott, this is a real bonus.

I am grateful to the Winnicott Trust, Mark Paterson and Associates, and the publishers who have given me permission to reproduce extracts from Winnicott's works.

I am indebted to many people who fired my interest in Winnicott's work when I first attended the Saturday series at The Squiggle Foundation—John Fielding, Stephen Haine, Sue Norrington, Val Richards, Laurence Spurling, and, especially,

Nina Farhi, former Director of The Squiggle Foundation. Nina's creative enthusiasm and particular ability to encourage the best in people are inspirational and exemplary for all of us connected with the Foundation's work. My gratitude also goes to Lindsay Wells, Chair of the Trustees, and to each of the Trustees of The Squiggle Foundation—Dee Fagin, Wille Henriques, Bryce MacKenzie-Smith, Ellen Noonan, Boris Rumney, and Joyce Wellings—for their financial and emotional support of this project.

Many colleagues and friends gave up their time and energy to read parts of the manuscript, and my deep gratitude goes to Julia Casterton, Nina Farhi, Rosemary Graham, Michel Gribinski, Marina Perris, Val Richards, Viqui Rosenberg, Diane Thurman, and John van Rooyen. Their comments and suggestions were invaluable. I am also indebted to both Amelie Noack and Jonathan Pedder, who meticulously read through the complete manuscript. Their comments made a significant difference to the final product.

Warm and special thank-yous to Jennifer Johns, Jonathan Pedder, and Ray Shepherd of The Winnicott Trust, who generously granted financial assistance at a crucial time to facilitate completion of the manuscript.

Special thanks must also go to Klara and Eric King of Communication Crafts for their excellent handling of the manuscript. Long telephone calls with Klara assisted my thinking on creating a text that was as "user-friendly" as possible. Many thanks also to Graham Sleight of Karnac Books.

Appreciation and many thanks to Caroline Dawnay of Peters, Fraser and Dunlop, for sound advice and skilful help.

Patients, trainees, supervisees, and participants of Squiggle events have unknowingly assisted my understanding of Winnicott's work, and I am grateful to them all.

Personal mentors are always present somewhere in my soul whilst studying Winnicott's texts—gratitude and warm thanks as ever to Rosalie Joffe, Christopher Bollas, and Marion Milner. The work of Madeleine Davis has constantly accompanied my research, and although we only met a few times before her untimely death, Madeleine's profound appreciation of Winnicott's work very much lives on and continues to influence many of us connected with The Squiggle Foundation.

And, finally, my deep appreciation goes to my family and friends for their continued collusion with my various obsessions—especially Ben, whose interruptions help focus my mind, and John, whose unwavering support is indispensable.

FOREWORD

Jonathan Pedder
Chairman, The Winnicott Trust

T he creation of this volume, *The Language of Winnicott,* arose out of Jan Abram's experience at The Squiggle Foundation and her active involvement in studying, discussing, and teaching Winnicott, both for The Squiggle Foundation and for many psychotherapy courses. Her work convinced her of the need for a volume such as this.

Although there are volumes attempting to do similar jobs for the whole of psychoanalysis (for instance, Laplanche and Pontalis) and for other major figures (such as Hinshelwood on Klein), none existed before now for Winnicott. This may, perhaps, be because of his extraordinary ability to choose everyday words for concepts that get to the very root of our selfhood. If one reads Winnicott carelessly, one may see him as being too simplistic, or too complex (or both at the same time . . .); even the most experi-

---

The Winnicott Trust, which owns the copyright of Donald Winnicott's writings, was set up by Clare Winnicott to continue editing his unpublished papers and to advance and promote education, training, and research in the field of Winnicott's work. At the time of Winnicott's death in 1971, about half his papers had been published; there were about a further 100 unpublished manuscripts, the bulk of which have since been published.

enced Winnicottians may at times need a road-map to find their way around his thought. This book fulfils that need, and does so most admirably. Jan Abram's instinctive knowledge of the needs of those studying Winnicott will be felt, as will her wide reading in and around the topics she discusses. She uses copious and apt quotations from the original papers to illuminate key themes in this work, while placing them in broader historical context. Her direct style of writing is also most welcome, mirroring as it does Winnicott's own ability to set down complex ideas using simple words.

Although this book was not primarily the initiative of The Winnicott Trust, on hearing of its conception the Trust has been delighted to help facilitate its birth. When I first read the draft manuscript, I was in the privileged position of being able regularly to observe a mother and her first baby interacting. Irresistibly many of Winnicott's ideas and expressions, as traced in his work, reminded me vividly of this mother and baby's interaction, and vice versa; as I observed the pair, I was reminded of the exposition of his work. Time and again he seemed to get it absolutely right, especially the way in which mother and baby create each other. Donald Winnicott said that there is no such thing as a baby . . . and there is no such thing as a mother (in isolation).

One might also say that there is no such thing as a book or a reader in isolation: each person will find different things in this volume, depending on what he or she brings to it. For the student who has not yet encountered Winnicott, this is a signpost to the riches that are waiting to be discovered; for the practitioner, it will be a source of new insights to be used in clinical practice; and for the scholar, it will be an invaluable resource for bibliographic and thematic data on Winnicott's work.

While considering the ways in which this book might be used, I was also reminded of the mutual creativity of the Squiggle Game, in which Winnicott and his child patient would alternately construct a drawing out of a line, each contributing towards the construction of something with meaning to both of them. So—ponder for a moment the two quotations that Jan gives us at the start of the book. One makes me think of the book; the other conjures up mother and baby—or is it the other way round? . . . your turn . . .

THE LANGUAGE
OF WINNICOTT

Come at the world creatively, create the world; it is only what you create that has meaning for you.

For most people the ultimate compliment is to be found and used.

["Communication between Infant and Mother, and Mother and Infant, Compared and Contrasted": D.W.W., 1968]

INTRODUCTION

Winnicott's writing can be deceptively simple to read. His use of ordinary, evocative language in the many talks and broadcasts he gave to lay audiences render his ideas immediately recognizable to the reader with no psychoanalytic background. However, underneath the apparent simplicity of a phrase or sentence lies a labyrinth of complex theory.

Between 1931 and 1970, Winnicott wrote over 600 papers. Some were theoretical and written for his psychoanalytical colleagues, but very many were talks and presentations he addressed to a broad spectrum of groups and organizations. Each paper is a unique explication of the many themes that preoccupied him in his work.

Papers written for a psychoanalytic audience introduce new developments in psychoanalytic theory and seminal concepts, although often expressed obliquely and/or even denied, particularly in the theoretical papers during the 1940s and early 1950s. The mixture of passion and tentativeness in his thought suggests an elusive duality, as if he feared creating theory that might turn

1

into dogma. In contrast, the papers for lay audiences carry a freedom of expression, where Winnicott's desire to communicate the
essence of human nature takes precedence over the development
of theory.

Winnicott's intellectual environment made a huge impact on
his thinking, which may explain the passionate and tentative
aspects of his presentation of theory. From 1935, the year in which
he qualified as a psychoanalyst, the British Psycho-Analytical
Society became his professional organization, and he was its
President on two separate occasions. The climate of the Society
was fraught with political tensions and in-fighting regarding the
correct understanding of Freud's theory of psychoanalysis and its
subsequent evolution. These disagreements both frustrated and
challenged Winnicott, and nearly all of his papers contain direct
and indirect personal statements to Melanie Klein and the
Kleinian group. In his later writings, from the late 1950s and particularly during the 1960s, he was unequivocal in his criticism of
what he perceived to be the Kleinians' refusal to acknowledge the
environment's impact on the mental health of the baby linked
with his vehement disagreement with the Kleinians' version of
Freud's "death instinct". Nevertheless, it is true to say that Winnicott never denied the importance of Melanie Klein's contribution
to psychoanalysis as well as to his own thinking.

Winnicott's own substantial contribution to psychoanalytic
thought may be condensed into three main areas: the mother–
infant relationship, primary creativity, and transitional phenomena—and running through all the concepts is the value attributed
to the sense of self.

Relationship

Winnicott had initially trained as a physician and subsequently
as a paediatrician, so that although he had been working with
mothers and babies for several years before training as a psychoanalyst, it was not until seven years post-qualification in 1942 that
he suddenly became aware, in the middle of a seminar, that
"there's no such thing as a baby"—". . . if you show me a baby you

certainly show me also someone caring for the baby. . . ." From that moment of realization, every aspect of Winnicott's work evolved within and around the specific nature of the mother–infant relationship, and all his thinking on emotional development is centred on this first relationship—"the environment–individual set-up". This took psychoanalysis away from viewing the individual in isolation into the realm of the Darwinian-flavoured emphasis of the environment's impact on the baby—the individual in relation to the m/other. Winnicott studied the minutiae of the good-enough mother's attention towards her baby, and this became for him an indispensable paradigm for the analytic setting. While never intending that the psychoanalytic relationship should be seen *only* as a replica of the early mother–infant relationship, he nevertheless recognized that the model of the good-enough mother–infant relationship could be transposed into therapeutic technique. Thus for Winnicott psychoanalysis became a holding environment that could facilitate all groups of patients, particularly those whose early environment had severely failed them, and who had hitherto not been seen as suitable patients for psychoanalytic treatment.

Primary creativity

Although Winnicott refers to instincts, he does not exactly clarify his own view of Freud's instinct theory, although he vehemently disagrees with the Kleinians' belief in the death instinct as innate. However, across the whole of his work runs a deep conviction in the human baby's drive towards health. This could be seen as Winnicott's version of the life instinct—primary or primitive creativity linked with the ruthless self—and in the late 1960s he refers to the "life force". This meant that for Winnicott psychopathology was evidence of the human baby's capacity to adapt to an early not-good-enough environment. Although the pathology, depending on its severity, would be at a cost to the sense of self, nevertheless it was the best option available to the baby at that very early stage of development, in the face of a failing environment. Therefore, if the clinician could offer a patient such an environment, which both symbolically and literally created aspects of the good-enough mother/infant relationship, there was a possibility that the early environmental failure could be mended.

Transitional phenomena

Winnicott's discovery of transitional phenomena emerged from his appreciation of how the baby separated from mother and developed a sense of self. For Winnicott the capacity to use the transitional space represented the ultimate in human development and signified the ability to "live creatively" and "feel real". This concept, linked with both the capacity for concern and the capacity to be alone, embellished and transformed the concept of transference. Winnicott's *sine qua non* of the analytic encounter became the analyst's ability to play rather than to interpret. In this setting, the analyst would limit interpretative comments and wait for the patient to discover the ability to play and to search for the answers within. This brought a new emphasis to psychoanalysis—it is not the analyst who knows the internal world of the analysand but, rather, the analysand.

THE ENTRIES

Each entry has its own contents list indicating the pertinent themes, followed by a brief definition of the word or phrase.

Sources are given at the end of each quotation and listed chronologically at the end of each entry; references to the volume in which each paper can be found (e.g. [W16]) relate to Harry Karnac's bibliographies at the end of the book.

The brief reference to the work of Freud, Jung, Klein, and others is intended to signpost the areas of similarity, difference, and/or debate.

In keeping with Winnicott's texts, the mother is "she" and the baby "he".

Aggression

Aggression in the individual begins, for Winnicott, in the womb and is synonymous with activity and motility. Early on in his work, Winnicott refers to "primary aggression" and states that instinctual aggressiveness is originally part of appetite.

Aggression changes its quality as the infant grows. This change absolutely depends on the kind of environment in which the infant finds himself. With good-enough mothering and a facilitating environment, aggression in the growing child becomes integrated. If the environment is not good enough, aggression manifests itself in a destructive, antisocial way.

Gradually, as Winnicott's work evolved, aggression as a concept—latterly "destruction"—came to play a central part in his theory of emotional development and is pivotal in all the most celebrated of his concepts—"the antisocial tendency", "creativity", "the good-enough mother", "transitional phenomena", "true and false self", and, towards the end of his career and probably most central of all, "the use of an object".

1   *The concept of aggression in psychoanalysis*

The notion of a separate aggressive drive was not taken up by Freud himself until 1920, in "Beyond the Pleasure Principle". In this paper Freud introduced his dualistic theory of the life and death instincts, although, as has been pointed out, he did this somewhat equivocally (Pedder, 1992).

Melanie Klein's work with very young children led her to amplify Freud's instinct theory, and she came to see aggression as the manifestation of the death instinct, with its derivatives, sadism, and envy. Aggression, therefore, according to Kleinian theory, is synonymous with envy, hate, and sadism, all of which are manifestations of the death instinct. Since the death instinct is innate, so too are envy, hate, and sadism in the new-born infant.

Melanie Klein's version of Freud's death instinct turned this theory, which Freud regarded with caution, into a certainty. The issue of Melanie Klein's (and her followers') rendering of the death instinct became one of the factors that led to the Controversial Discussions in the British Psycho-Analytical Society between 1941 and 1945 (King & Steiner, 1992). One of the criticisms directed at Klein during the "discussions" was that she was misinterpreting Freud to such an extent that her theories were seen as a repudiation of his.

Anna Freud and her followers, along with many other analysts, could not accept Klein's death instinct; some of them went so far, eventually, as to dispose of instinct theory altogether. There has also been some criticism of the translation of the German *"Todestrieb"* as death "instinct"; death "drive" is seen as a more accurate translation (Pedder, 1992).

Winnicott never makes clear his view of Freud's instinct theory, although he does use the word "instinct" to denote a biologically driven impulse. However, he does make clear his disagreement with the Kleinian "death instinct", because he believes that envy, sadism, and hate are signs of emotional growth that develop in the infant in relation to the external environment. It is the external environment, in Winnicott's theory of aggression, that influences the way in which the infant will deal with his innate aggression. In a good environment aggression becomes integrated in the individual personality as a useful energy related to work and play, whereas in a deprived environment aggression can turn into enactments of violence and destruction.

Disagreement in the British Psycho-Analytical Society over the value of the death instinct became a political issue amongst the different groups. Four papers written between 1959 and 1969 provide an account of Winnicott's thoughts and views on the continuation (to some extent) of the Controversial Discussions. They were published posthumously in *Psycho-Analytic Explorations* (W19, pp. 443–464), under the general heading, "Melanie Klein: On Her Concept of Envy." The tone of these papers is angry, and he pleads for more original thinking rather than a toeing of the party line.

> In our Society here, although we serve science, we need to make an effort every time we attempt to re-open matters which seem to have been settled. It is not only the inertia which belongs to the fear of doubt; it is also that we have loyalties. We associate specific ideas with peaks of achievement that mark the progress of our pioneers. In this way, when we look anew at the roots of aggression there are two concepts in particular, each of which must be thrown away deliberately, so that we may see whether we are better off without them. One is Freud's concept of a death instinct, a by-product of his speculations in which he seemed to be achieving a theoretical simplification that might be compared to the gradual elimination of detail in the technique of a sculptor like Michelangelo. The other is Melanie Klein's setting up of envy in the prominent place that she gave at Geneva in 1955.
>
> ["Roots of Aggression", 1968, p. 458]

Winnicott is referring to Melanie Klein's seminal paper, "Envy and Gratitude", and his main point is that envy comes about in the infant as a result of emotional development in relation to the environment and therefore cannot be described as something innate. In a paper, which was read in his absence by Enid Balint, written as one of the contributions to a Symposium on Envy and Jealousy in 1969, he writes:

> First I assume that we are not in this discussion concerned with envy and jealousy as these two words appear in nearly every clinical paper given in recent years by a Kleinian. Also I

claim that in present-day usage of these two terms envy is a
state of mind and belongs to a highly sophisticated mental
organization, while jealousy has the characteristic that its use
implies that the whole person has already begun to mobilise
revenge or theft.

["Symposium on Envy and Jealousy", p. 462]

In each of the four papers he makes a plea for the environment to
be taken into consideration.

My objection has to do with Mrs. Klein's determination to
make a complete statement of the individual development of
the human baby in terms of the baby alone without reference
to the environment. This, in my opinion, is impossible. . . .
Every tendency towards maturation is inherited and psychoanalysis is simply concerned with the interaction with what is
inherited and what is environmental.

["Symposium on Envy and Jealousy", p. 463]

And in the psychoanalytic world today, amongst all clinicians,
this debate about the interaction between the innate in the individual in relation to the environment still continues. (*see*
ENVIRONMENT: 1)

2   *Primary aggression*

Winnicott's earliest statement on aggression can be found in a
paper simply entitled "Aggression", which was a talk addressed
to teachers in 1939. It will not escape notice that 1939 marks the
beginning of the Second World War, although in this paper that
external reality is never mentioned by Winnicott.

Winnicott's fundamental views on aggression never really
change from this paper onwards, although his preoccupation with
the role of aggression in individual development leads him to
embellish and elaborate the ideas put forward in this first paper.

Winnicott supplies his audience of teachers with many examples of how primary aggression manifests itself in external
relationships; at the same time, he includes the idea of an inner
world where aggression manifests itself through fantasy.

One mother I know said, "When the baby was brought to me she went for my breast in a savage way, tore at the nipples with her gums, and in a few moments blood was flowing. I felt torn to pieces and terrified. It took me a long time to recover from the hate roused in me against the little beast, and I think this was a big reason why she never developed real confidence about good food."

Here is a mother's account of facts revealing her fantasy as well as what may have happened. Whatever this baby really did, it is certain that the majority of infants do not destroy the breasts that are offered them, though we have good evidence that they want to, and even that they believe they do destroy them by feeding from them.

["Aggression and Its Roots", 1939, pp. 86–87]

Winnicott introduces the idea of examining the internal worlds of both mother and infant in relation to the real event of feeding. The actual breast is not destroyed; the mother's feelings of being destroyed are due to her fantasies, linked with her own violent feelings towards her infant. [The mother's feelings of hate towards her new-born infant are explored by Winnicott eight years later, in 1947, in his paper, "Hate in the Countertransference" (*see* HATE: 7).] In this paper of 1939, though, focusing on the infant's experience of his own aggression, Winnicott continues to explore the fantasy of destruction involved in primary aggression along with an inhibition of the urge actually to destroy. This introduces Winnicott's differentiation between the destruction that occurs in fantasy from the destruction that is acted out. This notion is central to Winnicott's theory of the use of an object, which came to fruition in 1968:

If it is true, then, that the infant has a vast capacity for destruction it is also true that he has a vast capacity for protecting what he loves from his own destructiveness, and the main destruction must always exist in his fantasy. And the important thing to note about this instinctual aggressiveness is that although it soon becomes something that can be mobilised in the service of hate, it is originally a part of appetite, or of some other form of instinctual love. It is something that increases during excitement, and the exercise of it is highly pleasurable.

> Perhaps the word greed conveys more easily than any
> other the idea of original fusion of love and aggression,
> though the love here is confined to mouth-love.
>
> ["Aggression and Its Roots", pp. 87–88]

In his description of primary aggression, Winnicott uses the terms
"instinctual aggressiveness", "theoretical greed", "primary appe-
tite-love", and "mouth-love". He points out that all these aspects
of aggression in the new-born infant can be seen by the observer
(or felt by the mother) as "cruel, hurting, dangerous", but—and
this is crucial to Winnicott's theory—for the infant they are so *by
chance*. This links with Winnicott's continued difference of opinion
with Melanie Klein and her followers. He feels that naming an
emotion, such as innate envy, when observing the infant implies intention on the part of the infant. From his observation of
mothers and infants, Winnicott concludes that, at first, the infant
is not able to feel envy, because this belongs to a later stage of
emotional development.

This differentiation between intention and chance is made by
Winnicott two years prior to the Controversial Discussions and
seven years after Klein had designated envy as a distinct innate
instinct. To reiterate—Winnicott considers that early aggression in
the infant may be seen as hateful (envious or sadistic) by the observer but is at first *not intended to be so* by the infant and therefore
not yet part of the infant's emotional vocabulary.

For Winnicott, earliest aggression is part of appetite and
love—"mouth-love". Three years earlier, in his 1936 paper, "Appetite and Emotional Development", Winnicott had demonstrated
the link between the baby's appetite and his emotional development through observation of the infant's use of the spatula (*see*
SPATULA GAME). The way in which the infant of between 5 and 13
months relates to the spatula is a demonstration of how his innate
aggression has changed and developed, according to his relationship with mother, so that his attitude as he reaches out for the
spatula, touches it, picks it up, drops it, and mouths it will corre-
spond to his experience of the way his mother has held him, fed
him, loved him, and generally treated him. Here there is an implied emphasis that the mother determines the infant's health;
however, Winnicott was actually focusing on the communication

between mother and infant and how their unconscious inter-mutuality contributed to the infant's maturational processes. (*see* COMMUNICATION: 2)

3 *The baby's ruthlessness*

By 1945, Winnicott's thoughts on aggression have evolved consid-erably. This year marks not only the end of the Second World War, but also the end of the Controversial Discussions, when the British Psycho-Analytical Society divided into two groups—Freudians and Kleinians. Analysts who did not wish to be identified with one or the other faction came to be known as the Middle Group. This group later on named themselves the In-dependent Group, and although Winnicott did not wish to be part of any group, his work is most associated with the Independent tradition in British psychoanalysis, along with other clinicians such as Marion Milner, Michael Balint, Ronald Fairbairn, and, most notably today, Christopher Bollas and Charles Rycroft.

In his important and pivotal paper, "Primitive Emotional Development" (1945), many of the themes that continue to preoccupy Winnicott for the rest of his life are set out like a ground-plan for all his later speculation (Phillips, 1988, p. 76). He postulates the initiation of three processes at the beginning of life:

> There are three processes which seem to me to start very early: (1) integration, (2) personalization, (3), following these, the appreciation of time and space and other properties of reality—in short, realization.
> A great deal that we tend to take for granted had a begin-ning and a condition out of which it developed.
> ["Primitive Emotional Development", p. 149]

Although the above three processes may begin in the infant dur-ing the first 24 hours of life post-birth, Winnicott stakes a claim for what he terms the "primitive ruthless self". This ruthlessness oc-curs before the infant is able to feel concern, and so the ruthless self predates the concerned self. But the concerned self—the abil-ity to feel concern—depends for its development on the ruthless self being allowed to be expressed.

If one assumes that the individual is becoming integrated and personalized and has made a good start in his realization, there is still a long way for him to go before he is related as a whole person to a whole mother, and concerned about the effect of his own thoughts and actions on her.

We have to postulate an early ruthless object relationship. . . . The normal child enjoys a ruthless relation to his mother, mostly showing in play, and he needs his mother because only she can be expected to tolerate his ruthless relation to her even in play, because this really hurts her and wears her out. Without this play with her he can only hide a ruthless self and give it life in a state of dissociation.

["Primitive Emotional Development", p. 154]

Winnicott is not specific, in this paper, regarding the approximate age of the infant who is being ruthless with his mother. However, as we shall see, the ruthlessness that the infant and growing child demonstrates is an aspect of the first two years of life. The play associated with the ruthless self refers to a child from about 6 months onwards—an infant/child who is able to play. (*see* PLAYING: 4)

However, the ruthless aspect of the playing is the enactment of the early ruthless self at the time before object relationships. Here is a point of evolution in Winnicott's thought; in the 1945 paper, "Primitive Emotional Development", Winnicott refers to a ruthless object relationship that has to exist at the beginning of life. By 1952, in a short paper, "Anxiety Associated with Insecurity", Winnicott explains how he had found himself saying, in 1942, "There's no such thing as a baby!", and it is in the paper of 1952 that he is ready to postulate a time when mother and infant are merged, which precedes object relationship. The ruthlessness of the infant occurs during this time, which is the time of the infant's absolute dependence, when he has no ability to know of his dependency on his mother and his ruthless love for her. (*see* DEPENDENCE: 2; BEING: 3; HATE: 5)

It should be remembered that this is a time referred to by Winnicott as "pre-ruth" or "pre-concern". In other words, the infant has no awareness of his ruthlessness. Only as he starts to become aware is he able then to look back and say, "I was ruthless then". (*see* CONCERN: 6)

How this ruthless self is responded to by the mother is a crucial aspect of how aggression affects emotional development in the growing infant.

If the infant is obliged to hide his ruthless self because of an environment that cannot tolerate aggression, it will have to be dissociated—that is to say, not integrated, unacknowledged, and split off. And it is this dissociation that Winnicott explores in 1947 in one of his seminal papers, "Hate in the Countertransference". (*see* HATE: 1)

4   *The analyst's aroused hatred*

This paper of 1947 addresses the feelings of primitive aggression aroused in the analyst when working with borderline or psychotic patients, referred to by Winnicott as "research cases". (*see* HATE: 3)

The relevance to this entry is that Winnicott quotes Freud's paper, "Instincts and Their Vicissitudes" (1915c) in order to clarify and illustrate why he believes that the concepts of constitutional hate, sadism, and envy are untenable.

> "We might at a pinch say of an instinct that it 'loves' the object . . . so we become aware that the attitudes of love and hate cannot be said to characterize the relation of instincts to their objects, but are reserved for the relations of the ego as a whole to objects."
>
> . . . This I feel is true and important. Does this not mean that the personality must be integrated before an infant can be said to hate? However early integration may be achieved—perhaps integration occurs earliest at the height of excitement or rage—there is a theoretical earlier stage in which whatever the infant does that hurts is not done in hate. I have used the term "ruthless love" in describing this stage. Is this acceptable? As the infant becomes able to feel to be a whole person, so does the word hate develop meaning as a description of a certain group of his feelings.
>
> ["Hate in the Countertransference", pp. 200–201]

Continuing his debate with Melanie Klein, Winnicott argues that envy, hate, and sadism are emotions that require intention, and that the immature infant has not yet reached the capability of conscious intent. A whole person, for Winnicott, is the individual who has achieved "unit status" and is able to distinguish between "Me" and "Not-Me", inside and outside. (*see* EGO: 3; DEPRESSION: 3)

What emerges in Winnicott's developmental theory is that at the beginning aggression in the infant happens to be necessarily ruthless. This is the infant during the phase of absolute dependence. (*see* DEPENDENCE: 1, 2)

From the early 1950s onwards, Winnicott's thought on aggression develops in a way that provides psychoanalysis with an alternative perspective on the infant to that of Klein.

5   The evolution of aggression in the developing child

In the 1950–54 paper, "Aggression in Relation to Emotional Development", which is a combination of three papers, Winnicott's definitive statement on the role of aggression is expounded.

He begins by demarcating aggression at three different stages of ego development:

> A complete study would trace aggressiveness as it appears at the various stages of ego development:
>
> | Early | Pre-integration |
> |---|---|
> | | Purpose without concern |
> | Intermediate | Integration |
> | | Purpose with concern |
> | | Guilt |
> | Total person | Inter-personal relationships |
> | | Triangular situations, etc. |
> | | Conflict, conscious & unconscious |
>
> ["Aggression in Relation to Emotional Development", pp. 205–206]

It must be noted that although Winnicott—unlike Klein and Freud—distinguishes between the ego and the self, throughout his work his use of these terms is often contradictory and ambiguous. (*see* EGO: 1; SELF: 1)

Winnicott is quite explicit about his wish to replace Klein's term "depressive position", and at the same time he elaborates his ideas on the fate of aggression:

STAGE OF CONCERN

Now comes the stage described by Melanie Klein as the "depressive position" in emotional development. For my purpose I will call this the Stage of Concern. The individual's ego integration is sufficient for him to appreciate the personality of the mother figure, and this has the tremendously important result that he is concerned as to the results of his instinctual experiences, physical and ideational.

The stage of concern brings with it the capacity to feel guilty. Henceforth some of the aggression appears clinically as grief or a feeling of guilt or some physical equivalent, such as vomiting. The guilt refers to the damage which is felt to be done to the loved person in the excited relationship. In health the infant can hold the guilt, and so with the help of a personal, alive mother (who embodies a time factor) is able to discover his own personal urge to give and to construct and to mend. In this way much of the aggression is transformed into the social functions, and appears as such. In times of helplessness (as when no person can be found to accept a gift or to acknowledge effort to repair) this transformation breaks down, and aggression reappears. Social activity cannot be satisfactory except it be based on a feeling of personal guilt in respect of aggression.

ANGER

In my description there now comes a place for anger at frustration. Frustration, which is inevitable in some degree in all experience, encourages the dichotomy: 1. innocent aggressive impulses towards frustrating objects, and 2. guilt-productive aggressive impulses towards good objects. Frustration acts as a seduction away from guilt and fosters a defence mechanism, namely, the direction of love and hate along separate lines. If this splitting of objects into good and bad takes place, there is an easing of guilt feeling; but in payment the love loses some of its valuable aggressive component, and the hate becomes the more disruptive.

["Aggression in Relation to Emotional Development", pp. 206–207]

This last paragraph turns Klein's theory on its head. The baby in Klein's theory splits good and bad from the beginning (the paranoid–schizoid position), whereas here, though Winnicott's baby will come to split the good and the bad, this will be *as a result* of frustration. Klein's focus is on the infant's internal world; for Winnicott, the colouring of the infant's internal world is absolutely contingent on its relation to the outside world. (*see* BEING: 5; ENVIRONMENT: 1; PRIMARY MATERNAL PREOCCUPATION: 1)

As already stated above, Winnicott never accepts Klein's (life and death) instinct theory; instead, he discovers in his clinical work what he describes as two different roots of instinctual life: the aggressive root and the erotic root. What strikes Winnicott is

> . . . that when a patient is engaged in discovering the aggressive root the analyst is more exhausted by the process, one way or another, than when the patient is discovering the erotic root of the instinctual life.
> ["Aggression in Relation to Emotional Development", p. 214]

He is alluding to a difference in quality, but he is not clear as to his meaning of "erotic". Throughout Winnicott's work he rarely uses the word "erotic", and his theory is frequently seen as a "flight from the erotic" (Phillips, 1988, p. 152). It seems that, in addressing his colleagues of the British Psycho-Analytical Society at that time, he is frustrated by their pathologizing something that he sees as normal:

> . . . confusion exists through our using the term aggression sometimes when we mean spontaneity.
> ["Aggression in Relation to Emotional Development", p. 217]

Winnicott's propensity is always to look for health, as opposed to pathology, in the individual, but his idiosyncratic use of Freudian terminology, intermixed with the language from patients, can make some of the passages in this 1950–54 paper confusing and difficult to understand. The four key areas related to aggression are:

- the task of fusion
- the need for opposition
- the need for the reality of the external object to feel real
- the need for an object rather than pleasure

6   *The task of fusion*

Fusion was a term Freud used in relation to his theory of the instincts. Winnicott sees that the fusion of erotic and aggressive components should not be taken for granted; it should, instead, be celebrated as an achievement:

> We assume a fusion of aggressive and erotic components in health, but we do not always give proper significance to the pre-fusion era, and to the task of fusion. We may easily take fusion too much for granted, and in this way we get into futile arguments as soon as we leave the consideration of an actual case.
>
> It must be conceded that the task of fusion is a severe one, that even in health it is an uncompleted task, and that it is very common to find large quantities of unfused aggression complicating the psychopathology of an individual who is being analysed.
>
> . . . In severe disorders that involve failure at the point of fusion, we find the patient's relationship to the analyst aggressive and erotic in turn. And it is here that I am claiming that the analyst is more likely to be tired by the former than by the latter type of partial relationship.
>
> ["Aggression in Relation to Emotional Development", pp. 214–215]

Winnicott is referring to the parallels between the patient who regresses in analysis and the new-born infant. If the task of fusion has not occurred in the individual because of an early environmental failure, then it will have to be achieved within the transference relationship. (see REGRESSION: 7)

He does not clarify his precise meaning of "the patient's relationship to the analyst aggressive and erotic in turn", but we may assume that the "aggressive" links with the baby's ruthlessness which really does tire the mother. The erotic, in contrast, is linked with the "sensuous co-existence" of baby in an unintegrated state with his mother in her primary maternal preoccupation.

These two separate roots of instinctual life may also relate to Winnicott's thesis of "the stage of concern", which was written in 1963, almost ten years after the above quote. It is in the 1963 paper, "The Development of the Capacity for Concern", that Winnicott elaborates on the notion that for the infant there are two mothers: the object–mother and the environment–mother. The former is the mother experienced by the infant in his excited state and the latter the mother experienced differently by the infant in his quiet and peaceful state. The coming together of these two mothers in the infant's mind is a necessary developmental achievement that enables him to develop a sense of concern. Thus the "task of fusion" could be seen to be Winnicott's precursor theory which, by 1963 had evolved into the "task of bringing two mothers together". (see CONCERN: 3)

In addition, we may suppose that the tiredness of the mother with her infant who is going through the task of fusion and that of the analyst with the regressed patient who is also struggling to fuse the two roots of instinctual life is related to the hate engendered in the mother by her baby and in the analyst by the patient. Painful but necessary. (see HATE: 3, 7)

7   The need for opposition and the reality of the external object

> . . . the aggressive impulses do not give any satisfactory experience unless there is opposition. The opposition must come from the environment, from the Not-Me which gradually comes to be distinguished from the Me . . . in normal development opposition from outside brings along the development of the aggressive impulse.
>
> ["Aggression in Relation to Emotional Development", p. 215]

What he designated "primary aggression" in his earlier work Winnicott now refers to as "life force"—"the aliveness of tissues"—which, he states, is more or less the same in each individual foetus:

> The complication is that the amount of aggressive potential an infant carries depends on the amount of opposition that has been met with. In other words, opposition affects the conversion of life force into aggression potential. Moreover, excess of opposition introduces complications that make it impossible for the existence of an individual who, having aggressive potential, could achieve its fusion with the erotic.
>
> ["Aggression in Relation to Emotional Development", p. 216]

This last sentence refers to the disruption of emotional development from reactions to impingement (*see* ENVIRONMENT: 7). If the
external opposition is too intrusive, the baby can only react, rather
than respond. Reacting to impingements, in Winnicott's terminology, means that the infant's sense of self and continuity-of-being is
interrupted. Therefore the task of fusion is prevented. This is what
constitutes a violation of the self. (see ENVIRONMENT: 7; COMMUNICA-
TION: 10)

Winnicott stresses that the quantity—of what he is now calling
the "aggressive potential"—

> . . . is not dependent on biological factors (which determine
> motility and erotism) but is dependent on the chance of
> early environmental impingement, and therefore, often, on
> the mother's psychiatric abnormalities, and the state of the
> mother's emotional environment.
>
> ["Aggression in Relation to Emotional Development", pp. 217–218]

In the third part of this paper, entitled "The External Nature of
Objects", which was originally presented to a private group in
1954, Winnicott formulates a personality with three selves:

> The personality comprises three parts: a true self, with Me
> and Not-Me clearly established, and with some fusion of the
> aggressive and erotic elements; a self that is easily seduced
> along lines of erotic experience, but with the result of a loss of
> sense of real; a self that is entirely and ruthlessly given over to
> aggression. This aggression is not even organized to destruc-
> tion, but it has value to the individual because it brings a
> sense of real and a sense of relating, but it is only brought into
> being by active opposition, or (later) persecution.
>
> ["Aggression in Relation to Emotional Development", p. 217]

Never again does Winnicott refer specifically to these three selves
in one. However, by 1960, the development of his thinking on
dissociation related to the development of the sense of self
emerges in his paper, "Ego Distortion in Terms of True and False
Self". (see SELF: 4)

In Freud's theory of the instincts, the pleasure principle plays a
major part in the infant's need for the object—that is, the infant
seeks pleasure when reaching out for the object. Winnicott dis-

agrees with this, though he never categorically states that he is in disagreement with Freud. His disagreement is with Klein:

> The impulsive gesture reaches out and becomes aggressive when opposition is reached. There is reality in this experience, and it very easily fuses into the erotic experiences that await the newborn infant. I am suggesting: it is this impulsiveness, and the aggression that develops out of it, that makes the infant need an external object, and not merely a satisfying object.
>
> ["Aggression in Relation to Emotional Development", p. 217]

The final paragraph in this paper anticipates the most difficult and yet perhaps the most ingenious of Winnicott's concepts, a paper that he would still be working on almost until the day he died— "The Use of an Object and Relating Through Identifications":

> In adult and mature sexual intercourse, it is perhaps true that it is not the purely erotic satisfactions that need a specific object. It is the aggressive or destructive element in the fused impulse that fixes the object and determines the need that is felt for the partners actual presence, satisfaction, and survival.
>
> ["Aggression in Relation to Emotional Development", p. 218]

"The Use of an Object and Relating through Identifications" was written in 1968 and published in Winnicott's book, *Playing and Reality*. Before this paper came into being, though, and from 1954 onwards, Winnicott's themes on aggression emerged in many different papers, specifically in relation to depression and the depressive position, the sense of guilt and reparation, creativity, and the capacity for concern. (*see* ANTISOCIAL TENDENCY: 10; CONCERN: 8; CREATIVITY: 5; MOTHER: 8)

8   Ruthless love

Winnicott's 1954 paper, "The Depressive Position and Normal Development", starts off, as he states, as a personal account of Melanie Klein's "depressive position". (*see* CONCERN: 2)

He reiterates that at the beginning the infant's "instinctual love" is "ruthless". In a few words he introduces the idea that he will later develop in "The Use of an Object" and the papers in *Playing and Reality*, when he states that the ruthless love of the infant at the beginning helps to "place the object outside the self".

The "benign circle" that belongs to "the capacity for concern", and the idea of two mothers—the object–mother and the environment–mother—are introduced in this paper and further developed in the 1960s. (*see* CONCERN: 3, 5)

Four years later, in 1958, in a paper celebrating Freud's centenary, "ruthlessness" is positively connected with the artist's creativity. In an enigmatic paragraph subtitled "The Creative Artist", Winnicott applauds the "ruthless self" in the artist.

> Ordinary guilt-ridden people find this bewildering; yet they have a sneaking regard for ruthlessness that does in fact, in such circumstances, achieve more than guilt-driven labour.
> ["Psycho-Analysis and the Sense of Guilt", 1958, p. 26]

In May 1960, in a talk given to the Progressive League and entitled "Aggression, Guilt and Reparation", Winnicott continues to explore early ruthless love and its necessarily destructive nature:

> I wish to draw on my experience as a psychoanalyst to describe a theme which comes over and over again in analytic work and which is always of great importance. It has to do with one of the roots of constructive activity. It has to do with the relationship between construction and destruction.
> ["Aggression, Guilt and Reparation", p. 136]

This is followed by a tribute to Melanie Klein, who, according to Winnicott, "took up the destructiveness that there is in human nature and started to make sense of it in psychoanalytic terms".

9 *Tolerance of destructiveness leading to concern*

Winnicott points out in this 1960 paper how important it is for each person to understand that their primitive destructive urge belongs to their early love.

> Perhaps it is true to say that human beings cannot tolerate the destructive aim in their very early loving. The idea of it can be

tolerated however if the individual who is getting towards it has evidence of a constructive aim already at hand of which he or she can be reminded.

["Aggression, Guilt and Reparation", p. 139]

This constructive aim, he says, is an aspect of the sense of guilt:

We are dealing with one aspect of the sense of guilt. It comes from toleration of one's destructive impulses in primitive loving. Toleration of one's destructive impulses results in a new thing, the capacity to enjoy ideas, even with destruction in them, and the bodily excitements that belong to them, or that they belong to. This development gives elbow room for the experience of concern, which is the basis for everything constructive.

["Aggression, Guilt and Reparation", p. 142]

When Winnicott writes about the value of destruction, he is specifically referring to the destruction that goes on in unconscious fantasy, as opposed to destruction that is carried out overtly. It can be seen from a letter he wrote to a colleague in 1963 that he had been working out for himself the meaning of unconscious destruction on his internal journey to seeing its link with object relating and object usage. He describes one of the dreams he had which falls into three parts: in the first, he was part of the world that was being destroyed; in the second, he was the destroying agent; and in the third, he woke up from his dream:

. . . and I knew I had dreamed of being destroyed and of being the destroying agent. There was no dissociation, so the three I's were altogether in touch with each other. This felt to be immensely satisfactory although the work done had made tremendous demands on me.

["D.W.W's Dream Related to Reviewing Jung", 1963, p. 229]

For Winnicott, this dream was of "special importance" because he had become aware of the meaning of the role of aggression in relation to the stage of emotional development where object usage replaces object relating. "Primary aggression" and "ruthlessness" are aspects of a sort of primary destructiveness which, if the object/environment survives them, will lead the subject to be able to see the real world for what it is.

> I had an acute awareness in the third part of the dream and
> when awake that destructiveness belongs to relating to objects
> that are outside the subjective world or the area of omnipo-
> tence. In other words, first there is the creativeness that
> belongs to being alive, and the world is only a subjective
> world. Then there is the objectively perceived world and ab-
> solute destruction of it and all its details.
>
> ["D.W.W's Dream", p. 229]

At the beginning, the infant cannot distinguish Me from Not-me,
and objects (the environment) are subjectively perceived—object
relating. As the infant develops, depending on a facilitating environment and good-enough mother, he comes objectively to
perceive the world—object usage.

Winnicott is aware how difficult it is for the idea of destructiveness to be accepted.

> To help I wish to point out that I am referring to such things
> as eagerness.
>
> ["Comments on My Paper 'The Use of an Object' ", 1968, p. 240]

> ... one could profitably use the idea of the fire from the
> dragon's mouth. I quote from Pliny, who (in paying tribute to
> fire) writes, "Who can say whether in essence fire is construc-
> tive or destructive?" Indeed the physiological basis for what I
> am referring to is the first and subsequent breaths, out-breath-
> ing.
>
> ["Comments on My Paper", p. 239]

This is reminiscent of the philological origin of inspiration, which
is to breathe in; a conspiracy is a breathing together, and breath
(spirit) is holy in Judaeo–Christian culture.

> The paper I have presented gives psychoanalysis a chance to
> rethink this subject. In this vitally important early stage the
> "destructive" (fire–air or other) aliveness of the individual is
> simply a symptom of being alive, and has nothing to do with
> an individual's anger at the frustrations that belong to meet-
> ing the reality principle.
>
> As I have tried to state, the drive is destructive. Survival of
> the object leads on to object use, and this leads on to the sepa-
> ration of two phenomena:

1. fantasy and
2. actual placing of the object outside the area of projections.

Therefore this very early destructive urge has a vital positive function (when by survival of the object, it works) namely
the objectivisation of the object (the analyst in the transference).

["Comments on My Paper", p. 239]

Later on, Winnicott states that what he is calling the "destructive
drive" could have been called a "combined love–strife drive"—
not two distinct life and death instincts, but a combination of two
in one at the beginning.

Here is a similarity with Jung's theory. Jung does not focus on
aggression but, rather, refers to destructive and constructive processes in the psyche. He postulates a neutral nature of psychic
energy and undivided vital energy (also called life instinct), which
serves regressive as well as progressive processes; when it serves
the former, it leads to a dissolution or "death" of the ego, precipi-
tating psychic change or "re-birth". Creativity is related to being
able to tolerate this "death" process and its inherent tension of
opposites.

10 Survival: from object-relating to object-usage

Referring to the "fate of the destructive drive", Winnicott emphasizes the crucial part played by the environment which must
survive the subject's destruction. This will be how the individual
arrives at object usage:

The fate of this unity of drive cannot be stated without
reference to the environment. The drive is potentially
"destructive" but whether it is destructive or not depends on
what the object is like; does the object *survive*, that is, does it
retain its character, or does it *react*? If the former then there is
no destruction, or not much, and there is a next moment when
the baby can become and does gradually become aware of a
cathected object plus the *fantasy* of having destroyed, hurt,
damaged, or provoked the object. The baby in this extreme of
environmental provision goes on in a pattern of developing
personal aggressiveness that provides the backcloth of a con-

tinuous (unconscious) fantasy of destruction. Here we may use Klein's reparation concept, which links constructive play and work with this (unconscious) *fantasy backcloth* of destruction or provocation (perhaps the right word has not been found). But destruction of an object that survives, has not reacted or disappeared, leads on to use.

["The Use of an Object in the Context of *Moses and Monotheism*", p. 245]

The infant who is able to perceive the world objectively has had the experience of the object surviving his destructiveness (primary aggression). This means that the object stays more or less the same and does not retaliate by rejection or punishment. The mother who is not good enough and cannot respond to the infant's spontaneous gesture does not survive and consequently impinges on her infant's emotional development. One consequence of this kind of impingment is that the infant is in danger of developing a compliant, false self, or worse. (*see* ENVIRONMENT: 4, 7; MOTHER: 6)

In some notes written in 1965 and published in 1969, Winnicott provides an illustration of the difference between a literal enactment of destruction and a destruction in fantasy.

For example: the antisocial person who enters an art gallery and slashes a picture by an old master is not activated by love of the painting and in fact is not being as destructive as the art-lover is when preserving the picture and using it fully and in unconscious fantasy destroying it over and over again. Nevertheless the vandal's one act of vandalism affects society, and society must protect itself. This rather crude example may serve to show the existence of a wide difference between the destructiveness that is inherent in object-relating, and the destructiveness that stems from an individual's immaturity.

["Notes Made on a Train, Part 2", p. 232]

In other words, for Winnicott there is a destruction that is healthy and one that is pathological. Healthy destruction is unconscious and in fantasy, and it signifies integration and emotional maturity. Pathological, acting-out destruction indicates an aggression that has not been integrated into the personality and remains split off—this belongs to emotional immaturity.

In a much-quoted passage from "The Use of an Object and Relating through Identifications", Winnicott illustrates how the journey from object-relating to object usage is achieved through unconscious destruction.

> This change (from relating to usage) means that the subject destroys the object. From here it could be argued by an arm-chair philosopher that there is therefore no such thing in practice as the use of an object: if the object is external, then the object is destroyed by the subject. Should the philosopher come out of his chair and sit on the floor with his patient, however, he will find that there is an intermediate position. In other words, he will find that after "subject relates to object" comes "subject destroys object" (as it becomes external); and then may come *"object survives destruction by the subject"*. But there may or may not be survival. A new feature thus arrives in the theory of object-relating. The subject says to the object: "I destroyed you", and the object is there to receive the communication. From now on the subject says: "Hullo object!" "I destroyed you." "I love you." "You have value for me because of your survival of my destruction of you." "While I am loving you I am all the time destroying you in (uncon-scious) *fantasy*." Here fantasy begins for the individual. The subject can now *use* the object that has survived. It is impor-tant to note that it is not only that the subject destroys the object because the object is placed outside the area of omnipo-tent control. It is equally significant to state this the other way round and to say that it is the destruction of the object that places the object outside the area of the subject's omnipotent control. In these ways the object develops its own autonomy and life, and (if it survives) contributes-in to the subject, ac-cording to its own properties.
>
> ["Use of an Object and Relating", pp. 89–90]

It is worth noting another fundamental difference between Winni-cott and Klein: the object that is destroyed is not repaired by the subject, but, rather, because of the object's survival, it is made whole, separate and external, in the subject's perception:

> The assumption is always there, in orthodox theory, that ag-gression is reactive to the encounter with the reality principle, whereas here it is the destructive drive that creates the quality of externality. This is central in the structure of my argument. . . . There is no anger in the destruction of the ob-

ject to which I am referring, though there could be said to be joy at the object's survival.

["Use of an Object and Relating", p. 93]

Towards the end of this paper, Winnicott clarifies his meaning of the word "use":

I wish to conclude with a note on using and usage. By "use" I do not mean "exploitation". As analysts, we know what it is like to be used, which means that we can see the end of the treatment, be it several years away. Many of our patients come with this problem already solved—they can use objects and they can use us and can use analysis, just as they have used their parents and their siblings and their homes. However, there are many patients who need us to be able to give them a capacity to use us. This for them is the analytic task. In meeting the needs of such patients, we shall need to know what I am saying here about our survival of their destructiveness. A backcloth of unconscious destruction of the analyst is set up, and we survive it or, alternatively, here is yet another analysis interminable.

["Use of an Object and Relating", p. 94]

In the last few years of his life Winnicott's main preoccupation was with the themes belonging to the role of the destructive drive in object-relating and object-usage. The ultimate of healthy development is the capacity to find and use the object. And for Winnicott to be used by the other was a compliment.

For most people the ultimate compliment is to be found and used, and I suppose therefore that these words could represent the communication of the baby with the mother.
> I find you;
> You survive what I do to you as I come to
>   recognise you as not–me;
> I use you;
> I forget you;
> But you remember me;
> I keep forgetting you;
> I lose you;
> I am sad.

["Communication between Infant and Mother, and Mother and Infant, Compared and Contrasted", 1968, p. 103]

If there is one paper that brings together the whole of Winnicott's forty years of thinking on the issues related to aggression, it is "The Use of an Object and Relating through Identifications", which was presented to the New York Psychoanalytic Society in 1968. The main tenet of the paper, as may be seen from the above, is that aggression—in this paper "destruction"—is an essential aspect of ordinary emotional development. However, Winnicott's use of paradox, his coinage of everyday words such as "destruction" and "survival", and his invention of new word combinations such as "object-relating" and "object-usage" make the paper difficult to understand for anybody not versed in his work. The New York Society's initial response to this paper has its own painful story (see Goldman, 1993, pp. 197–212; Kahr, 1996, pp. 118–120).

The lack of understanding on the part of the New York Society that Winnicott experienced had led him to write two more short papers in relation to the use of an object concept (in *Psycho-Analytic Explorations*, W19, pp. 238–246). The second of these papers, "The Use of an Object in the Context of *Moses and Monotheism*", dated January 1969, unusually features the importance of the father (described in *Psycho-Analytic Explorations*, pp. 217–218).

11   *The death instinct and the father*

Published posthumously, it is in "The Use of an Object in the Context of *Moses and Monotheism*" that Winnicott comments on the legacy of Freud's death instinct. In relation to Winnicott's last statements on the way aggression develops in the infant, two main points are examined:

- the part played by the actual father in terms of the development of the infant's ability to integrate;
- the part played by the environment in the aetiology of psychosis.

Winnicott wishes to relieve Freud of the burden of his instinct theory, stating that work with psychotics had to lead to a different conclusion:

To warn the reader I should say that I have never been in love with the death instinct and it would give me happiness if I could relieve Freud of the burden of carrying it forever on his Atlas shoulders. . . . It is always possible that the death instinct formulation was one of the places where Freud was near to a comprehensive statement but could not make it because, while he knew all we know about human psychology back to repression of the id in relation to cathected objects, he did not know what borderline cases and schizophrenics were going to teach us in the three decades after his death.

["The Use of an Object in the Context of *Moses*", p. 242]

And then Winnicott unusually refers to the importance of the father's role. There is nothing really new in terms of Winnicott's thoughts on the function of the father. He was always aware of the significance of the parents' partnership and its impact on the growing child (*see* MOTHER: 6, 7, 8, 9). However, in this paper, a little more than a year before his death, it is the father's role as the third that is emphasized—not just the father and who he is as a person in relation to the mother, but also the father whom mother holds in her mind whilst mothering.

. . . what is there in the actual presence of the father, and the part he plays in the experience of the relationship between him and the child and between the child and him? What does this do for the baby? For there is a difference according to whether the father is there or not, is able to make a relationship or not, is sane or insane, is free or rigid in personality.

If the father dies this is significant, and when exactly in the baby's life he dies, and there is a great deal too to be taken into account that has to do with the imago of the father in the mother's inner reality and its fate there.

["The Use of an Object in the Context of *Moses*", p. 242]

Winnicott postulates the existence of a father who is always, therefore, a whole object for the infant.

. . . the third person plays or seems to me to play a big part. The father may or may not have been a mother-substitute, but at some time he begins to be felt to be there in a different role, and it is here I suggest that the baby is likely to make use of the father as a blue-print for his or her own integration when just becoming at times a unit. . . .

In this way one can see that the father can be the first glimpse for the child of integration and of personal wholeness. . . .

It is easy to make the assumption that because the mother starts as a part object or as a conglomeration of part objects the father comes into ego-grasp in the same way. But I suggest that in a favourable case the father starts off whole (i.e.: as father, not as mother surrogate) and later becomes endowed with a significant part object, that he starts off as an integrate in the ego's organization and in the mental conceptualisation of the baby.

["Use of an Object in the Context of *Moses*", pp. 242–243]

Winnicott's implication is that the good-enough environment depends on a mother adapting to her infant's needs while a father, or third, is always present in her mind as well as there in his own right in relation both to mother and infant. (*see* ENVIRONMENT: 8)

REFERENCES

1939 Aggression and Its Roots   [W13]

1945 Primitive Emotional Development   [W6]

1947 Hate in the Countertransference   [W6]

1950–54   Aggression in Relation to Emotional Development   [W6]

1958 Psychoanalysis and the Sense of Guilt   [W9]

1960 Aggression, Guilt and Reparation   [W13]

1963 The Development of the Capacity for Concern   [W9]

1963 D.W.W.'s Dream Related to Reviewing Jung   [W19]

1965 Notes Made on a Train, Part 2   [W19]

1968 Comments on My Paper "The Use of an Object"   [W19]

1968 Communication between Infant and Mother, and Mother and Infant, Compared and Contrasted   [W16]

1968 Roots of Aggression   [W19]

1968 The Use of an Object and Relating through Identifications [W10]

1969 Contribution to a Symposium on Envy and Jealousy   [W19]

1969 The Use of an Object in the Context of *Moses and Monotheism* [W19]

Alone (the capacity to be)

1   *Ego-relatedness*
2   *I am alone*
3   *Withdrawal and loneliness*

T he capacity to be alone is based on the paradox of being alone in the presence of another and signifies health and the ultimate of emotional maturity.

The experience of being alone in the presence of the other is rooted in the early mother–infant relationship, which Winnicott names "ego-relatedness"— and later in his work "object-relating". This refers to the time when the mother is in a state of primary maternal preoccupation and the infant is in the phase of absolute dependence.

The capacity to be alone should not be confused with the withdrawn state.

The sense of loneliness, on the other hand, indicates a lack of the experience of having been alone in the presence of an important m/other.

1   Ego-relatedness

"The Capacity to Be Alone" was presented to the British Psycho-Analytical Society in 1957 and subsequently first published in 1958 in the *International Journal of Psycho-Analysis*. Although many of Winnicott's themes contribute to the thesis of this paper, the theme of the ability to be alone is explored only here.

The capacity to be alone is based on a paradox.

> Although many types of experience go to the establishment of the capacity to be alone, there is one that is basic, and without a sufficiency of it the capacity to be alone does not come about; *this experience is that of being alone, as an infant and small child, in the presence of mother.* Thus the basis of the capacity to be alone is a paradox; it is the experience of being alone while someone else is present."
>
> ["The Capacity to Be Alone", p. 30]

The possibility that the capacity to be alone will develop in the baby depends on how he is held, particularly in the first two years. (*see* HOLDING: 4, 5)

In 1956, a year before the above paper was written, Winnicott introduced the term "ego-relatedness" in two papers—"Primary Maternal Preoccupation" and "The Antisocial Tendency". Ego-relatedness refers to the time when mother and baby are merged. During this time of merger, when the baby sees the mother, he sees himself, and when the mother sees her infant, she remembers (unconsciously) her own early days and weeks, and this enables her to identify with her infant's needs, so that it is as if she sees herself. This is the mother in a state of primary maternal preoccupation. These very early moments, days, and weeks are a vital starting point for the healthy emotional development of the individual. (*see* BEING: 4, 5; PRIMARY MATERNAL PREOCCUPATION)

In the above paper of 1957, Winnicott explores the nature of ego-relatedness within the context of the established Freudian theory of the primal scene and Kleinian theory of the good internal object.

In Freud's primal scene, the ability to be alone means that the infant/toddler is able to tolerate the fact of the parents' intercourse. And in Klein's good-internal-object language, being alone implies that the good internal object has been internalized and established in the infant's inner world.

By placing his idea of the capacity to be alone in both Freudian and Kleinian theory, Winnicott uses the different emphases of both (Oedipus and internal object relationships) in order to gain understanding from his audience. At the same time, he is quietly dispensing with "well-worn psychoanalytic phraseology" to make way for his own language and his own emphasis—namely, the phenomena of the very early mother–infant relationship.

2 *I am alone*

In studying the phrase "I am alone", Winnicott points to three different stages of emotional development, always stressing the importance of the environment:

> First there is the word "I", implying much emotional growth. The individual is established as a unit. Integration is a fact. The external world is repudiated and an internal world has become possible. . . .
>
> Next come the words "I am", representing a stage in individual growth. By these words the individual not only has shape but also life. In the beginnings of "I am" the individual is (so to speak) raw, is undefended, vulnerable, potentially paranoid. The individual can only achieve the "I am" stage because there exists an environment which is protective; the protective environment is in fact the mother preoccupied with her own infant and orientated to the infant's ego requirements through her identification with her own infant. There is no need to postulate an awareness of the mother on the part of the infant at this stage of "I am".
>
> Next I come to the words "I am alone". According to the theory that I am putting forward this further stage does indeed involve an appreciation on the part of the infant of the mother's continued existence. By this I do not necessarily mean an awareness with the conscious mind. I consider, however, that "I am alone" is a development from "I am", dependent on the infant's awareness of the continued existence of a reliable mother whose reliability makes it possible

for the infant to be alone and to enjoy being alone, for a limited period.

[*"The Capacity to Be Alone", p. 33*]

The "I" stage represents the self-emergence from the environment–individual set-up (the time of merger), when the infant
begins to be able to differentiate between Me and Not-me (*see*
BEING: 3). The "I am" stage occurs between the ages of 3 and 6
months and relates to the developmental achievement of Klein's
depressive position and Winnicott's stage of concern (*see* CONCERN:
6). "I am alone", therefore, may start to occur in the infant from
about the age of 6 months onwards, but the reliable presence of
mother has to continue for an establishment of the capacity.

Winnicott wishes to emphasize the crucial aspect of ego-
relatedness.

> It will be seen that I attach a great importance to this relation-
> ship, as I consider that it is the stuff out of which friendship is
> made. It may turn out to be the matrix of transference. . . .
>
> I think it will be generally agreed that id-impulse is signifi-
> cant only if it is contained in ego living. An id-impulse either
> disrupts a weak ego or else strengthens a strong one. It is
> possible to say that id-relationships strengthen the ego when
> they occur in a framework of ego-relatedness. If this be ac-
> cepted, then an understanding of the importance of the
> capacity to be alone follows. It is only when alone (that is to
> say, in the presence of someone) that the infant can discover
> his own personal life. The pathological alternative is a false
> life built on reactions to external stimuli. When alone in the
> sense that I am using the term, and only when alone, the
> infant is able to do the equivalent of what in an adult would
> be called relaxing. The infant is able to become unintegrated,
> to flounder, to be in a state in which there is no orientation, to
> be able to exist for a time without being either a reactor to an
> external impingement or an active person with a direction of
> interest or movement. The stage is set for an id-experience. In
> the course of time there arrives a sensation or an impulse. In
> this setting the sensation or impulse will feel real and be truly
> a personal experience. . . .
>
> It is only under these conditions that the infant can have
> an experience which feels real. A large number of such expe-

riences form the basis for a life that has reality in it instead of futility. The individual who has developed the capacity to be alone is constantly able to rediscover the personal impulse, and the personal impulse is not wasted because the state of being alone is something which (though paradoxically) always implies that someone else is there.

[*"The Capacity to Be Alone"*, pp. 33–34]

By id-experience Winnicott means physiological impulses (like hunger), to which the mother, because of her ability to identify with the infant, is able to respond. The quality of response by the environment to meet the infant's need transforms the id-experience, thereby strengthening the sense of self. The cumulative effect of the countless repetitions of the mother meeting the infant's needs means that he is enabled to *feel real* and *live creatively*. (*see* COMMUNICATION: 2; CREATIVITY: 4; EGO: 2; HOLDING: 2; SELF: 5)

Winnicott does not make it clear why he wishes to refer to the early mother/infant relationship as "ego-relatedness", and in the "Summary" of his paper he does, in fact, say that the term may be for temporary use. Indeed, in his later work he drops this term; it is replaced with the term "object relating"—the precursor to "object usage". (*see* AGGRESSION: 10)

3   Withdrawal and loneliness

The capacity to be alone must not be mistaken for the state of withdrawal. The individual who has to withdraw from relationships with others has, in Winnicott's theory, experienced gross impingements from the beginning and has had to withdraw in order to preserve the core self from violation (*see* COMMUNICATION: 12). Withdrawal constitutes a relating to subjective objects that facilitates the sense of feeling real, and Winnicott points out that there is an aspect of withdrawal that is healthy. However, withdrawal is also an insulation that, like the autistic state, does not help to enrich and develop the sense of self, even though the sense of feeling real may be present. So whilst the individual who spends a great deal of time alone may appear to have reached the capacity to be alone, in relation to Winnicott's thesis, the withdrawn state may well demonstrate an *incapacity* to be alone. (*see* COMMUNICATION: 9, 11; ENVIRONMENT: 9; REGRESSION: 14)

Likewise, the individual who experiences intense loneliness has also experienced impingement through a lack of the experience of ego-relatedness with a mother who is able to be reliably present because she is in identification with her infant.

> It will be appreciated that actually to be alone is not what I am discussing. A person may be in solitary confinement, and yet not be able to be alone. How greatly he must suffer is beyond imagination.
>
> ["The Capacity to Be Alone", p. 30]

Winnicott also sees the capacity to be alone in the presence of another as a necessary development during the course of a psychotherapy.

> In almost all our psycho-analytic treatments there come times when the ability to be alone is important to the patient. Clinically this may be represented by a silent phase or a silent session, and this silence, far from being evidence of resistance, turns out to be an achievement on the part of the patient. Perhaps it is here that the patient has been able to be alone for the first time.
>
> ["The Capacity to Be Alone", p. 29]

For the patient and analyst to *be* in a session is thus an achievement. To be unintegrated, to free associate, to surrender, to flounder are all signs that the capacity to be alone is being reached. (*see* BEING: 7; SELF: 11)

REFERENCE

1958   The Capacity to Be Alone   [W9]

Antisocial tendency

A ntisocial tendency is a term inextricably linked with deprivation. The antisocial act (stealing, bedwetting, etc.) is an enactment that signifies an environmental failure at the time of
relative dependence.

In Winnicott's thesis, the antisocial tendency indicates that
the infant had experienced a good-enough environment during the
time of absolute dependence that was subsequently lost. Therefore
the antisocial act is a sign of hope that the individual will rediscover
the good experience of the time before the loss occurred.

The antisocial tendency is not a diagnosis and applies to both
children and adults.

Winnicott makes a distinction between the antisocial tendency
and delinquency, although both stem from the same root—deprivation.

1   *The evacuation experience*

Winnicott's discovery that the antisocial tendency was a sign of
hope evolved from his work during the Second World War, when
he became Consultant Psychiatrist for the Government Evacuation
Scheme in a reception area outside London. The impact on Winnicott of this experience gave rise to many talks and broadcasts
during the war and post-war, where the themes linked with separation and deprivation of home life are explored. Some of these
talks were posthumously published along with other papers written some time after the war and are to be found in the collection
entitled *Deprivation and Delinquency* (W13).

In the introduction to this collection of papers, Clare Winnicott, who had first met and worked with Winnicott during this
period, describes something of Winnicott's process of discovery
whilst working with deprived children and adolescents.

> Although the circumstances in which Winnicott found him-
> self were abnormal because of the war time, the knowledge
> gained from the experience has general application because
> deprived children who become delinquent have basic prob-
> lems which are manifested in predictable ways whatever the
> circumstances. Moreover, the children who became Winni-
> cott's responsibility were those who needed special provision
> because they could not settle in ordinary homes. In other
> words, they were already in trouble in their own home. . . .
>
> The evacuation experience had a profound effect on Winni-
> cott because he had to meet in a concentrated way the
> confusion brought about by the wholesale break-up of
> family life, and he had to experience the effect of separation
> and loss, and of destruction and death. The personal re-
> sponses in bizarre and delinquent behaviour that followed
> had to be managed and encompassed and gradually under-
> stood by Winnicott working with a staff team at local level.
> The children he worked with had reached the end of the line;
> there was nowhere else for them to go and how to hold them
> became the main preoccupation of all those trying to help
> them. . . .
>
> There is no doubt that working with deprived children
> gave a whole new dimension to Winnicott's thinking and to
> his practice, and affected his basic concepts on emotional

growth and development. Quite early on his theories about
the drives behind the antisocial tendency began to take shape
and to be expressed.

[Clare Winnicott, 1984, pp. 1–3]

Clare Winnicott describes how their joint collaboration was re-
corded and subsequently used as vital information that contributed to the passing of the Children Act in 1948.

Clare Winnicott's words at the end of the introduction are
salutary. The antisocial tendency as a concept is relevant not only
to evacuees during the war, but to society and to all individuals
who have not experienced a strong holding environment at crucial
stages of their emotional development.

> Although these writings are of historical interest, they do not
> belong to history, but to the ever-present encounter between
> the antisocial elements in society and the forces of health and
> sanity which reach out to reclaim and recover what has been
> lost. The complexity of this encounter cannot be overesti-
> mated. The point of interaction between the care givers and
> the cared for is always the focus for therapy in this field or
> work, and it requires constant attention and support from the
> professional experts involved, and enlightened backing from
> the responsible administrators. Today, as always, the practical
> question is how to maintain an environment that is humane
> enough, and strong enough, to contain both the care givers
> and the deprived and delinquent who desperately need care
> and containment, but who will do their best to destroy it
> when they find it.
>
> [Clare Winnicott, 1984, p. 5]

2   Delinquency and normal antisocial behaviour

In 1946, just a year after the end of the war, Winnicott talked to an
audience of magistrates. This paper, entitled "Some Psychological
Aspects of Juvenile Delinquency", attributes the delinquent's act to
early emotional deprivation. By introducing the Freudian unconscious, Winnicott is hoping to convey to his audience that antisocial
behaviour is the product of an unconscious communication.

Before exploring the aspects of deprivation in the delinquent, Winnicott illustrates the normality of the antisocial act in emotional development, even in a good home.

> What is the normal child like? Does he just eat and grow and smile sweetly? No, that is not what he is like. A normal child, if he has confidence in father and mother, pulls out all the stops. In the course of time he tries out his power to disrupt, to destroy, to frighten, to wear down, to waste, to wangle, and to appropriate. Everything that takes people to the courts (or to the asylums, for that matter) has its normal equivalent in infancy and early childhood, in the relation of the child to his own home. If the home can stand up to all the child can do to disrupt it, he settles down to play; but business first, the tests must be made, and especially so if there is some doubt as to the stability of the parental set-up and the home (by which I mean more than house). At first the child needs to be conscious of a framework if he is to feel free, and if he is to be able to play, to draw his own pictures, to be an irresponsible child.
> ["Some Psychological Aspects", p. 115]

Winnicott explains why the child needs to be like this and refers to the essential quality of a strong and loving environment. The parents' response to the infant's primary aggression is all part and parcel of this theory. (*see* AGGRESSION: 3, 4, 6)

> Why should this be? The fact is that the early stages of emotional development are full of potential conflict and disruption. The relation to external reality is not yet firmly rooted; the personality is not yet well integrated; primitive love has a destructive aim, and the small child has not yet learned to tolerate and cope with instincts. He can come to manage these things, and more, if his surroundings are stable and personal. At the start he absolutely needs to live in a circle of love and strength (with consequent tolerance) if he is not to be too fearful of his own thoughts and of his imaginings to make progress in his emotional development.
> ["Some Psychological Aspects", p. 115]

This is a picture of the child who has had a good-enough start— a facilitating environment. The parents' toleration of the infant's aggression is key to the infant's ability to grow. This is what will lead the individual to a sense of freedom to move. The child who is given no boundaries will not feel free—on the contrary, he will feel anxious.

> Now what happens if the home fails a child before he has got the idea of a framework as part of his own nature? The popular idea is that, finding himself "free" he proceeds to enjoy himself. This is far from the truth. Finding the framework of his life broken, he no longer feels free. He becomes anxious, and if he has hope he proceeds to look for a framework elsewhere than at home. The child whose home fails to give a feeling of security looks outside his home for the four walls; he still has hope, and he looks to grandparents, uncles and aunts, friends of the family, school. He seeks an external stability without which he may go mad. . . .
>
> The antisocial child is merely looking a little farther afield, looking to society instead of to his own family or school to provide the stability he needs if he is to pass through the early and quite essential stages of his emotional growth.
>
> ["Some Psychological Aspects", pp. 115–116]

If the unconscious communication of the antisocial act is not understood by the environment, then the child's antisocial behaviour is in danger of developing into delinquency. Winnicott differentiates between delinquency and the antisocial tendency. For the delinquent, it may already be too late for treatment.

> By the time the boy or girl has become hardened because of the failure of the communication, the antisocial act not being recognised as something that contains an S O S, and when secondary gains have become important, and great skill has been achieved in some antisocial activity, then it is much more difficult to see (what is still there, nevertheless) the S O S that is a signal of hope in the boy or girl who is antisocial.
>
> ["Delinquency as a Sign of Hope", 1967, p. 90]

The individual who is likely to become a criminal has lost touch with the sense of the original deprivation, and the antisocial way of life keeps the psychic pain at bay. However, as Winnicott points out, if the root of the criminal act is acknowledged, appropriate treatment and rehabilitation may be worked out, as opposed to punishment, which will only serve to harden the defence.

The point is that punishment and force only leads to compliance and false-self living. In a 1963 paper—"Morals and Education"—Winnicott illustrates what he means:

> Professor Niblett in the opening lecture of this series referred to the headmaster Keate who said to a child: "You will believe in the Holy Ghost by 5 o'clock this afternoon or I will beat you till you do," and in this way Professor Niblett led on to the idea of the futility of teaching values or religion by force. I am trying to open up this important theme and to examine the alternatives. My main point is that there does exist a good alternative, and that this good alternative is not to be found in a more and more subtle teaching of religion. The good alternative has to do with the provision of those conditions for the infant and child that enable such things as trust and "belief in", and ideas of right and wrong, to develop out of the working of the individual child's inner processes.
>
> ["Morals and Education", pp. 93–94]

In this same 1963 paper—originally presented to the University of London Institute of Education—Winnicott makes a brief reference to wickedness as the manifestation of the antisocial tendency.

> Wickedness belongs to the clinical picture produced by the antisocial tendency. . . . Briefly the antisocial tendency represents the hopefulness in a deprived child who is otherwise hopeless, hapless and harmless; a manifestation of the antisocial tendency in a child means that there has developed in the child some hopefulness, hope that a way may be found across a gap. This gap is a break in the continuity of environmental provision, experienced at a stage of relative dependence. In every case there has been experienced a break in the continuity of the environmental provision, and one that resulted in a hold-up of maturational processes and a painful confusional clinical state in the child. . . . The wickedness goes if the gap is bridged. This is an over-simplification but it must suffice. Compulsive wickedness is about the last thing to be cured or even stopped by moral education. The child knows in his bones that it is *hope* that is locked up in the wicked behaviour, and that *despair* is linked with compliance and false socialization. For the antisocial or wicked person the moral educator is on the wrong side.
>
> ["Morals and Education", pp. 103–104]

The father's function in relation to the holding environment is an important factor in dealing with the antisocial element of all babies and children. The paper—"Some Psychological Aspects of Juvenile Delinquency"—was written as early as 1946, and yet it can be seen that the issues of the indestructible environment to do with the father's authority are part of what in the 1960s—and in 1968 in particular ("The Use of an Object and Relating Through Identifications")—becomes the object's survival and the subject's need for the object's survival to gain psychological health. (*see* AGGRESSION: 10)

> When a child steals sugar he is looking for the good mother, his own, from whom he has a right to take what sweetness is there. In fact this sweetness is his, for he invented her and her sweetness out of his own capacity to love, out of his own primary creativity. . . . He is also looking for his father, one might say, who will protect mother from his attacks on her, attacks made in the exercise of primitive love. When a child steals outside his own home he is still looking for his mother, but he is seeking with more sense of frustration, and increasingly needing to find at the same time the paternal authority that can and will put a limit to the actual effect of his impulsive behaviour, and to the acting out of the ideas that come to him when he is in a state of excitement. In full-blown delinquency it is difficult for us as observers, because what meets us is the child's acute need for the strict father, who will protect mother when she is found. The strict father that the child evokes may also be loving, but he must first be strict and strong. Only when the strict and strong father figure is in evidence can the child regain his primitive love impulses, his sense of guilt, and his wish to mend. Unless he gets into trouble, the delinquent can only become progressively more and more inhibited in love, and consequently more and more depressed and depersonalised, and eventually unable to feel the reality of things at all, except the reality of violence.
>
> ["Some Psychological Aspects", pp. 116–117]

In this respect, the hardened criminal may need this violent way of life as the only way to feel real. The antisocial act is essentially a sign of hope for the individual performing the act. The hope is that the lost boundary (the father's authority) will be rediscovered. The individual is searching for the environment that will say *no*, not in a punitive way, but in a way that will create a sense of security. In Winnicott's thesis of the use of an object, the object must survive for the infant to develop a true sense of self.

> Delinquency indicates that some hope remains. You will see that it is not necessarily an illness of the child when he behaves antisocially, and antisocial behaviour is at times no more than an S.O.S. for control by strong, loving, confident people. Most delinquents are to some extent ill, however, and the word illness becomes appropriate through the fact that in many cases the sense of security did not come into the child's life early enough to be incorporated into his beliefs. While under strong management, an antisocial child may seem to be all right; but give him freedom and he soon feels the threat of madness. So he offends against society (without knowing what he is doing) in order to re-establish control from outside.
>
> ["Some Psychological Aspects", pp. 116–117]

Winnicott's thesis that the environment has failed the delinquent means that thought needs to be given to the treatment. Winnicott believes that every infant has the right to a good-enough environment. Therefore children and adolescents who have never had this right exercised need to be compensated for this loss through therapy and, if necessary, management.

> Apart from being neglected (in which case they reach the Juvenile Courts as delinquents) they can be dealt with in two ways. They can be given personal psychotherapy, or they can be provided with a strong stable environment with personal care and love, and gradually increasing doses of freedom. As a matter of fact, without this latter the former (personal psychotherapy) is not likely to succeed. And with the provision of a suitable home-substitute, psychotherapy may become unnecessary, which is fortunate because it is practically never available. . . .
>
> Personal psychotherapy is directed towards enabling the child to complete his or her emotional development. This means many things, including establishing a good capacity for feeling the reality of real things, both external and internal, and establishing the integration of the individual personality.
>
> ["Some Psychological Aspects", p. 118]

Throughout the whole of Winnicott's work, the nature of the environment never ceases to be important, emotionally and physically. For the developing child, though, and particularly at the beginning, it is the environment that contributes to setting up a pattern of expectations inside. The child or adolescent displaying an antisocial tendency has lost the containing boundary of the environment and is unconsciously driven to find it.

> The antisocial tendency is characterized by an element in it which compels the environment to be important. The patient through unconscious drives compels someone to attend to management. It is the task of the therapist to become involved in this the patient's unconscious drive, and the work is done by the therapist in terms of management, tolerance, and understanding.
>
> ["The Antisocial Tendency", 1956, p. 309]

It is quite clear from Winnicott's early writings that he always stresses the importance of environmental continuity and stability as laying down the grounds for mental health (*see* ENVIRONMENT: 1). In the papers written after the Second World War, a continuity of management is strongly recommended for children requiring residential care, either because they had no family or because their home had failed them:

> There are two broad categories of children in peacetime: children whose homes do not exist or whose parents cannot form a stable background in which a child can develop, and children with an existing home which, nevertheless, contains a mentally ill parent. Such children appear in our peacetime clinics, and we find they need just what the children who were difficult to billet needed. Their home environment has failed them. Let us say that what these children need is *environmental stability, personal management, and continuity* of management. We assume an ordinary standard of physical care.
>
> ["Children's Hostels in War and Peace", 1948, p. 74]

Winnicott subsequently stresses that continuity of management and environmental stability is dependent on the staff's ability to bear the emotional burden a child in distress will cause.

> To ensure personal management the staffing of a hostel must be adequate, and the wardens must be able to stand the emo-

tional strain that belongs to the proper care of any child, but especially to the care of children whose own homes have failed to bear such strain. Because of this the wardens need constant support from psychiatrist and psychiatric social worker. The children (unselfconsciously) look to the hostel, or failing that to society in a wider sense, to provide the framework for their lives that their own homes have failed to give them. Inadequate staffing not only makes personal management impossible, but also it leads to ill health and breakdowns in the staff, and therefore interferes with continuity of personal relationship, which is essential in this work"

["Children's Hostels in War and Peace", p. 74]

The emphasis on the psychological contribution made by the environment to the physical and psychological health of the individual characterizes the whole of Winnicott's work. Thus the sense of "being" in the individual depends on the holding and facilitating environment—*and* the ability to hold comes from the carer's unconscious memory of having been held (*see* HOLDING; ENVIRONMENT; PRIMARY MATERNAL PREOCCUPATION).

3   *The need to steal*

On 20 June 1956, Winnicott read his paper, "The Antisocial Tendency", to the British Psycho-Analytical Society. It has become his definitive statement on the theme of deprivation at the time of relative dependence and includes recommendations for treatment.

From the start of this paper, Winnicott sets out to illustrate how the antisocial tendency can be discerned in the extreme acting-out individual as well as in the individual who by all accounts appears to have a good home but needs to steal because of an experience of deprivation. In the first case illustration, Winnicott's adolescent patient is eventually sent to an approved school because he cannot be contained enough in psychotherapy; in the second case, Winnicott helps a friend by suggesting, over lunch, a simple interpretation she can make to her son, who is going through a phase of stealing. This not only works for the child concerned, but also for the mother, Winnicott's friend.

In considering this case it must be remembered that I had known the mother very well during her adolescence and to some extent had seen her through an antisocial phase of her own. She was the eldest in a large family. She had a very good home but very strong discipline was exerted by the father, especially at the time when she was a small child. What I did therefore had the effect of a double therapy, enabling this young woman to get insight into her own difficulties through the help that she was able to give to her son. When we are able to help parents to help their children we do in fact help them about themselves.

["Antisocial Tendency", p. 308]

Winnicott is pointing out that it is relatively straightforward to help both children and their parents at the early stages of the antisocial tendency, if the therapeutic intervention takes account of the unconscious communication of the hope of finding what is felt to be lost.

The deprived child who behaves in an antisocial way is in fact more hopeful than the child who cannot behave badly. For the latter, hope has gone, and the child has become defeated.

The antisocial tendency implies hope. Lack of hope is the basic feature of the deprived child who, of course, is not all the time being antisocial. In the period of hope the child manifests an antisocial tendency. This may be awkward for society, and for you if it is your bicycle that is stolen, but those who are not personally involved can see the hope that under-lies the compulsion to steal. Perhaps one of the reasons why we tend to leave the therapy of the delinquent to others is that we dislike being stolen from?

["Antisocial Tendency", p. 309]

Because the antisocial act evokes such hatred and anger in most people, Winnicott stresses the importance of understanding that it is an expression of profound need, and therefore adults need to be able to appreciate its significance.

The understanding that the antisocial act is an expression of hope is vital in the treatment of children who show the anti-social tendency. Over and over again one sees the moment of hope wasted, or withered, because of mismanagement or intolerance. This is another way of saying that the treatment of the antisocial tendency is not psychoanalysis but management, a going to meet and match the moment of hope.

["Antisocial Tendency", p. 309]

Winnicott is well aware of how intensely people's hatred can be mobilized by the antisocial act. In this sense, the problems of the management of the psychotic patient parallel the management of children and adolescents with challenging behaviour. (*see* HATE: 2)

Winnicott distinguishes between privation and deprivation. Privation means that the child has no experience of anything that is good; deprivation, on the other hand, refers to an individual who has, somewhere, a sense of what is good—that is, the unconscious memory of having been loved.

> When there is an antisocial tendency there has been a true deprivation (not a simple privation); that is to say, there has been a loss of something good that has been positive in the child's experience up to a certain date, and that has been withdrawn; the withdrawal has extended over a period of time longer than that over which the child can keep the memory of the experience alive. The comprehensive statement of deprivation, one that includes both the early and the late, both the pinpoint trauma and the sustained traumatic condition and also both the near normal and the clearly abnormal.
>
> ["Antisocial Tendency", p. 309]

What has happened to the infant/child in terms of the failure of the environment will affect the extent of the deprived feelings. There is thus a spectrum to the antisocial tendency, in terms of aetiology as well as expression.

4   Two trends: destructive and object-seeking

Along the spectrum, however, there exist two trends, each with its own aim.

> There are always two trends in the antisocial tendency although the accent is sometimes more on one than on the other. One trend is represented typically in stealing, and the other in destructiveness. By one trend the child is looking for

something, somewhere, and failing to find it seeks it else-
where, when hopeful. By the other the child is seeking that
amount of environmental stability which will stand the strain
resulting from impulsive behaviour. This is a search for an
environmental provision that has been lost, a human attitude,
which, because it can be relied on, gives freedom to the individual to move and to act and to get excited.

In examining the near-normal and (in terms of individual
development) the early roots of the antisocial tendency I wish
to keep in mind all the time these two trends: object-seeking
and destruction.

["Antisocial Tendency", p. 310]

It is the destructive trend that relates to the unconscious search for
the mother's body and arms—the infant's first environment.

It is particularly because of the second of these trends that the
child provokes total environmental reactions, as if seeking an
ever-widening frame, a circle which had as its first example
the mother's arms or the mother's body. One can discern a
series—the mother's body, the mother's arms, the parental
relationship, the home, the family including cousins and near
relations, the school, the locality with its police-stations, the
country with its laws.

["Antisocial Tendency", p. 310]

This is reminiscent of Winnicott's environment–mother of the
infant's early life—the mother of the infant's quiet times of
unintegration (see BEING: 1), whereas the mother of the excited
times—the object–mother—is initially experienced by the baby as
separate and different from the environment–mother. The coming-together of these two mothers in the infant's mind contributes
to the developmental stage of the capacity for concern (see CON-
CERN: 3). The deprived child, who has not only had a real
environmental deprivation but has also been deprived of the opportunity of bringing the two mothers together, thus cannot yet
reach the important stage of concern (see DEPRESSION: 4, 6). Stealing
an object is, therefore, seen as the act of seeking both object– and
environment–mother.

Stealing is at the centre of the antisocial tendency, with the
associated lying.

The child who steals an object is not looking for the object stolen but seeks the mother over whom he or she has rights. These rights derive from the fact that (from the child's point of view) the mother was created by the child. The mother met the child's primary creativity, and so became the object that the child was ready to find.

["Antisocial Tendency", p. 311]

This last sentence refers to the mother's function of object-presenting. The good-enough mother provides the environment that facilitates the infant's sense of omnipotence—that is, he is God, creator of the world. (see CREATIVITY: 2; DEPENDENCE: 9; MOTHER: 12)

The child/adolescent displaying an antisocial tendency has lost the sense of omnipotence and the necessary environment to fuse "aggressive motility roots" (instincts) with the libidinal roots (object-seeking). (see AGGRESSION: 6)

When there is at the time of the original deprivation some fusion of aggressive (or motility) roots with the libidinal the child claims the mother by a mixture of stealing and hurting and messing, according to the specific details of that child's emotional developmental state. When there is less fusion the child's object-seeking and aggression are more separated off from each other, and there is a greater degree of dissociation in the child. This leads to the proposition that the nuisance value of the antisocial child is an essential feature, and is also, at its best, a favourable feature indicating again a potentiality for recovery of lost fusion of the libidinal and motility roots.

["Antisocial Tendency", p. 311]

The antisocial tendency is a normal strand of emotional development, at the beginning of life, which usually goes unnoticed. Nuisance value implies that there is a communication from the infant that needs to be acknowledged and registered by the mother.

In ordinary infant care the mother is constantly dealing with the nuisance value of her infant. For instance, a baby commonly passes water on the mother's lap while feeding at the breast. At a later date this appears as a momentary regression in sleep or at the moment of waking and bed-wetting results. Any exaggeration of the nuisance value of an infant may indicate the existence of a degree of deprivation and antisocial tendency.

The manifestation of the antisocial tendency includes stealing and lying, incontinence and the making of a mess generally. Although each symptom has its specific meaning and value, the common factor for my purpose in my attempt to describe the antisocial tendency is the nuisance value of the symptoms. This nuisance value is exploited by the child, and is not a chance affair. Much of the motivation is unconscious, but not necessarily all.

["Antisocial Tendency", p. 311]

The roots of the antisocial tendency derive from the very beginning of life in the context of the mother–infant relationship, and the "first signs of deprivation are so common that they pass for normal". Greediness is one of the first signs of a "degree of deprivation and some compulsion towards seeking for a therapy in respect of this deprivation, through the environment" ("Antisocial Tendency", pp. 311–312). This implies that the environment is responsible for the sense of deprivation the infant feels, which compels him to seek compensation from the environment.

At the point of emotional development when the infant needs to unite or fuse the motility instinctual roots with the libidinal, the mother is required by the infant, for her ego-support, because at this stage the infant's ego is too weak to carry out the task of integration. If the mother does not supply the ego-support at this crucial moment, then the infant is let down and experiences deprivation. This is the "time of the original deprivation".

There is one special point that I wish to make. At the basis of the antisocial tendency is a good early experience that has been lost. Surely, *it is an essential feature that the infant has reached to a capacity to perceive that the cause of the disaster lies in an environmental failure.* Correct knowledge that the cause of the depression or disintegration is an external one, and not an internal one, is responsible for the personality distortion and for the urge to seek for a cure by new environmental provision. The state of ego maturity enabling perception of this kind determines the development of an antisocial tendency instead of a psychotic illness. A great number of antisocial compulsions present and become successfully treated in the early stages by the parents.

["Antisocial Tendency", p. 313]

For Winnicott, the aetiology of psychosis lies in the earliest failure of the environment during the time of absolute dependence. A failure at this time means that the mother has not been able to identify with her infant and therefore has not been in the state of primary maternal preoccupation that is required for the infant's strong development. But the roots of the antisocial tendency refer to the time *after* absolute dependency, when the failure occurs in the time of relative dependence. It is during this time of dependency needs that the infant is beginning to become aware of his dependency, and if he is let down, he will experience deprivation. When and if things change and he perceives a chance that he may recover the holding he misses, then he becomes hopeful. It is this hope that motivates the antisocial act. (*see* DEPENDENCE: 1, 2; AGGRESSION: 7)

5   *The hopeful moment*

Winnicott provides a list of what is happening to the infant or child at the moment of hope:

> In the hopeful moment the child:
> • Perceives a new setting that has some elements of reliability.
> • Experiences a drive that could be called object-seeking.
> • Recognizes the fact that ruthlessness is about to become a feature and so
> • Stirs up the immediate environment in an effort to make it alert to danger, and organized to tolerate nuisance.
>
> If the situation holds, the environment must be tested and retested in its capacity to stand the aggression, to prevent or repair the destruction, to tolerate the nuisance, to recognize the positive element in the antisocial tendency, to provide and preserve the object that is to be sought and found.
>
> In a favourable case . . . the favourable conditions may in the course of time enable the child to find and love a person, instead of continuing the search through laying claims on substitute objects that had lost their symbolic value.

In the next stage the child needs to be able to experience despair in a relationship, instead of hope alone. Beyond this is the real possibility of a life for the child. When the wardens and staff of a hostel carry a child through all the processes they have done a therapy that is surely comparable to analytic work.

["Antisocial Tendency", p. 314]

In 1957, 11 years after Winnicott had written "The Antisocial Tendency", he gave a paper entitled "Delinquency as a Sign of Hope", at the Borstal Assistant Governors' Conference. The stress in this paper, illustrating Winnicott's evolution of thought, is not so much about the search for the lost object, but about the *capacity to search,* and reach out. This capacity contains the conviction at a deep level that there is something that can be found. In terms of development this capacity is linked with the search for the sense of self. (*see* SELF: 11)

. . . it is necessary to see that we are talking about two aspects of this one thing, the antisocial tendency. I would like to relate one of these to the relationship between the small child and the mother and the other to the later development which is the child's relation to the father. The first one has to do with the fact that the mother in her adaptation to the small child's needs enables the child creatively to find objects. She initiates the creative use of the world. When this fails, the child has lost contact with objects, has lost the capacity creatively to find anything. At the moment of hope the child reaches out and steals an object. This is a compulsive act and the child does not know why he or she does it. Often the child feels mad because of having a compulsion to do something without knowing why. Naturally the fountain pen stolen from Woolworths is not satisfactory: it is not the object that was being sought, and in any case *the child is looking for the capacity to find,* not for an object.

["Delinquency as a Sign", pp. 92–93]

Winnicott warns that police investigation and punishment as ways of dealing with the young person will only exacerbate the problem, because the true communication will not have been heard. He argues for a dual response from society of both management and therapy. The young offender needs an appropriately safe and structured setting (management) as well as one-to-one treatment (psychotherapy). The therapy is an important part of the process of rehabilitation, because the antisocial act is an unconscious request from the adolescent or child to go back to a state *before* the moment of deprivation. The antisocial act signifies a potential reinstatement of something good.

> The question is what is this hope? What does the child hope to do? It is difficult to answer this question. The child, without knowing it, hopes to be able to take someone who will listen back to the moment of deprivation or to the phase in which deprivation became consolidated into an inescapable reality. The hope is that the boy or girl will be able to re-experience in relation to the person who is acting as psychotherapist the intense suffering that followed immediately the reaction to deprivation. The moment that the child has used the support that the therapist can give to reach back to the intense suffering of that fateful moment or period of time, there follows a memory of the time before the deprivation. In this way the child has reached back either to the lost capacity to find objects or to the lost security of the framework. The child has reached back to a creative relationship to external reality or to the period in which spontaneity was safe, even if it involved aggressive impulses. This time the reaching back has been done without stealing and without aggression, because it is something that happens automatically as a result of the child's arrival at what had previously been intolerable: the suffering reactive to the deprivation. By suffering I mean acute confusion, disintegration of the personality, falling forever, a loss of contact with the body, complete disorientation and other states of this nature. Once one has taken a child to this area and the child has come through to remember it and what went before, then one has no difficulty whatever in understanding why it is that antisocial children must spend their lives looking for help of this kind. They cannot get on with their own lives until someone has gone back with them and enabled them to remember by reliving the immediate result of the deprivation.
>
> ["Delinquency as a Sign", pp. 98–99]

In other words, the moment of deprivation must occur in the transference relationship. The therapist's ability to meet and match the moment of hope means that she (the therapist) is able to provide the holding environment that will eventually lead to the patient's ability to integrate.

6   The antisocial tendency and psychoanalysis

The concept of the antisocial tendency breaks new ground in the psychoanalytic theory of emotional development. Hitherto, Freud had attributed crime to an unconscious sense of guilt linked with the Oedipus complex: the criminal committed the crime to relieve the unbearable unconscious feelings of guilt—his sense of guilt was then attached to an external crime. The external crime (antisocial act) was therefore a distraction or enactment of the fantasied internal crime—parricide and/or incest. The relief came about from the enactment and subsequent punishment (Freud, 1916d).

As has been illustrated above, Winnicott stresses that the external environment plays a crucial role to the person who commits a crime, and that its aetiology is rooted in the early mother–infant relationship. Deprivation, for Winnicott, occurs as a result of the loss of the necessary ego-support to the infant at the time of relative dependence. The antisocial act

> . . . compels the environment to be important. The patient through unconscious drives compels someone to attend to management.
>
> ["Antisocial Tendency", p. 309]

Masud Khan, in his Introduction to *Through Paediatrics to Psychoanalysis* (W6), points out that for Freud "every symptom carries wish-fulfilment in it", whereas "Winnicott extends it further to show how every antisocial behaviour carries in it the statement of the unmet need at its source".

For Khan the importance of Winnicott's contribution of the concept of the antisocial tendency is its value regarding psychoanalytic patients. Khan came to realize that what he at first saw as resistance or negative therapeutic reaction in his patients could in fact be seen in a more positive light as a communication from the patient regarding his deprivation.

If the analyst is able to recognize the patient's deprivation and "meet and match the moment of hope", there is subsequently a chance that the patient will rediscover the good experience that had been lost to him.

The patient who displays a strong antisocial tendency in the analytic relationship has difficulty with symbolizing and is forced to enact his distress. If the analyst reads the antisocial act as the sign of hope, the patient's communication will be at last received, and there is a chance that the enactments will lead on to the patient's ability to symbolize and thus make use of the transitional space. (*see* TRANSITIONAL PHENOMENA)

REFERENCES

1946 Some Psychological Aspects of Juvenile Delinquency   [W13]
1948 Children's Hostels in War and Peace   [W13]
1956 The Antisocial Tendency   [W6]
1963 Morals and Education   [W9]
1967 Delinquency as a Sign of Hope   [W14]

Being (continuity of)

T he continuity of being may be described as a state or feeling
that comes about as a result of the infant's subjective experience of being merged with a good-enough mother. Winnicott
also describes this sense of "being" as the "centre of gravity", which
has to occur in the very early weeks of the infant's state of absolute
dependence and is only possible if the mother is in a state of primary
maternal preoccupation.

Being belongs to the true self and the inherited potential. Being is
linked with unintegration, which is the precursor of the ability to relax
and enjoy. The ability to "be" derives from the experience of a
holding environment at the very start. From the experience of "being"
can develop the capacity to "live creatively" and "play", which are
aspects of integration and lead on to doing.

Winnicott places the experience of "being" with the female
element—and he also states that, at the heart of being, culture is
located.

1   *The centre of gravity*

Winnicott's use of the word "being" and the phrase "continuity of being" developed during the last decade of his life and work. That is not to say that it was a new idea, but simply that he specifies and locates an internal subjectivity. This way of describing the state of being, inside the baby, brings an existential flavour to Winnicott's work, although this was not something that he wished to turn his theory into. As early as 1949, in a broadcast entitled "The Ordinary Devoted Mother", later published in 1966, Winnicott draws a distinction between his thoughts and existentialism:

> There is the beginning of everything, and it gives meaning to very simple words like *being*.
>
> We could use a Frenchified word *existing* and talk about existence, and we can make this into a philosophy and call it existentialism, but somehow or other we like to start with the word *being* and then with the statement *I am*. The important thing is that *I am* means nothing unless *I* at the beginning *am along with another human being* who has not yet been differentiated off. For this reason it is more true to talk about *being* than to use the words *I am*, which belong to the next stage. It cannot be overemphasized that being is the beginning of everything, without which *doing* and *being done to* have no significance.
>
> ["The Ordinary Devoted Mother", pp. 11–12]

Winnicott appears to dismiss the value of existential philosophy by placing his emphasis of existence on the early mother–infant relationship. Yet it is this "Frenchified" dimension of Winnicott's work that precisely extends and sometimes radically alters psychoanalytic theory (with its consequent ramifications for technique), and, whether Winnicott wished to or not, his theory of emotional development does make a significant contribution to philosophical areas of inquiry.

In a short paper presented to the British Psycho-Analytical Society in 1952, "Anxiety Associated with Insecurity", the heart of Winnicott's concept of "being" is presented. Being emanates from the notion of a "centre of gravity". Here is an important distinction between Winnicott's theory and Klein's. Where Klein said that object relations start from the beginning of life, Winnicott saw the beginning of object relations emerging out of the early weeks, where the mother and infant were as one—an environmental–individual set-up.

> What then precedes the first object relationship? For my own part I have had a long struggle with this problem. It started when I found myself saying in this Society (about ten years ago) and I said it rather excitedly and with heat: *"There is no such thing as a baby"*. I was alarmed to hear myself utter these words and tried to justify myself by pointing out that if you show me a baby you certainly show me also someone caring for the baby, or at least a pram with someone's eyes and ears glued to it. One sees a "nursing couple".

> In a quieter way today I would say that before object relationships the state of affairs is this: that the unit is not the individual, the unit is an environment–individual set-up. The centre of gravity of the being does not start off in the individual. It is in the total set-up. By good-enough child care, technique, holding, and general management the shell becomes gradually taken over and the kernel (which has looked all the time like a human baby to us) can begin to be an individual. The beginning is potentially terrible because of the anxieties I have mentioned and because of the paranoid state that follows closely on the first integration, and also on the first instinctual moments, bringing to the baby, as they do, a quite new meaning to object relationships. The good-enough infant care technique neutralizes the external persecutions, and prevents the feelings of disintegration and loss of contact between psyche and soma.

> In other words, without a good-enough technique of infant care the new human being has no chance whatever. With a good-enough technique the centre of gravity of being in the environment–individual set-up can afford to lodge in the centre, in the kernel rather than in the shell. The human being now developing an entity from the centre can become localized in the baby's body and so can begin to create an external world at the same time as acquiring a limiting membrane and an inside. According to this theory there was no external world at the beginning although we as observers could see an infant in an environment.

> ["Anxiety Associated with Insecurity", pp. 99–100]

Primary narcissism, like many Freudian terms, changes its emphasis and meaning according to the writer's interpretation and use of its theory. Winnicott uses the term infrequently, but when he does he is referring to the early states of mother and infant before object relations exist.

The mother who is in a state of primary maternal preoccupation is taken over by a preoccupation with her infant, because of her intense identification with his predicament. This enables her to provide a psychological as well as physical protection for her baby. (*see* PRIMARY MATERNAL PREOCCUPATION: 1, 2, 3, 4)

Merging, for Winnicott, means that both mother and infant are as one, although the healthy mother has an awareness of herself and on behalf of her infant (*see* EGO: 4). The merging state for the infant means that he is not yet able to distinguish between Me and Not-me. He sees his mother's face and believes her face to be his. This state of reverie between mother and infant is linked with Winnicott's theories of mutuality, the necessity of illusion, and communicating with subjective objects. (*see* COMMUNICATION: 9, DEPENDENCE: 9, MOTHER: 4, SELF: 3)

Early on, Winnicott describes the state of "being" as a state of unintegration and describes what he means in some notes written in 1948, in preparation for a talk.

> . . . in the quiet moments let us say that there is no line but just lots of things they separate out, sky seen through trees, something to do with mother's eyes all going in and out, wandering round. Some lack of need for any integration. . . . That is an extremely valuable thing to be able to retain. Miss something without it. Something to do with being calm, restful, relaxed and feeling one with people and things when no excitement is around.
>
> [quoted in Davis & Wallbridge, 1981, p. 39]

The ability to relax and surrender in this way will depend entirely on an environment—mother's arms, which can absolutely be trusted in. The ability to unintegrate and relax is paradoxically a sign of integration and maturity. (*see* ALONE: 2)

In 1960, the accumulation of Winnicott's work with babies and their mothers results in his paper, "The Theory of the Parent–Infant Relationship." In this he focuses on the crucial aspects of the effect of a good-enough environment on the continuity-of-being in the infant. Winnicott elaborates on details of parental care and how they contribute to the infant's realization of his sense of well-being. (*see* HOLDING: 4; SELF: 5)

> With "the care it receives from its mother" each infant is able to have a personal existence, and so begins to build up what might be called a *continuity of being*. On the basis of this continuity of being the inherited potential gradually develops into an individual infant. If maternal care is not good enough then the infant does not really come into existence, since there is no continuity of being; instead the personality becomes built on the basis of reactions to environmental impingement.
> ["Parent–Infant Relationship", p. 54]

A life built on the cumulative effect of reactions to impingement results in false-self living, which is no life at all. (*see* SELF: 7)

However, there is a healthy false self that exists in order to protect the core/true self.

2   The true incommunicado self

Winnicott assumes the existence of a core self from the beginning of life. This core self can only come into being in an authentic and alive way if it is *protected* and allowed to remain *isolated*. This notion of the isolate self is one that Winnicott starts to explore in his paper, "The Theory of the Parent–Infant Relationship".

> Another phenomenon that needs consideration at this phase is the hiding of the core of the personality. Let us examine the concept of a central or true self. The central self could be said to be the inherited potential which is experiencing a continuity of being, and acquiring in its own way and at its own speed a personal psychic reality and a personal body-scheme. It seems necessary to allow for the concept of the isolation of this central self as a characteristic of health. Any threat to this isolation of the true self constitutes a major anxiety at this early stage, and defences of earliest infancy appear in relation to failures on the part of the mother (or in maternal care) to ward off impingements which might disturb this isolation.
> ["Parent–Infant Relationship", p. 46]

The theme of the isolate aspect of the true self is elaborated by Winnicott in 1963, in one of his greatest papers: "Communicating and Not Communicating Leading to a Study of Certain Opposites". (*see* COMMUNICATION: 12)

> I am putting forward and stressing the importance of the idea of the *permanent isolation of the individual* and claiming that at the core of the individual there is no communication with the not-me world either. . . .
>
> This theme of the individual as an isolate has its importance in the study of infancy and of psychosis, but it also has importance in the study of adolescence. The boy and girl at puberty can be described in many ways, and one way concerns *the adolescent as an isolate*. This preservation of personal isolation is part of the search for identity, and for the establishment of a personal technique for communicating which does not lead to violation of the central self. This may be one reason why adolescents on the whole eschew psychoanalytic treatment, though they are interested in psychoanalytic theories. They feel that by psychoanalysis they will be raped, not sexually but spiritually. In practice the analyst can avoid confirming the adolescent's fears in this respect, but the analyst of an adolescent must expect to be tested out fully and must be prepared to use communication of indirect kind, and to recognize simple non-communication.
>
> ["Communicating and Not Communicating", p. 190]

Earlier on in this paper, Winnicott postulates that society's fear of psychoanalysis is associated with the violation of the self.

> We can understand the hatred people have of psychoanalysis which has penetrated a long way into the human personality, and which provides a threat to the human individual in his need to be secretly isolated. The question is: how to be isolated without having to be insulated?
>
> ["Communicating and Not Communicating", p. 187]

This paradoxical and important question is linked with the themes of violation of the self and withdrawal states. (*see* ALONE: 3)

Respect and appreciation for the patient's need *not* to communicate is a radical notion in psychoanalysis where the tradition has been for the patient to talk about *everything*.

3   Creative apperception

Creative apperception is the name Winnicott gives to the infant's subjective experience, from the beginning, of his mother and his environment.

> It is creative apperception more than anything else that makes the individual feel that life is worth living. Contrasted with this is a relationship to external reality which is one of compliance, the world and its details being recognized but only as something to be fitted in with or demanding adaptation.
>
> ["Creativity and Its Origins", 1971, p. 65]

The infant who develops from the centre of gravity and therefore is lodged in the kernel (his own sense of self) as opposed to the shell (his mother's narcissistic need for herself to be seen) is able to apperceive creatively. It is this and only this that leads to a sense of self and of feeling real. This sense lends meaning to life and makes living worth while. It is this that most preoccupied Winnicott during his last decade. (*see* CREATIVITY: 6 SELF: 11)

For Winnicott, there is a sequence from apperception to perception. The baby, if he could, would say:

> When I look I am seen, so I exist.
> I can now afford to look and see.
> I now look creatively and what I apperceive I also perceive.
> In fact I take care not to see what is not there to be seen (unless I am tired).
>
> ["Mirror-Role of Mother and Family
> in Child Development", 1971, p. 114]

The crucial sentence here in terms of "being" is "When I look I am seen, so I exist". The infant depends on being seen (needs adapted to) by mother in order to feel alive. Looking and being seen are the focus of primary identification. From the sense-of-being and being-seen emerges a space in which to dream and to play. (*see* CREATIVITY: 1; MOTHER: 4, 9; PLAYING: 1; TRANSITIONAL PHENOMENA: 5)

Winnicott's above sequence relates to the process in the healthy individual that overlaps with silent communicating and relating to subjective objects. This sort of self-relationship establishes and enriches the sense of feeling real. (*see* COMMUNICATION: 4, 9)

4   *Being and the female element*

In one paper, "Creativity and its Origins"—a combination of two papers written within the last few years of his life—Winnicott refers to "male and female elements". He places "doing" with the male element and "being" with the female element. In this way, his theory of emotional development includes the crucial nature of the father and the third area. (*see* TRANSITIONAL PHENOMENA: 7)

> I wish to say that the element that I am calling "male" does traffic in terms of active relating or passive being related to. . . . My suggestion is that, by contrast, the pure female element relates to the breast (or to the mother) in the sense of the *baby becoming the breast (or mother), in the sense that the object is the subject.* . . . Here in this relatedness of pure female element to "breast" is a practical application of the idea of the subjective object, and the experience of this paves the way for the objective subject—that is, the idea of a self, and the feeling of real that springs from the sense of having an identity.
>
> However complex the psychology of the sense of self and of the establishment of an identity eventually becomes as a baby grows, *no sense of self emerges except on the basis of this relating in the sense of* BEING. This sense of being is something that antedates the idea of being-at-one-with, because there has not yet been anything else except identity. Two separate persons can *feel* at one, but here at the place that I am examining the baby and the object *are* one. The term primary identification has perhaps been used for just this that I am describing and I am trying to show how vitally important this first experience is for the initiation of all subsequent experiences of identification.
>
> Projective and introjective identifications both stem from this place where each is the same as the other.
>
> ["Creativity and Its Origins", pp. 79–80]

And what was once, in the 1950s, called ego-relatedness is now termed "object-relating", at the centre of which is *being:*

> In the growth of the human baby, as the ego begins to organize, this that I am calling the object-relating of the pure female element establishes what is perhaps the simplest of all experiences, the experience of *being.* Here one finds a true continuity

of generations, being which is passed on from one generation
to another, via the female element of men and women and of
male and female infants. ... It is a matter of the female elements in both males and females.

[*"Creativity and Its Origins"*, p. 80]

Winnicott points out that psychoanalysis has neglected this aspect
of what he calls the female element—the capacity to be.

Psychoanalysts have perhaps given special attention to this
male element or drive aspect of object-relating, and yet have
neglected the subject–object identity to which I am drawing
attention here, which is at the basis of the capacity to be.
The male element *does* while the female element *is*. Here
would come in those males in Greek myth who tried to be at
one with the supreme goddess. Here also is a way of stating
a male person's very deeply-seated envy of women whose
female element men take for granted, sometimes in error.

[*"Creativity and Its Origins"*, p. 81]

This last sentence relates to Winnicott's thesis of WOMAN. Envy
of women based on a fantasy that they possess the female element
is linked with the "fear of WOMAN". The fear of WOMAN, which
may exist in men as well as women, is due to the unacknowledged
fact that we were all once absolutely dependent on a woman. (*see*
DEPENDENCE: 2, 3, 4)

Whilst Winnicott berates psychoanalysis for not paying attention to the female element, at the same time he fails to
acknowledge that his distinction of male and female elements is
parallel to Jung's original ideas of Eros and Logos. Jung asserts
that both can coexist in a single individual of either sex, and Eros
is attributed to the female and denotes the psychic principle of
relatedness, whereas Logos, attributed to the male, is seen as dynamic and describes the psychic principle of differentiation.

A discussion of the female element is impossible, for Winnicott, without reference to a good-enough mother, who is able to
offer a facilitating environment.

I now return to the consideration of the very early stage in
which the pattern is being laid down by the manner in which
the mother in subtle ways handles her infant. I must refer in
detail to this very special example of the environmental fac-

tor. Either the mother has a breast that *is*, so that the baby can also *be* when the baby and mother are not yet separated out in the infant's rudimentary mind; or else the mother is incapable of making this contribution, in which case the baby has to develop without the capacity to be, or with a crippled capacity to be.

["Creativity and Its Origins", p. 81–82]

In a message clearly directed at the Kleinians, who believe that envy is innate, Winnicott wishes to stress his long-standing theoretical disagreement with Melanie Klein and to point out that envy arises out of a *failure* of the environment. The experience of a tantalizing mother—sometimes good, sometimes bad, but never good enough—is the worst mother of all. (*see* MOTHER: 12)

The mother who is able to do this very subtle thing that I am referring to does not produce a child whose "pure female" self is envious of the breast, since for this child the breast is the self and the self is the breast. Envy is a term that might become applicable in the experience of a tantalizing failure of the breast as something that IS.

["Creativity and Its Origins", pp. 81–82]

Object-relating (ego-relatedness) in terms of the pure female element is nothing to do with instinct or drive.

The study of the pure distilled uncontaminated female element leads us to BEING, and this forms the only basis for self discovery and a sense of existing (and then on to the capacity to develop an inside, to be a container, to have a capacity to use the mechanisms of projection and introjection and to relate to the world in terms of introjection and projection).

["Creativity and Its Origins", p. 82]

5   *What life is all about*

Winnicott does not seem to be able to emphasize enough that *being* is at the centre of any subsequent experience in life. In fact if the individual has not had the opportunity to simply *be*, his future does not augur well in terms of the emotional quality of his life. The likelihood is that this individual will feel empty.

> ... I find that the characteristic of the female element in the
> context of object-relating is identity, giving the child the basis
> for being, and then, later on, a basis for a sense of self. But I
> find that it is here, in the absolute dependence on maternal
> provision of that special quality by which the mother meets or
> fails to meet the earliest functioning of the female element,
> that we may seek the foundation for the experience of being.
> ... Now I want to say: "After being—doing and being done
> to. But first, being".
>
> ["Creativity and Its Origins", pp. 84–85]

The ability to *do*, therefore, is based on the capacity to *be*. The search
and discovery of the sense of self, in the context of therapy, is all to
do with finding an identity.

In 1967, Winnicott poses a question—one that would have
been more familiar to philosophers than to psychoanalysts—in his
paper, "The Location of Cultural Experience":

> We have to tackle the question of *what life itself is about*. Our
> psychotic patients force us to give attention to this sort of
> basic problem. ... When one speaks of a man one speaks of
> him *along with* the summation of his cultural experiences. The
> whole forms a unit.
>
> I have used the term cultural experience as an extension of
> the idea of transitional phenomena and of play without being
> certain that I can define the word "culture". The accent indeed
> is on experience. In using the word culture I am thinking of
> the inherited tradition. I am thinking of something that is in
> the common pool of humanity, into which individuals and
> groups of people may contribute, and from which we may all
> draw *if we have somewhere to put what we find*.
>
> ["Location of Cultural Experience", pp. 98–99]

For Winnicott, culture belongs to the very heart of the merged
experience of mother and infant at the beginning, *along with and
including* the fact of contingency—the context in which the mother
finds herself. (*see* CREATIVITY: 3)

But, the infant who does *not* have the experience of a good-
enough mother is prevented from developing and discovering the
capacity to be. This is the infant who will experience what Winnicott refers to as unthinkable anxiety, primitive agonies, and
annihilation. (*see* ENVIRONMENT: 6)

Anxiety in these early stages of the parent–infant relationship relates to the threat of annihilation, and it is necessary to explain what is meant by this term.

In this place which is characterized by the essential existence of a holding environment, the "inherited potential" is becoming itself a "continuity of being". The alternative to being is reacting, and reacting interrupts being and annihilates. Being and annihilation are the two alternatives. The holding environment therefore has as its main function the reduction to a minimum of impingements to which the infant must react with resultant annihilation of personal being. Under favourable conditions the infant establishes a continuity of existence and then begins to develop the sophistications which make it possible for impingements to be gathered into the area of omnipotence.

["Parent–Infant Relationship", p. 47]

Here again a spectrum can be implied. At one end there is being, which is related to health and integration and an ability to be, subsequent to doing; at the other end are the primitive agonies, where there is only crude reacting and an inability to distinguish between inside and outside, Me and Not-me. In this case, there is always a chance that psychotherapy will facilitate the regression necessary to discover the centre of gravity within the transference relationship from which to begin to be. (*see* SELF: 11)

REFERENCES

1952 Anxiety Associated with Insecurity   [W6]
1960 The Theory of the Parent–Infant Relationship   [W9]
1963 Communicating and Not Communicating Leading to a Study of Certain Opposites   [W9]
1966 The Ordinary Devoted Mother   [W16]
1967 The Location of Cultural Experience   [W10]
1971 Creativity and Its Origins   [W10]
1971 Mirror-Role of Mother and Family in Child Development [W10]

Communication

*C*ommunication, according to Winnicott, starts with the transmission of feeling states between mother and infant— mutuality. The mother's feelings about her unborn infant begin imaginatively in her being from babyhood. The infant senses his mother's feelings towards him from the womb.

Winnicott differentiates between certain qualities of communication that vary according to each stage of the infant's development.

At the heart of Winnicott's theory of communication is the paradoxical notion of an incommunicado/isolate self that is non-communicating. It must never be communicated with; if, however, communication starts to "seep through", a violation occurs, and the individual must set up a defence system to seal and protect the core/ true self.

1   Non-verbal symbolization

It was in the last decade of his life that Winnicott explored the meaning of communication, which added to and elaborated on many areas of his work—early mother–infant relationship, object-

69

relating, the transition from subjectively perceived objects to objectively perceived objects, and the creative communication of the
transitional area. (*see* BEING: 2, 3; CREATIVITY: 2, 3; HOLDING: 4; MOTHER:
12; PRIMARY MATERNAL PREOCCUPATION: 2)

With the focus on unconscious communication, Winnicott considers that the ability to communicate does not rely, initially, on
language acquisition, but on a preverbal interaction through "mutuality". Therefore, the infant's ability to play and symbolize *precedes*
the time he begins to use words.

> . . . the mother may or may not talk to her baby; it doesn't
> matter, the language is not important.
>
> Just here you will want me to say something about the
> inflections that characterize speech, even at its most sophisti-
> cated. An analyst is at work, as it is called, and the patient is
> verbalizing and the analyst is interpreting. It is not just a mat-
> ter of verbal communication. The analyst feels that a trend in
> the patient's material that is being presented calls for verbali-
> sation. Much depends on the way the analyst uses the word,
> and therefore on the attitude that is at the back of the interpre-
> tation. A patient dug her nails into the skin of my hand at a
> moment of intense feeling. My interpretation was: "Ow!" This
> scarcely involved my intellectual equipment at all, and it was
> quite useful because it came *immediately* (not after a pause for
> reflection) and because it meant to the patient that my hand
> was alive, that it was part of me, and that I was there to be
> used. Or, shall I say, I can be used if I survive.
>
> ["Communication between Infant and Mother, and Mother
> and Infant", Compared and Contrasted", p. 95]

By the time his paper, "Communication between Infant and
Mother, Mother and Infant, Compared and Contrasted", was written in 1968, Winnicott had arrived at his theory of the use of an
object, presented in the same year. Object-usage comes about from
the survival of the object. (*see* AGGRESSION: 10)

The ironic tone of this paper will not go unnoticed, along with
another radical notion for psychoanalysis. It is not that words are
unimportant—rather, that they may sometimes be irrelevant.

> Although psychoanalysis of suitable subjects is based on
> verbalization, nevertheless every analyst knows that along

with the content of interpretations the attitude is reflected in
the nuances and in the timing and in a thousand ways that
compare with the infinite variety of poetry.

["Communication between Infant and Mother", p. 95]

Keats points out that poetry, like medicine, is healing. Winnicott
values the *way in which* meaning is conveyed in the analytic session:

> For instance, the non-moralistic approach, which is basic to
> psychotherapy and to social work, is communicated not in
> words, but in the non-moralistic quality in the worker. It's the
> positive of the music-hall song whose refrain goes: "It's not
> exactly what she says, it's the nasty way she says it".
>
> In terms of baby-care, the mother who feels like it can dis-
> play a moralistic attitude long before words like "wicked"
> make sense to the baby. She may enjoy saying: "Damn you,
> you little bugger" in a nice way, so that she feels better
> and the baby smiles back, pleased to be burbled at. Or, more
> subtly still, what about: "Hushabye baby on the tree tops,"
> which isn't very nice verbally, but forms a quite sweet lullaby?
>
> ["Communication between Infant and Mother", p. 96]

It was in 1947 that Winnicott, in his paper, "Hate in the Countertransference", observed that each mother hated her baby from the
start, and he provided a list of 18 reasons for this. His thesis of
hate includes the necessity of the baby's subjective experience of
his mother's hate as well as her love. (*see* HATE: 6)

> It is even possible for a mother to show her baby, who has no
> language yet, that she means: "God will strike you dead if
> you mess yourself when I've just cleaned you up" or the quite
> different: "You can't do that there 'ere!" which involves a
> direct confrontation of wills and personalities.
>
> ["Communication between Infant and Mother", pp. 95–96]

2 The experience of mutuality

Primary maternal preoccupation—the tuning-in to her infant of
the good-enough mother—came to be referred to by Winnicott
as "mutuality"—it is akin to Daniel Stern's work on affect "attune-

ment" (Stern, 1985). For Winnicott, mutuality belongs to preverbal communication:

> From birth a baby can be seen to take food. Let us say that the baby finds the breast and sucks and ingests a quantity suffi- cient for satisfaction of instinct and for growth. This can be the same whether the baby has a brain that will one day develop as a good one or whether the baby's brain is in fact defective or damaged. What we need to know about is the communication that goes or does not go with the feeding process. It is difficult to be sure of such matters by the instrument of infant-observa- tion, though it does seem that some babies watch the mother's face in a meaningful way even in the first weeks. At 12 weeks, however, babies can give us information from which we can do more than guess that communication is a fact.

ILLUSTRATION 1

Although normal babies vary considerably in their rate of development (especially as measured by observable phenom- ena), it can be said that at 12 weeks they are capable of play such as this: Settled in for a (breast) feed, the baby looks at the mother's face and his or her hand reaches up so that in play the baby is feeding the mother by means of a finger in her mouth.

It may be that the mother has played a part in the establish- ment of this play detail, but even though this is true it does not invalidate the conclusion that I draw from the fact that this kind of playing can happen.

I draw the conclusion from this that, whereas all babies take in food, there does not exist a communication between the baby and the mother except in so far as there develops a mutual feeding situation. The baby feeds and the baby's expe- rience includes the idea that the mother knows what it is like to be fed.

If this happens for all to see at 12 weeks, then in some way or other it can (but need not) be true in some obscure way at an earlier date.

["The Mother–Infant Experience of Mutuality", 1969, p. 255]

So, the unconscious communication and feeling states between mother and infant are intrinsically linked with the mother's ability to identify with her baby (to merge). The baby whose mother is involved in this intense identification with him benefits from the experience of feeling understood. (*see* BEING: 3)

Winnicott suggests that the experience of mutuality is dependent on both mother, for her identification with infant, and infant, for his inner potential to grow. For the baby, this constitutes an achievement.

> In this way we actually witness a *mutuality* which is the beginning of a communication between two people; this (in the baby) is a developmental achievement, one that is dependent on the baby's inherited processes leading toward emotional growth and likewise dependent on the mother and her attitude and her capacity to make real what the baby is ready to reach out for, to discover, to create.
>
> ["Mother–Infant Experience", p. 255]

If the baby is to develop well, he really does depend on a mother who will facilitate his capacity to create the world. (*see* CREATIVITY: 2)

At this point, Winnicott links his comments in a footnote to Sechehaye's work on "symbolic realization"—"which means enabling a real thing to become a meaningful symbol of mutuality in a specialized setting" ("Mother–Infant Experience", p. 255). This work needs to be carried out for the patient who has been deprived of the experience of creating the world because of an early environmental failure. (*see* ENVIRONMENT: 3, 4; SELF: 8)

Winnicott goes on to explore the different individual experience in mother and baby in their mutual task of communication on a variety of levels.

> At this point it is necessary to interpolate a reference to the obvious fact that the mother and the baby come to the point of mutuality in different ways. The mother has been a cared-for baby; also she has played at babies and at mothers; she has perhaps experienced the arrival of siblings, cared for younger babies in her own family or in other families; and she has perhaps learned or read about baby care and she may have strong views of her own on what is right and wrong in baby management.
>
> The baby, on the other hand, is being a baby for the first time, has never been a mother, and has certainly received no instruction. The only passport the baby brings to the customs

barrier is the sum of the inherited features and inborn tendencies toward growth and development.

Consequently, whereas the mother can identify with the
baby, even with a baby unborn or in process of being born,
and in a highly sophisticated way, the baby brings to the
situation only a developing capacity to achieve cross-identifications in the experience of mutuality that is made a fact. This
mutuality belongs to the mother's capacity to adapt to the
baby's needs.

["Mother–Infant Experience", p. 256]

"Cross-identifications" is a term Winnicott uses in his later
years. It appears in three papers published in *Playing and Reality*
(W10)—"Creativity and Its Origins", "Contemporary Concepts of
Adolescent Development and Their Implications for Higher Education", and "Interrelating apart from Instinctual Drive and in
Terms of Cross-identifications"—as well in some posthumously
published papers in *Psycho-Analytic Explorations* (W19). The term
basically refers to the ability to tune in and empathize with the
other. (*see* CREATIVITY: 7)

To this last sentence—"This mutuality belongs to the mother's
capacity to adapt to the baby's needs"—Winnicott adds a footnote:

The word "need" has significance here just as "drive" has
significance in the area of satisfaction of instinct. The word
"wish" is out of place as it belongs to sophistication that is not
to be assumed at this stage of immaturity that is under consideration.

["Mother–Infant Experience", p. 256]

This differentiation of "needs" and "wishes" is linked to the relevant phases of emotional development and applies particularly
to psychoanalytic work carried out with regressed patients and
those who regress to dependency during analysis. (*see* DEPENDENCE:
1, 4; REGRESSION: 9)

Following on from here, Winnicott wishes to "enter the deep
waters of mutuality that does not directly relate to drives or to
instinct tension". He is alluding to two distinct types of mutuality,
one belonging to need and the other to wishes. Mutuality without
instinct-tension belongs to the patient's needs and to the area of
"regression to dependence":

Like so much of what we know of these very early babyhood experiences, this example derives from the work that has to be done in the analysis of older children or of adults when the patient is in a phase, long or short, in which regression to dependence is the main characteristic of the transference. Work of this kind always has two aspects, the first being the positive discovery in the transference of early types of experience that were missed out or distorted in the patient's own historical past, in the very early relationship to the mother; and the second being the patient's use of the therapist's failures in technique. These failures produce anger, and this has value because the anger brings the past into the present. At the time of the initial failure (or relative failure) the baby's ego-organisation was not organised sufficiently for so complex a matter as anger about a specific matter.

["Mother–Infant Experience", p. 257]

This component of the analyst's mistakes and failures needing to take place in the transference is explored further by Winnicott in 1963 in his paper, "Dependence in Infant-Care, in Child-Care, and in the Psycho-Analytic Setting". (*see* DEPENDENCE: 7)

3   *The controversy of touching patients during treatment*

In the clinical examples given in Winnicott's 1969 paper, "The Mother–Infant Experience of Mutuality", he makes quite a specific criticism of the "analyst with a rigid analytic morality that does not allow touch". Winnicott points out the importance of touch in those cases where the patient's mother had continually failed her infant at a crucial moment of development:

ILLUSTRATION 3

This example is taken from the analysis of a woman of 40 years (married, two children) who had failed to make full recovery in a six-year analysis with a woman colleague. I agreed with my colleague to see what analysis with a man might produce, and so started a second treatment.

The detail I have chosen for description has to do with the absolute need this patient had, from time to time, to be in contact with me. (She had feared to make this step with a woman analyst because of the homosexual implications).

A variety of intimacies were tried out, chiefly those that belong to infant feeding and management. There were violent episodes. Eventually it came about that she and I were together with her head in my hands.

Without deliberate action on the part of either of us there developed a rocking rhythm. The rhythm was rather a rapid one, about 70 per minute (c.f. heart beat), and I had to do some work to adapt to this rate. Nevertheless, there we were with *mutuality* expressed in terms of a slight but persistent rocking movement. We were *communicating* with each other without words. This was taking place at a level of development that did not require the patient to have maturity in advance of that which she found herself possessing in the regression to dependence of the phase of her analysis.

This experience, often repeated, was crucial to the therapy, and the violence that had led up to it was only now seen to be a preparation and a complex test of the analyst's capacity to meet the various communicating techniques of early infancy.

This shared rocking experience illustrates what I wish to refer to in the early stages of baby care. The baby's instinctual drives are not specifically involved. The main thing is a communication between the baby and the mother in terms of the anatomy and physiology of live bodies. The subject can easily be elaborated, and the significant phenomena will be the crude evidences of life, such as the heartbeat, breathing movements, breath warmth, movements that indicate a need for change of position, etc.

["Mother–Infant Experience", p. 258]

It is as if Winnicott becomes, in this interaction with his patient, a midwife who facilitates the mother's pushing and the baby's movement forward.

However, this emphasis on touch is an area of controversy amongst clinicians working in the analytic tradition. Some say that *any* form of touch is too sexually arousing for the patient. But there are many others who have been working out how to adapt the technique particularly for the patient who is regressed or becomes regressed in the transference relationship.

The difficulties related to whether or not the analyst should touch the patient in the therapeutic hour are illustrated in two papers of leading psychoanalysts of the Independent tradition: Jonathan Pedder and Patrick Casement. In his 1976 paper, Pedder explains why he decided that touch was the most appropriate intervention for his patient, and Casement, in his 1982 paper, explains why he resisted the patient's request to hold her hand.

In 1969, like many clinicians working with extremely deprived and regressed patients, Winnicott believed he was adapting to a need, and therefore in the case cited in the 1969 paper he chose to touch his patient in a way that seemed to him most appropriate. His attitude to touching patients was criticized in some quarters of the analytic world; it is still open to debate whether or not this may be the right kind of technique for certain patients. (*see* REGRESSION: 9)

4   Two categories of babies

Winnicott makes reference to two categories of babies—those who have experienced a reliable environment and those who have not. The babies who know about reliability receive a "silent" communication from their mothers' holding, and the babies whose mothers are not able to hold them receive a traumatic communication that constitutes a "gross impingement". (*see* ENVIRONMENT: 7)

> I have tried elsewhere to develop the theme of the developmental processes in the babies that need, for their becoming actual, the mother's holding. The "silent" communication is one of reliability which, in fact, protects the baby from *automatic reactions* to impingement from external reality, these reactions breaking the baby's line of life and constituting traumata. A trauma is that against which an individual has no organised defence so that a confusional state supervenes, followed perhaps by a re-organisation of defences, defences of a more primitive kind than those which were good enough before the occurrence of the trauma.
>
> Examination of the baby being held shows that communication is either silent (reliability taken for granted) or else traumatic (producing the experience of unthinkable or archaic anxiety).

   This divides the world of babies into two categories:

1. Babies who have not been significantly "let down" in infancy, and whose belief in reliability leads towards the acquisition of a personal reliability which is an important ingredient of the state which may be termed "towards independence". These babies have a line of life and retain a capacity to move forward and backward (developmentally) and become able to take all the risks because of being well insured.

2. Babies who have been significantly "let down" once or in a pattern of environmental failures (related to the psychopathologic state of the mother or mother-substitute). These babies carry with them the experience of unthinkable or archaic anxiety. They know what it is to be in a state of acute confusion or the agony of disintegration. They know what it is like to be dropped, to fall forever, or to become split into psychosomatic disunion.

   In other words, they have experienced trauma, and their personalities have to be built round the re-organisation of defences following traumata, defences that must needs retain primitive features such as personality splitting.

                              ["Mother–Infant Experience", pp. 259–260]

This "splitting" refers to the defensive splitting of the true and false self. The "silent communications" of the isolated core self presented in Winnicott's 1963 paper, "Communicating and Not Communicating Leading to a Study of Certain Opposites", refer to the *necessary* splitting that is characteristic of healthy babies of the first category. For these babies, there is a choice between communicating and the right *not* to communicate that relates to the pathological split of the babies who have suffered violation of the self and as a consequence are limited in choice. (*see* COMMUNICATION: 10)

5   *To communicate or not to communicate*

Winnicott's central statement on communication is that every individual is an isolate, and therefore the right not to communicate must be respected. This point is based on one of Winnicott's famous paradoxes—"It is a joy to be hidden and disaster not to be found" ("Communicating and Not Communicating", p. 186).

The paper, "Communicating and Not Communicating Leading to a Study of Certain Opposites", was presented in 1963, when Winnicott was 67. It marked his final preoccupations, the fruit of forty years of his emotional investigation, observation, and analysis of the mother–infant relationship and its use as a paradigm for the analyst–analysand relationship.

The extension and elaboration of the themes pertinent to that most crucial of all relationships of the individual at the beginning of life opens out into the topic of the individual's self-communication and the necessity for an "incommunicado", private, secret self. It is this secret self that not only has the right *not* to communicate but, essentially, "it must never be communicated with or be influenced by external reality" ("Communicating and Not Communicating", p. 187).

Winnicott begins this 1963 paper by quoting a line from Keats: "Every point of thought is the centre of an intellectual world", and he states that his paper "contains only one idea". This one idea is hinted at in the second paragraph and clearly relates to Winnicott's present subjective experience.

> Starting from no fixed place I soon came, while preparing this paper . . . to staking a claim, to my surprise, to the right not to communicate. This was a protest from the very core of me to the frightening fantasy of being infinitely exploited. In another language this would be the fantasy of being swallowed up. In the language of this paper it is the *fantasy of being found*.
> ["Communicating and Not Communicating", p. 179]

Subsequently, in order to explore the theme of the right not to communicate, Winnicott makes reference to the early stages of emotional development, revisiting his formulations on object-relating (hitherto ego-relatedness). This provides him with the opportunity of re-presenting the notion of the infant creating the object. This was written still five years before his presentation of "The Use of an Object and Relating Through Identifications", in which he was to examine the journey from object-relating to object-usage. (*see* AGGRESSION: 10)

> The infant experiencing omnipotence under the aegis of the facilitating environment *creates and re-creates the object*, and the

process gradually becomes built in, and gathers a memory backing.

Undoubtedly that which eventually becomes the intellect does affect the immature individual's capacity to make this very difficult transition from relating to subjective objects to relating to objects objectively perceived. . . .

In health the infant creates what is in fact lying around waiting to be found. But in health *the object is created, not found*. This fascinating aspect of normal object-relating has been studied by me in various papers, including the one on "Transitional Objects and Transitional Phenomena" (1951). A good object is no good to the infant unless created by the infant. Shall I say, created out of need? Yet the object must be found in order to be created. This has to be accepted as a paradox. . . .

["Communication between Infant and Mother", pp. 180–181]

The force of aggression in the infant needs to be responded to by the environment—mother, extended family, and society—in a non-retaliatory way. It is this response that will determine the infant's ability to arrive at a stage of emotional maturity and to distinguish between Me and Not-me. (*see* AGGRESSION: 5)

The two trends in communicating and not communicating Winnicott sees as a dilemma, particularly for the artist.

In the artist of all kinds I think one can detect an inherent dilemma, which belongs to the co-existence of two trends, the urgent need to communicate and the still more urgent need not to be found.

["Communication between Infant and Mother", p. 185]

This heartfelt sentence no doubt relates to Winnicott's personal dilemma as writer and communicator.

6   The function of dissatisfaction

In order to arrive at the ability to distinguish between Me and Not-me, the infant has to achieve a developmental task in terms of perception. Winnicott refers to two types of perception, one subjective, the other objective. The subjectively perceived object refers to the time when the infant believes that what he sees when he looks at his mother's face is himself (that's Me). As he becomes aware of the difference between his own body and external objects (that's Not-me), so he starts to perceive objectively.

However, to make the journey from perceiving subjective objects (that's Me) to objects objectively perceived (that's Not-me) a bridge—a period between the two perceptions—is required. So, before arriving at the stage of being able to perceive the world objectively, the sense of omnipotence (I created this object out of my need, therefore I am God) needs to have been established (*see* MOTHER: 8). One crucial aspect of this in-between stage is the experience of dissatisfaction:

> There is another point that has importance if one considers the location of the object. The change of the object from "subjective" to "objectively perceived" is jogged along less effectually by satisfactions than by dissatisfactions. The satisfaction to be derived from a feed has less value in this respect of the establishment of object-relating than when the object is, so to speak, in the way. Instinct-gratification gives the infant a personal experience and *does but little to the position of the object*; I have had a case in which satisfaction eliminated the object for an adult schizoid patient, so that he could not lie on the couch, this reproducing for him the situation of the infantile satisfactions that eliminated external reality or the externality of objects. I have put this in another way, saying that the infant feels "fobbed off" by a satisfactory feed, and it can be found that a nursing mother's anxiety can be based on the fear that if the infant is not satisfied then the mother will be attacked and destroyed. After a feed the satisfied infant is not dangerous for a few hours. . . .
>
> Per contra, the infant's experienced aggression, that which belongs to muscle erotism, to movement, and to irresistible forces meeting immovable objects, this aggression, and the ideas bound up with it, lends itself to the process of placing the object, to placing the object separate from the self, in so far as the self has begun to emerge as an entity.
>
> ["Communicating and Not Communicating", p. 181]

The infant has to have a sense that it was due to his effort—his energetic sucking—that he received the milk (created the object). This kind of satisfaction leads on to the sense of feeling real, rather

than the kind of satisfaction that occurs *without* his effort, which is
a fobbing-off satisfaction.

The function of the type of dissatisfaction that enables the infant
to develop a sense of self in relation to the world is also linked with
the process of disillusionment in Winnicott's work. (*see* MOTHER: 11)

7   The need to refuse the good object

Winnicott draws attention to another aspect of the intermediate
stage of healthy development: the journey from the subjective Me
experience to the objective Not-me experience—that is, the ability
to say no:

> There is an intermediate stage in healthy development in
> which the patient's most important experience in relation to
> the good or potentially satisfying object is the refusal of it. The
> refusal of it is part of the process of creating it.
>
> ["Communicating and Not Communicating", p. 182]

This paradox of creating the object in the act of refusing it brings
about a difference in the purpose of communication throughout
the journey:

> THEORY OF COMMUNICATION
>
> These matters, although I have stated them in terms of object-
> relating, do seem to affect the study of communication,
> because naturally there comes about a change in the purpose
> and in the means of communication *as the object changes over*
> from being subjective to being objectively perceived, in so far
> as the child gradually leaves the area of omnipotence as a
> living experience. In so far as the object is subjective, *so far is it*
> *unnecessary for communication with it to be explicit.* In so far as
> the object is objectively perceived, communication is either
> explicit or dumb. Here then appear two *new* things, the indi-
> vidual's use and enjoyment of modes of communication, and
> the individual's non-communicating self, or the personal core
> of the self that is a true isolate. . . .
>
> ["Communicating and Not Communicating", p. 182]

The healthy baby who benefits from the reliable environment has
the choice of communicating or not communicating. The ability to

make this choice emerges from the early mother–infant relationship and links with Winnicott's exploration of two mothers in one—the environment–mother and the object–mother—in his paper, "The Development of the Capacity for Concern". (*see* CONCERN: 3)

8 Two opposites of communication

Having established the difference in quality between communication in babies and further on in emotional development, Winnicott delineates two types of non-communication:

> Two opposites of communication are:
> 1 A simple not-communicating
> 2 A not-communicating that is active or reactive
>
> It is easy to understand the first of these. Simple not-communicating is like resting. It is a state in its own right, and it passes over into communicating, and reappears as naturally.
> ["Communication between Infant and Mother", p. 183]

The simple not-communicating refers to the quiet moments of unintegration and being between mother and infant, which is the precursor of relaxing. (*see* BEING: 4)

The "not-communicating that is active" belongs to health and comes from choice. The "not-communicating that is reactive" belongs to pathology and arises out of an environment that has not been good enough and consequently has failed to facilitate growth.

> In the psychopathology . . . the facilitation has failed in some respect and in some degree, and in the matter of object-relating the infant has developed a split. By one half of the split the infant relates to the presenting object, and for this purpose there develops what I have called a false or compliant self. By the other half of the split the infant relates to a subjective object, or to mere phenomena based on body experiences, these being scarcely influenced by an objectively perceived world. (Clinically do we not see this in autistic rocking movements, for instance; and in the abstract picture that is a cul-de-sac communication, and that has no general validity?)
> ["Communicating and Not Communicating", p. 183]

Babies who suffer gross impingements have to create a defence structure that splits the personality. Winnicott sees this kind of split as a necessary result of environmental traumatic impingement. His 1960 paper, "Ego Distortion in Terms of True and False Self", complements the aspects he explores related to true and false communication that emanate from the true and the false self. (*see* SELF: 6, 9)

9   *The sense of feeling real*

Winnicott's thesis contains the notion that the "cul-de-sac" communication of pathology (the not-communicating that is reactive)—illustrated by withdrawn states, for example—actually helps the individual to feel real, whereas communication belonging to the false self does not feel real because it is detached or split-off from the true self, and therefore there is no communication with subjective objects:

> There seems to be no doubt that for all its futility from the observer's point of view, the cul-de-sac communication (communication with subjective objects) carries all the sense of real. *Per contra*, such communication with the world as occurs from the false self does not feel real; it is not a true communication because it does not involve the core of the self, that which could be called the true self.
>
> ["Communicating and Not Communicating", p. 184]

From the observer's point of view, an individual may be successful in the world, but success based on the false self leads to an intensification of the sense of emptiness and despair. This relates to the intellectual false self referred to by Winnicott in 1960. (*see* SELF: 8)

Winnicott is suggesting something quite new: the split or dissociation that is obvious in pathology (withdrawal) has a corresponding parallel in the healthy individual—indeed, it *is part of health.*

> It is easy to see that in the cases of slighter illness, in which there is some pathology and some health, there must be expected an active non-communication (clinical withdrawal)

because of the fact that communication so easily becomes linked with some degree of false or compliant object-relating; silent or secret communication with subjective objects, carrying a sense of real, must periodically take over to restore balance.

I am postulating that in the healthy (mature, that is, in respect of the development of object-relating) person there is a need for something that corresponds to the state of the split person in whom one part of the split communicates silently with subjective objects. There is room for the idea that significant relating and communicating is silent.

[right] ["Communicating and Not Communicating", p. 184]

It is specifically this silent communicating with subjective objects that Winnicott links with the "establishment of feeling real". And this is all part and parcel of creative apperception and the ability to be. (*see* BEING: 3)

10   *Violation of the self*

The complex notion of the ability to create a self-division between non-communicating and communicating in health is linked with Winnicott's thesis of violation of the self. As he leads up to his subject of violation in the 1963 "Communicating and Not Communicating" paper, he provides two brief clinical examples of two female patients.

The patient said that in childhood (nine years) she had a stolen school book in which she collected poems and sayings, and she wrote in it "My private book". On the front page she wrote: "What a man thinketh in his heart, so is he". In fact her mother had asked her: "Where did you get this saying from?" This was bad because it meant that the mother must have read her book. It would have been all right if the mother had read the book but had said nothing.

Here is a picture of a child establishing a private self that is not communicating, and at the same time wanting to communicate and to be found. It is a sophisticated game of hide-and-seek in which *it is a joy to be hidden but disaster not to be found.*

[right] ["Communicating and Not Communicating", p. 186]

This memory of one of Winnicott's patients came about through her association to a dream she had of being invaded. Her childhood memory showed Winnicott how violated his patient had felt by her mother's intrusion on her core self (represented by the secret book).

The second clinical illustration depicts for Winnicott the way in which his patient needs to relate to subjective objects through the writing of poetry, regardless of whether or not the poetry will be read by anyone else.

> When she needs to form a bridge with childhood imagination it has to be crystallized out in a poem. She would get bored to write an autobiography. She does not publish her poems or even show them to anybody because although she is fond of each poem for a little while she soon loses interest in it. She has always been able to write poems more easily than her friends because of a technical ability which she seems to have naturally. But she is not interested in the question: are the poems really good? or not? that is to say: would other people think them good?
>
> ["Communicating and Not Communicating": p. 187]

This illustration takes Winnicott to the crux of the paper that could be said to represent the very heart of his life's oeuvre.

> I suggest that in health there is a core to the personality that corresponds to the true self of the split personality; I suggest that this core never communicates with the world of perceived objects, and that the individual person knows that it must never be communicated with or be influenced by external reality. This is my main point, the point of thought which is the centre of an intellectual world and of my paper. Although healthy persons communicate and enjoy communicating, the other fact is equally true, that *each individual is an isolate, permanently non-communicating, permanently unknown, in fact unfound.*
>
> In life and living this hard fact is softened by the sharing that belongs to the whole range of cultural experience. At the centre of each person is an incommunicado element, and this is sacred and most worthy of preservation. Ignoring for the moment the still earlier and shattering experiences of failure of the environment–mother, I would say that the traumatic experiences that lead to the organization of primitive defences

belong to the threat to the isolated core, the threat of its being
found, altered, communicated with. The defence consists in a
further hiding of the secret self, even in the extreme to its
projection and to its endless dissemination. . . .

. . . Rape, and being eaten by cannibals, these are mere
bagatelles as compared with the violation of the self's core,
the alteration of the self's central elements by communication
seeping through the defences. For me this would be the sin
against the self. We can understand the hatred people have of
psychoanalysis which has penetrated a long way into the human personality, and which provides a threat to the human
individual in his need to be secretly isolated. The question is:
how to be isolated without having to be insulated?

["Communicating and Not Communicating", p. 187]

To state that psychological violation of the self is far worse than
rape and the eating of human flesh is a moot point, but this is the
way in which Winnicott seems to wish to accentuate just how
powerful he believes this kind of violation to be.

He subsequently postulates three strands of communication in
healthy development.

In the best possible circumstances growth takes place and the
child now possesses three lines of communication: communication that is *forever silent*, communication that is *explicit*, indirect and pleasurable, and this third or *intermediate* form of
communication that slides out of playing into cultural experience of every kind.

["Communicating and Not Communicating", p. 188]

11 *Implications for psychoanalytic technique*

The vital question of "how to be isolated without having to be
insulated" has major implications for healthy and creative living,
as well as the technique and practice of psychotherapy. This is one
of Winnicott's notable contributions to the technique of psychoanalysis.

In practice then there is something we must allow for in our
work, the patient's non-communicating as a positive contribution. We must ask ourselves, does our technique allow for the

patient to communicate that he or she is not communicating? For this to happen we as analysts must be ready for the signal: "I am not communicating", and be able to distinguish it from the distress signal associated with a failure of communication. There is a link here with the idea of being alone in the presence of someone, at first a natural event in child-life, and later on a matter of the acquisition of a capacity for withdrawal without loss of identification with that from which withdrawal has occurred. This appears as the capacity to concentrate on a task.

["Communicating and Not Communicating", p. 188]

This alters the brief of psychoanalysis, for where Freud advocated the need for the patient to free-associate and "tell all", here Winnicott advocates that the mother/analyst should respect the need of the infant's/patient's private self *not* to "tell all" and *not* to communicate.

And Winnicott elaborates and emphasizes this difference because of the dangers he sees as being inherent in psychoanalysis if the right to remain silent is not respected by the analyst. The unusual nature of Winnicott's message relates to his understanding of the difference between a patient who can use language (and consequently the transitional area) and one where words are not useful, because the patient has not yet reached the ability to symbolize. (*see* TRANSITIONAL PHENOMENA: 3)

In the clear-cut psycho-neurotic case there is no difficulty because the whole analysis is done through the intermediary of verbalization. Both the patient and the analyst want this to be so. But it is only too easy for an analysis (where there is a hidden schizoid element in the patient's personality) to become an infinitely prolonged collusion of the analyst with the patient's negation of non-communication.... In such an analysis a period of silence may be the most positive contribution the patient can make, and the analyst is then involved in a waiting game. One can of course interpret movements and gestures and all sorts of behavioural details, but in the kind of case I have in mind the analyst had better wait.

["Communicating and Not Communicating", p. 189]

Winnicott urges the analyst to wait and give the patient space to arrive at his own interpretations, particularly whilst the analyst is in the process (in the patient's experience) of becoming an object objectively perceived.

> . . . at the place when the analyst has not changed over from a subjective object to one that is objectively perceived, then psychoanalysis is dangerous, and the danger is one that can be avoided if we know how to behave ourselves. If we wait we become objectively perceived in the patient's own time, but if we fail to behave in a way that is facilitating the patient's analytic process (which is the equivalent of the infant's and the child's maturational process) we suddenly become not-me for the patient, and then we know too much, and we are dangerous because we are too nearly in communication with the central still and silent spot of the patient's ego-organization.
>
> For this reason we find it convenient even in the case of a straightforward psycho-neurotic case to avoid contacts that are outside the analysis. In the case of the schizoid or borderline patient this matter of how we manage extra-transference contacts becomes very much a part of our work with the patient.
>   ["Communicating and Not Communicating", p. 189]

This relates to the necessity of boundaries that provide a safe frame in the analytic relationship.

Winnicott, using a paradoxical inversion of Freudian interpretation that implies the analyst knowing, advocates the analyst's *not knowing*, as a useful experience for the patient.

> Here one could discuss the purpose of the analyst's interpreting. I have always felt that an important function of the interpretation is the establishment of the *limits* of the analyst's understanding.
>   ["Communicating and Not Communicating", p. 189]

The patient like the baby, also needs to arrive at a disillusionment with the analyst as part of the journey towards symbolization and self-awareness.

12   Isolation and adolescence

On re-iterating the topic of the individual as isolate, Winnicott uses the adolescent as the prime example of the isolation that belongs to each individual.

This theme of the individual as an isolate has its importance in the study of infancy and of psychosis, but it also has importance in the study of adolescence. The boy and girl at puberty can be described in many ways, and one way concerns *the adolescent as an isolate*. This preservation of personal isolation is part of the search for identity, and for the establishment of a personal technique for communicating which does not lead to violation of the central self. This may be one reason why adolescents on the whole eschew psychoanalytic treatment, though they are interested in psychoanalytic theories. They feel that by psychoanalysis they will be raped, not sexually but spiritually. In practice the analyst can avoid confirming the adolescent's fears in this respect, but the analyst of an adolescent must expect to be tested out fully and must be prepared to use communication of indirect kind and to recognize simple non-communication.

At adolescence when the individual is undergoing pubertal changes and is not quite ready to become one of the adult community there is a strengthening of the defences against being found, that is to say being found before being there to be found. That which is truly personal and which feels real must be defended at all cost, and even if this means a temporary blindness to the value of compromise. Adolescents form aggregates rather than groups, and by looking alike they emphasize the essential loneliness of each individual.

["Communication between Infant and Mother", p. 190]

The difference between compromise and compliance is something the adolescent has to learn (*see* SELF: 11). Winnicott's main point in this particular paper is the existential isolation of each individual.

REFERENCES

1963 Communicating and Not Communicating Leading to a Study of Certain Opposites   [W9]

1968 Communication between Infant and Mother, and Mother and Infant, Compared and Contrasted   [W16]

1969 The Mother–Infant Experience of Mutuality   [W19]

Concern

C oncern is the word used by Winnicott to emphasize the positive aspects of the sense of guilt. The "stage of concern" is approached as the infant begins to feel concern for his mother, towards whom his ruthless love has been hitherto directed. The infant's capacity to feel concern for his mother marks the developmental achievement of the journey from pre-ruth to ruth.

The overlapping features of Winnicott's stage of concern are ambivalence, the benign circle, contributing-in, and innate morality.

1   The depressive position

In 1935, when Winnicott qualified as a psychoanalyst, Melanie Klein was working on one of her major theoretical developments, which came to be known as the "depressive position". This term has become part of Kleinian vocabulary and is of as great a theoretical importance as Freud's Oedipus complex. Winnicott, amongst many others, whilst recognizing the components of the theory as crucial in relation to emotional development, neverthe-

less did not like the term and had his own way of describing this
stage of development.

Throughout many of Winnicott's papers of the 1950s, it can be
discerned that he was working out his personal theoretical contribution to this particular stage of emotional development in the
infant pertinent to relative dependence, notably in his paper of
1954, "The Depressive Position in Normal Emotional Development" and, later, in 1958, in "Psychoanalysis and the Sense of
Guilt". The evolving ideas put forward in these papers come to
fruition in 1963, in "The Development of the Capacity for Concern"; Winnicott is now ready to replace Klein's depressive
position with his stage of concern.

2   A personal view of the depressive position

In "The Depressive Position in Normal Development", Winnicott
sets out to provide his personal view of the tenets of Klein's "depressive position". His emphasis is on "normal" and on the
developmental achievements of the depressive position.

Early on in the paper Winnicott criticizes the term and offers
an alternative, to indicate health rather than illness.

> The term depressive position is a bad name for a normal pro-
> cess, but no one has been able to find a better. My own
> suggestion was that it should be called *"the Stage of Concern"*. I
> believe this term easily introduces the concept. . . .
>
> It has often been pointed out that a term that implies illness
> ought not to be used where a normal process is being de-
> scribed. The term depressive position seems to imply that
> infants in health pass through a stage of depression, or mood
> illness. Actually this is not what is meant.
>
> ["Depressive Position", pp. 264–265]

Winnicott stresses that depression is a symptom of ill health and
has nothing to do with normal healthy development and the
depressive position (*see* DEPRESSION: 1). The use of the word
"depressive" thus poses a puzzle—one that Winnicott wishes to
explore in terms of the infant's ruthless love (primary aggression)

for his mother, which within a facilitating environment will change to ruth and concern. (*see* AGGRESSION: 3, 8)

> At first the infant (from our point of view) is ruthless; there is no concern yet as to results of instinctual love. This love is originally a form of impulse, gesture, contact, relationship, and it affords the infant the satisfaction of self-expression and release from instinct tension; more it places the object outside the self.
>
> It should be noted that the infant does not feel ruthless, but looking back (and this does occur in regressions) the individual can say: I was ruthless then! The stage is one that is pre-ruth.
>
> ["Depressive Position", p. 265]

Winnicott sees the infant's journey from pre-ruth to ruth as the most vital aspect of emotional development. It is this journey that characterizes the stage of concern:

> At some time or other in the history of the development of every normal human being there comes the change over from pre-ruth to ruth. No one will question this. The only thing is, when does this happen, how, and under what conditions? The concept of the depressive position is an attempt to answer these three questions. According to this concept the change from ruthlessness to ruth occurs gradually, under certain definite conditions of mothering, during the period around five to twelve months, and its establishment is not necessarily final until a much later date; and it may be found, in an analysis, that it has never occurred at all.
>
> The depressive position, then, is a complex matter, an inherent element in a non-controversial phenomenon, that of the emergence of every human individual from pre-ruth to ruth or concern.
>
> ["Depressive Position", pp. 266–267]

This journey from pre-ruth to ruth involves the infant in a great deal of work. This work can begin once the infant is able to see the mother as other than himself. Winnicott describes this as the attainment of "unit status". This is when the infant arrives at the point of distinguishing between "Me" and "Not-me".

3   *Two aspects of mother*

The infant who achieves "unit status" has to become aware that
the two mothers in his fantasy are one and the same. In this 1954
paper, Winnicott refers to these two mothers as the mother of the
quiet phases and the mother of the excited phases. (By 1963, these
two mothers are called the "environment–mother" and the
"object–mother", respectively.)

The mother's function during this time continues to be vital for
the infant, as she has to adapt to the infant's needs and appreciate
that the infant who ruthlessly attacks her has no intention of hurting her. It is instinct, a biological drive like hunger, that makes the
infant ruthless. (*see* AGGRESSION: 2, 3)

> The infant, being a whole person, is able to identify with the
> mother, but there is not clear distinction yet for the baby be-
> tween what is intended and what really happens. Functions
> and their imaginative elaborations are not yet clearly distin-
> guished as fact and fantasy. It is astonishing what the baby
> has to accomplish at just about this time.
>
> ["Depressive Position", pp. 266–267]

And Winnicott provides an example to illustrate the baby's task:

> Let us now think in terms of a day, with the mother holding
> the situation, assuming that at some point early in the day the
> baby has an instinctual experience. For simplicity's sake I
> think of a feed, for this is really at the basis of the whole
> matter. There appears a cannibalistic ruthless attack, which
> partly shows in the baby's physical behaviour, and which
> partly is a matter of the infant's own imaginative elaboration
> of the physical function. The baby puts one and one together
> and begins to see that the answer is one, and not two. The
> mother of the dependent relationship (anaclitic) is also the
> object of instinctual (biologically driven) love.
>
> ["Depressive Position", pp. 267–268]

4   *Two types of anxiety*

This biologically driven instinct, which causes the infant to be
ruthless without intent, also creates anxiety in him. In this 1954
paper Winnicott writes about two types of depressive anxiety. (By

1963 he will have stopped using the word "depressive" as an ad-
junct and simply refers to "anxiety".)

The first type of anxiety relates to the baby's perception that
the mother is not the same after the feed as she was before his
"cannibalistic ruthless attack". Winnicott puts the baby's experience of this first type of anxiety into words:

> If we like we can use words to describe what the infant feels
> and say: there is a hole, where previously there was a full
> body of richness.
>
> ["Depressive Position", p. 268]

The second type of anxiety is related to the infant's growing awareness of how he feels inside, because it is during this
stage of development that he is working out the difference
between Me and Not-me. These two types of anxiety put the
infant into a developmental struggle.

> ... this infant, after the feed, besides being apprehensive
> about the imagined hole in the body of the mother is also very
> much caught up in the struggle within the self, a struggle
> between what is felt to be good, that is to say self-supportive,
> and what is felt to be bad, that is to say persecutory to the self.
>
> ["Depressive Position", p. 269]

The successful outcome of the infant's struggle will depend on (a)
how his mother holds him and (b) the mode in which she *receives*
his "gifts". (*see* HOLDING: 2)

> All the while the mother is holding the situation in time.
> Thus, the infant's day proceeds, physical digestion and also a
> corresponding working-through take place in the psyche.
> This working-through takes time and the infant can only
> await the outcome, passively surrendered to what is going on
> inside. In health this personal inner world becomes the infi-
> nitely rich core of the self.
>
> Towards the end of this day in the life of any healthy infant
> as a result of inner work done, the infant has good and bad to
> offer. The mother takes the good and the bad, and she is sup-
> posed to know what is offered as good and what is offered as
> bad. Here is the first giving, and without this giving there is
> no true receiving. All these are very practical everyday mat-
> ters of infant care, and indeed of analysis.
>
> ["Depressive Position", p. 269]

These "practical everyday matters", which are the giving and tak-ing between mother and infant, are absolutely essential for the infant to bring the two mothers (quiet/environment and excited/object) together in his mind, which is at the very centre of the work of integration. (*see* EGO: 3)

Winnicott emphasizes that it is the part the mother plays in the interaction at this stage, which will make all the difference.

> The infant that is blessed with a mother who survives, a mother who knows a gift gesture when it is made, is now in a position to do something about that hole, the hole in the breast or body, imaginatively made in the original instinctual moment. Here come in the words reparation and restitution, words which mean so much in the right setting, but which can easily become cliches if used loosely. The gift gesture may reach to the hole, if the mother plays her part.
>
> ["Depressive Position", p. 270]

5   The benign circle

The infant's struggle to distinguish between the two mothers in relation to how he feels builds up into a sequential dynamic, which is necessarily constantly repeated. Winnicott names this phenomenon the "benign circle" and provides a useful list of its aspects:

> There is now set up a benign circle. Among all the complica-tions we can discern
> - A relationship between infant and mother complicated by instinctual experience.
> - A dim perception of the effect (hole).
> - An inner working-through, the results of experience being sorted out.
> - A capacity to give, because of the sorting out of the good and the bad within.
> - Reparation.
>
> The result of a day-after-day reinforcement of the benign circle is that the infant becomes able to tolerate the hole (result of instinct love). Here then is the beginning of *guilt* feeling.

This is the only true guilt, since implanted guilt is false to the self. Guilt starts through the bringing together of the two mothers, and of quiet and excited love, and of love and hate, and this feeling gradually grows to be a healthy and normal source of activity in relationships. . . .

In the operation of the benign circle, concern becomes tolerable to the infant through a dawning recognition that, given time, something can be done about the hole, and the various effects of id impulse on the mother's body.

["Depressive Position", p. 270]

In subsequent papers, in particular in "Psycho-Analysis and the Sense of Guilt" (1958) and "The Development of the Capacity for Concern" (1963), aspects of the benign circle are elaborated.

In 1958 the emphasis is on the responsibility the infant begins to feel towards his mother, along with a recognition of the age at which the infant is reaching this stage of development:

. . . this important phase of development is composed of innumerable repetitions spread over a period of time. There is a benign circle of (i) instinctual experience, (ii) acceptance of responsibility which is called guilt, (iii) a working through, and (iv) a true restitutive gesture. . . .

I suggest that we are talking about the first year of the infant's life, and in fact about the whole period in which the infant is having a clearly human two-body relationship with the mother. . . . By the age of six months an infant can be seen to have a highly complex psychology, and it is possible that the *beginnings* of the depressive position are to be found by this age.

["Psycho-Analysis and Sense of Guilt", p. 24]

By 1963, in "The Development of the Capacity for Concern", Winnicott was ready to replace Klein's theory with his own. In this paper his definitive statement on the aspects of emotional development at this crucial time constitutes an original contribution to the theory of psychoanalysis. The emphasis is on health and normal maturational processes in the infant, always in relation to his environment.

The inter-relationship between mother and infant at this stage is by 1963 referred to as "destruction" rather than ruthless attack. It is to this "destruction" that Winnicott refers more and more in his work during the 1960s, and in this paper his evolving ideas on primary aggression can be discerned, leading up to his 1968 paper, "The Use of an Object and Relating Through Identifications". (*see* AGGRESSION: 10)

> The word "concern" is used to cover in a positive way a phenomenon that is covered in a negative way by the word "guilt". A sense of guilt is anxiety linked with the concept of ambivalence, and implies a degree of integration in the individual ego that allows for the retention of good object-imago along with the idea of a destruction of it. Concern implies further integration, and further growth, and relates in a positive way to the individual's sense of responsibility, especially in respect of relationships into which the instinctual drives have entered.
>
> ["Development of Capacity", p. 73]

6   Ambivalence

Ambivalence is a developmental achievement indicating the acknowledgement of loving and hating the same person at the same time. This ambivalence amounts to the baby's awareness that the mother of the quiet times is the same as the mother of the excited times.

At the beginning of his dawning awareness of the two mothers in his mind related to his own ambivalence, the infant is particularly vulnerable. His mother must also let go and allow him to separate. Winnicott is reminded of Humpty Dumpty:

> This state of affairs, precarious at first, could be nicknamed the "humpty-dumpty stage", the wall on which Humpty Dumpty is precariously perched being the mother who has ceased to offer her lap.
>
> ["Development of Capacity", p. 73]

Following on from Winnicott's outline of two aspects of the same mother in 1954 (see CONCERN: 3), he now offers terms to describe these aspects, while at the same time wishing to avoid sounding dogmatic:

> It is helpful to postulate the existence for the immature child of two mothers—shall I call them the object–mother and the

environment–mother? I have no wish to invent names that become stuck and eventually develop a rigidity and an obstructive quality, but it seems possible to use these words "object mother" and "environment mother" in this context to describe the vast difference that there is for the infant between two aspects of infant-care, the mother as object, or owner of the part-object that may satisfy the infant's urgent needs, and the mother as the person who wards off the unpredictable and who actively provides care in handling and in general management. . . .

In this language it is the environment–mother who receives all that can be called affection and sensuous co-existence; it is the object–mother who becomes the target for excited experience backed by crude instinct-tension. It is my thesis that concern turns up in the baby's life as a highly sophisticated experience in the coming-together in the infant's mind of the object–mother and the environment–mother. The environmental provision continues to be vitally important here, though the infant is beginning to be able to have that inner stability that belongs to the development of independence.

["Development of Capacity", p. 76]

Winnicott's intention is to break down the components of this stage of development involving weaning and separation. He concentrates on the infant's destruction (referred to earlier on as "primary aggression"), which leads on to the sense of guilt, responsibility, and concern. This destruction (in fantasy) involves, for the infant, both a need to possess and a need to protect.

The fantasy that goes with full-blooded id-drives contains attack and destruction. It is not only that the baby imagines that he eats the object, but also that the baby wants to take possession of the contents of the object. If the object is not destroyed, it is because of its own survival capacity, not because of the baby's protection of the object. This is one side of the picture.

The other side of the picture has to do with the baby's relation to the environment–mother, and from this angle there may come so great a protection of the mother that the child becomes inhibited or turns away. Here is a positive element in the infant's experience of weaning and one reason why some infants wean themselves.

["Development of Capacity", p. 76]

This idea of protection is an important one and essentially liberating because it draws a boundary between the responsibility of the subject and the responsibility of the object. For example, it is not the infant's responsibility if the mother is persecuted by his crying. However, if the mother *is* continually persecuted by her infant's needs because of her own difficulties, the infant is likely to grow up convinced that he is responsible for his mother's feelings.

7   The function of contributing-in

With a stress on the good-enough environment, Winnicott describes the infant's technique of dealing with ambivalence:

> In favourable circumstances there builds up a technique for the solution of this complex form of ambivalence. The infant experiences anxiety, because if he consumes the mother he will lose her, but this anxiety becomes modified by the fact that the baby has a contribution to make to the environment–mother. There is a growing confidence that there will be opportunity for contributing-in, for giving to the environment–mother, a confidence which makes the infant able to hold the anxiety. The anxiety held in this way becomes altered in quality and becomes a sense of guilt. . . .
>
> When confidence in this benign circle and in the expectation of opportunity is established, the sense of guilt in relation to the id-drives becomes further modified, and we then need a more positive term, such as "concern". The infant is now becoming able to be concerned, to take responsibility for his own instinctual impulses and the functions that belong to them. This provides one of the fundamental constructive elements of play and work. But in the developmental process, it was the opportunity to contribute that enabled concern to be within the child's capacity.
>
> ["Development of Capacity", p. 77]

Again, Winnicott is clear that the mother not only has to survive the infant's ruthless need of her, but also has to be there to *receive* the "gift gesture"—the "spontaneous gesture". In effect, it is her ability to receive that is part and parcel of her survival. For the instant, the receiving of his gift transforms his anxiety into concern. (This is to become a major feature of Winnicott's thesis, "the use of an object".) (*see* AGGRESSION: 10)

If the mother has difficulty in receiving the infant's gesture, the infant is less likely to develop an integrated capacity for concern:

> Briefly, failure of the object–mother to survive or of the environment–mother to provide reliable opportunity for reparation leads to a loss of the capacity for concern, and to its replacement by crude anxieties and by crude defences, such as splitting, or disintegration. We often discuss separation-anxiety, but here I am trying to describe what happens between mothers and their babies and between parents and their children when there is *no* separation, and when external continuity of child-care is *not* broken. I am trying to account for things that happen when separation is avoided.
>
> ["Development of Capacity", p. 77]

Here, Winnicott's thesis, like so many of his theories, is paradoxical. For him separation anxiety is not concerned with fear of separation, but, rather, with the difficulties of *not* being able to become separate.

8   The time dimension

Part of the mother's responsibility in her holding function is to take care of time:

> A feature that may be noted, especially in respect of the concept of anxiety that is "held", is that integration *in time* has become added to the more static integration of the earlier stages. Time is kept going by the mother, and this is one aspect of her auxiliary ego-functioning; but the infant comes to have a personal time-sense, one that lasts at first only over a short span.
>
> ["Development of Capacity", p. 77]

This time dimension contributes also to the continuity of being— a very central experience for the infant to have, in order to grow. The time feature of the mother–infant relationship is elaborated in

1967 in Winnicott's paper, "The Location of Cultural Experience". (see CREATIVITY: 3)

9   Innate morality

In 1962, in a lecture series entitled "The Young Child at Home and at School", Winnicott presented to an audience at the University of London Institute of Education his thoughts about the teaching of morality. It was subsequently published in *Moral Education in a Changing Society* (Niblett, 1963), and in 1965 in *The Maturational Processes and The Facilitating Environment* (W9), under the title, "Morals and Education".

Morality and immorality are, for Winnicott, bound up with true and false self living. (His paper, "Ego Distortion in Terms of True and False Self" was written just two years earlier, in 1960.)

> The fiercest morality is that of early infancy, and this persists as a streak in human nature that can be discerned throughout an individual's life. Immorality for the infant is *to comply at the expense of the personal way of life.* For instance, a child of any age may feel that to eat is wrong, even to the extent of dying for the principle. Compliance brings immediate rewards and adults only too easily mistake compliance for growth. The maturational processes can be by-passed by a series of identifications, so that what shows clinically is a false, acting self, a copy of someone perhaps; and what could be called a true or essential self becomes hidden, and becomes deprived of living experience.
>
> ["Morals and Education", p. 102]

Winnicott's thesis in this paper and in the whole of his work is that the teaching of morality means nothing if the child has not first developed his own inner sense of concern. In other words, the capacity for concern in the infant is the foundation of the adult's sense of morality and ethics, which are a part of emotional maturity and health:

> ... moral education follows naturally on the arrival of morality in the child by the natural developmental processes that good care facilitates.
>
> ["Morals and Education", p. 100]

10 *Wickedness*

If the infant has not had the opportunity to contribute-in and is not able therefore to develop his sense of concern, he may become "wicked", which, in this context, is linked with the antisocial tendency. (see ANTISOCIAL TENDENCY: 2)

> Compulsive wickedness is about the last thing to be cured or even stopped by moral education. The child knows in his bones that it is *hope* that is locked up in the wicked behaviour, and that *despair* is linked with the compliance and false socialization. For the antisocial or wicked person the moral educator is on the wrong side.
>
> ["Morals and Education", p. 104]

Winnicott's words on morality are characteristic of his whole attitude in terms of a trust in the infant's developmental tendencies when supported by ordinary, caring parents.

Winnicott's theory of the stage of concern contributes a further embellishment to Klein's depressive position, by emphasizing the role played by the environment. Central to Winnicott's theory is the mother's acknowledgement of her baby's gift gesture and her capacity to receive the gift.

This paradigm is extended in the psychoanalytic setting to the analyst's ability to receive the analysand's "gift". Christopher Bollas elaborates this theme in his paper, "The Psychoanalyst's Celebration of the Analysand" (1989b).

REFERENCES

1954–55 The Depressive Position in Normal Emotional Development [W6]

1958 Psycho-Analysis and the Sense of Guilt [W9]

1963 The Development of the Capacity for Concern [W9]

1963 Morals and Education [W9]

Creativity

For Winnicott, at the heart of living creatively is the infant's illusion of omnipotence—that is, that he is God and creates the world. This derives from the mother who, in her state of primary preoccupation, is able to provide exactly what the infant needs, and thus the infant feels that he creates the objects that are offered.

The creative act (painting, dancing, etc.) is not the same as living creatively.

1   The place of creativity

Winnicott's theory of creativity is different from those of Freud and Klein, in that he places the roots of creativity at the very beginning of life and at the heart of the mother–infant relationship. Briefly, for Freud creativity in the adult is linked with his theory of sublimation, and for Melanie Klein creativity is associated with the reparative aspects of her theory of the depressive position (which occurs some weeks or months after birth).

During the 1950s, Winnicott's evolving thoughts on the pivotal function of the mother in relation to her infant before and just after birth, place creativity at the centre of the first relationship and at the beginning. In 1953, Winnicott, with Masud Khan, reviewed W. R. D. Fairbairn's publication, *Psychoanalytic Studies of the Personality*. Winnicott's thesis of primary creativity begins to emerge in this review. Referring to Fairbairn's work, he writes:

> In his theory primary psychic creativity is not a human property; an infinite series of introjections and projections form the infant's psychic experience. Fairbairn's theory here lines up with the theory given us by Melanie Klein, which also allows no tribute to be paid to the idea of primary psychic creativity.
>
> In strictly Freudian theory this point can be said not to have arisen, since the place in clinical work at which the question of primary creativity comes up for consideration has not been reached. The analyst is concerned with the whole range of reality and phantasy associated with inter-personal relationships and the gradual attainment of maturity in the instinctual elements in these relationships; nevertheless no claim is being made that these matters cover the entire range of human experience. It would seem that only comparatively recently have analysts begun to feel the need for a hypothesis that would allow for areas of infancy experience and of ego development that are not basically associated with instinctual conflict and where there is intrinsically a psychic process such as that which we have here termed "primary (psychic) creativity".
>
> ["Review of *Psychoanalytic Studies*", p. 420]

For Winnicott, primary creativity is essentially an innate drive towards health and is inextricably linked with several of his major themes:

- the necessity of illusion in the early days and weeks of the infant's relating to his mother, which leads to the sense of omnipotence. (*see* BEING: 3; HOLDING: 4; PRIMARY MATERNAL PREOCCUPATION: 2)

- the mother's ability to respond to the infant's spontaneous gesture and thus facilitate the development of the sense of self emanating from the true self. (*see* SELF: 5)

- the role of primary aggression and the infant's requirement for an object (both the object–mother and environment–mother) to survive his ruthless love. (*see* AGGRESSION: 2, 3, 8, 9; CONCERN: 3, 4; MOTHER: 3, 4; TRANSITIONAL PHENOMENA: 3)

2   *The newborn infant as creator of the world*

In 1951, in his paper, "Transitional Objects and Transitional Phenomena", Winnicott refers to the infant's ability for creative activity that creates the breast:

> . . . the breast is created by the infant over and over again out of the infant's capacity to love or (one can say) out of need. A subjective phenomenon develops in the baby, which we call the mother's breast.

A footnote is added here:

> {I include the whole technique of mothering. When it is said that the first object is the breast, the word "breast" is used, I believe, to stand for the technique of mothering as well as for the actual flesh.}
>
> The mother places the actual breast just where the infant is ready to create, and at the right moment.
>
> ["Transitional Objects", pp. 238–239]

This placing of the object at the right place and at the right moment is something the mother is able to do only if she is in a state of primary maternal preoccupation, which means that she is identified with the infant and therefore at a very deep level attempts to find out what he needs. (*see* MOTHER: 8)

In this paper, Winnicott focuses on the relationship between the infant's subjectivity and his struggle with objectively perceiving the world:

> From birth, therefore, the human being is concerned with the problem of the relationship between what is objectively perceived and what is subjectively conceived of, and in the solution of this problem there is no health for the human being who has not been started off well enough by the mother. *The intermediate area to which I am referring is the area that is*

allowed to the infant between primary creativity and objective per-
ception based on reality-testing. The transitional phenomena
represent the early stages of the use of illusion, without which
there is no meaning for the human being in the idea of a
relationship with an object that is perceived by others as external to that being.

["Transitional Objects", p. 239]

Seventeen years later, in 1968, Winnicott clarifies the meaning and
value of the infant's experience of omnipotence by paraphrasing
the mother's message to her infant when she performs the task of
object-presenting:

> We have to say that the baby created the breast, but could not
> have done so had not the mother come along with the breast
> just at that moment. The communication to the baby is: "Come
> at the world creatively, create the world; it is only what you
> create that has meaning for you." Next comes: "the world is in
> your control." From this initial *experience of omnipotence* the
> baby is able to begin to experience frustration and even to
> arrive one day at the other extreme from omnipotence, that is
> to say, having a sense of being a mere speck in a universe, in a
> universe that was there before the baby was conceived of and
> conceived by two parents who were enjoying each other. Is it
> not from *being God* that human beings arrive at the humility
> proper to human individuality?
>
> ["Communication between Infant and Mother, and Mother and Infant,
> Compared and Contrasted", p. 101]

3   Cultural experience and its location

In 1967, Winnicott explored the theme of what he refers to as
"cultural experience". Characteristically, particularly at this time
in his life and work, Winnicott pursued "The Location of Cultural
Experience", which is the paper's title. Winnicott's theory of the
"use of an object" is already in preparation in this paper, and a
year later, in 1968, at the age of 72, he presented his paper, "The
Use of an Object and Relating through Identifications".

Essentially, the cultural experience begins in the early seques-
tered relationship of the nursing couple. As long as the environ-

ment is facilitating and good enough the infant will have the illusion of "being God", and *on the basis* of this experience, he will
begin to develop and work through a disillusioning process that he
in fact is *not* God. To help him journey from illusion to disillusion,
the healthy infant or young child will use a transitional object. Both
parents' attitude to the transitional object is crucial. (*see* TRANSI-
TIONAL PHENOMENA: 3, 4)

> I have claimed that when we witness an infant's employment
> of a transitional object, the first not-me possession, we are
> witnessing both the child's first use of a symbol and the first
> experience of play. An essential part of my formulation of
> transitional phenomena is that we agree never to make the
> challenge to the baby: did you create this object, or did you
> find it conveniently lying around? That is to say, an essential
> feature of transitional phenomena and objects is a quality in
> our attitude when we observe them.
>   The object is a symbol of the union of the baby and the
> mother (or part of the mother). This symbol can be located. It
> is at the place in space and time where and when the mother
> is in transition from being (in the baby's mind) merged in
> with the infant and alternatively being experienced as an ob-
> ject to be perceived rather than conceived of. The use of an
> object symbolizes the union of two now separate things, baby
> and mother, *at the point in time and space of the initiation of their
> state of separateness.*
>
>   ["Location of Cultural Experience", pp. 96–97]

Here Winnicott is referring to the infant's growing ability to
distinguish between Me and Not-me; this is illustrated by emphasizing the element of time:

> It is perhaps worth while trying to formulate this in a way
> that gives the time factor due weight. The feeling of the
> mother's existence lasts x minutes. If the mother is away more
> that x minutes, then the imago fades, and along with this the
> baby's capacity to use the symbol of the union ceases. The
> baby is distressed, but this distress is soon *mended* because the
> mother returns in $x+y$ minutes. In $x+y$ minutes the baby has
> not become altered. But in $x+y+z$ minutes the baby has be-
> come *traumatized*. In $x+y+z$ minutes the mother's return does
> not mend the baby's altered state. Trauma implies that the

baby has experienced a break in life's continuity, so that primitive defences now become organized to defend against a repetition of "unthinkable anxiety" or a return of the acute confusional state that belongs to disintegration of nascent ego structure.

We must assume that the vast majority of babies never experience the $x+y+z$ quantity of deprivation. This means that the majority of children do not carry around with them for life the knowledge from experience of having been mad. Madness here simply means a *break-up* of whatever may exist at the time of a *personal continuity of existence*. After "recovery" from $x+y+z$ deprivation a baby has to start again permanently deprived of the root which could provide *continuity with the personal beginning*. This implies the existence of a memory system and an organization of memories.

["Location of Cultural Experience", p. 97]

Winnicott's emphasis is how the mother must act on behalf of her infant in order to protect him from a break in the continuity-of-being. (*see* CONCERN: 5; ENVIRONMENT: 1, 2)

By contrast, from the effects of $x+y+z$ degree of deprivation, babies are constantly being *cured* by the mother's localized spoiling that mends the ego structure. This mending of the ego structure re-establishes the baby's capacity to use a symbol of union; the baby then comes once more to allow and even to benefit from the separation. *This is the place that I have set out to examine*, the separation that is not a separation but a form of union.

["Location of Cultural Experience", pp. 97–98]

If the infant has gradually become used to being actually separated from his mother for no more than $x + y$ minutes, then he is able to *remember* her and *keep her in mind*. This very much links with Winnicott's concept of the infant's capacity to be alone (see ALONE: 2). But how does this link with the location of culture?

The stress in Winnicott's theory of culture is placed on the infant's subjective experience of his mother's comings and goings, as well as his sense of her idiom, in conjunction with his inherited tendencies. The latter refer to his—the baby's—idiom: that is, the essential characteristics that are unique to his personality and disposition. The actual customs, language, and so on that relate to each specific society emerge out of this early culture:

> I have used the term cultural experience as an extension of the idea of transitional phenomena and of play without being certain that I can define the word "culture". The accent indeed is on experience. In using the word culture I am thinking of the inherited tradition. I am thinking of something that is in the common pool of humanity, into which individuals and groups of people may contribute, and from which we may all draw *if we have somewhere to put what we find*.
>
> There is a dependence here on some kind of recording method. No doubt a very great deal was lost of the early civilizations, but in the myths that were a product of oral tradition there could be said to be a cultural pool giving the history of human culture spanning six thousand years. This history through myth persists to the present time in spite of the efforts of historians to be objective, which they can never be, though they must try.
>
> ["Location of Cultural Experience", p. 99]

Winnicott is referring to the handing-down from one generation to the next, not just of the customs and traditions of a given society, but of their symbolic and emotional meaning. Of course, each family has its own myths and stories in the context of each society, which also plays its part in the individual psyche of each infant:

> . . . in any cultural field *it is not possible to be original except on a basis of tradition*. Conversely, no one in the line of cultural contributors repeats except as a deliberate quotation, and the unforgivable sin in the cultural field is plagiarism. The interplay between originality and the acceptance of tradition as the basis for inventiveness seems to me to be just one more example, and a very exciting one, of the interplay between separation and union.
>
> ["Location of Cultural Experience", p. 99]

Winnicott continually wishes to emphasize the nature of creativity in terms of *living* and *being alive* and *feeling real*:

> . . . what is life about? You may cure your patient and not know what it is that makes him or her go on living. It is of first importance for us to acknowledge openly that absence

of psychoneurotic illness may be health, but it is not life. Psychotic patients who are all the time hovering between living and not living force us to look at this problem, one that really belongs *not to psychoneurotics but to all human beings*. I am claiming that these same phenomena that are life and death to our schizoid or borderline patients appear in our cultural experiences. It is these cultural experiences that provide the continuity in the human race that transcends personal existence. I am assuming that cultural experiences are in direct continuity with play, the play of those who have not yet heard of games.

["Location of Cultural Experience", p. 100]

Central to Winnicott's theory of the location of cultural experience is the subject's ability to "remember", unconsciously, the mother's protection and good object-presenting at the early moments of life. This experience is internalized and thus creates an internal resource from which to live creatively.

4   Creative living is doing

Just as playing and being belong to the early mother–infant relationship, so, too, does creative living originate here. In a very late paper of Winnicott's, written in 1970, just before his death, he elaborates further the themes of creativity and creative living:

Whatever definition we arrive at, it must include the idea that life is worth living or not, according to whether creativity is or is not a part of an individual person's living experience.

To be creative a person must exist and have a feeling of existing, not in conscious awareness, but as a basic place to operate from.

Creativity is then the doing that arises out of being. It indicates that he who is, is alive. Impulse may be at rest, but when the word "doing" becomes appropriate, then already there is creativity.

. . . Creativity, then, is the retention throughout life of something that belongs properly to infant experience: the ability to create the world.

["Living Creatively", pp. 39–40]

And on the basis of the sense of having created the world is built everything else that is meaningful. There can be no disillusionment without first of all having had the illusion, no weaning unless first of all there was the good feed, no doing unless first of all there was being. The foundation of creative living is creative apperception, which, in turn, is based on the experience of having been merged with mother. It is precisely this experience of "keeping mother in mind" that develops into remembering and becomes the place of cultural experience. Here there is a silent communication with subjective objects in the individual's internal world. This is the incommunicado element of each personality and is crucial to making life feel meaningful and worth living. (*see* BEING: 2; COMMUNICATION: 9)

5   *Creativity and the artist*

To live creatively is both something and nothing to do with the artist.

> I must make clear the distinction between creative living and being artistically creative.
>
> In creative living you or I find that everything we do strengthens the feeling that we are alive, that we are ourselves. One can look at a tree (not necessarily at a picture) and look creatively. If you have ever had a depression phase of the schizoid sort (and most have), you will know this in the negative. How often I have been told: "There is a laburnum outside my window and the sun is out and I know intellectually that it must be a grand sight, for those who can see it. But for me this morning (Monday) there is no meaning in it. I cannot feel it. It makes me acutely aware of not being myself real".
>
> Although allied to creative living, the active creations of letter writers, writers, poets, artists, sculptors, architects, musicians, are different. You will agree that if someone is engaged in artistic creation, we hope he or she can call on some special talent. But for creative living we need no special talent.
>
> ["Living Creatively", pp. 43–44]

This idea is elaborated in Winnicott's paper entitled "Playing: Creative Activity and the Search for the Self" (1971). Here, Winnicott posits that in the artist the urge to create is the search for the creative apperception that is bound up and linked with the location of culture and the baby's feeling of being merged with mother. For it is only from this feeling that the true sense of self can start to grow.

> In a search for the self the person concerned may have produced something valuable in terms of art, but a successful artist may be universally acclaimed and yet have failed to find the self that he or she is looking for. The self is not really to be found in what is made out of products of body or mind, however valuable these constructs may be in terms of beauty, skill, and impact. If the artist (in whatever medium) is searching for the self, then it can be said that in all probability there is already some failure for that artist in the field of general creative living. The finished creation never heals the underlying lack of sense of self.
>
> ["Playing: Creative Activity", pp. 54–55]

6   Searching for the self

In "Playing: Creative Activity and the Search for the Self", Winnicott goes back to Freud's technique of free association with his own individual embellishments. For him, it is the holding environment and the reliability of the setting that can enable the patient to search for the self. However, this search must emerge naturally and in the patient's own time, out of formlessness:

> The person we are trying to help needs a new experience in a specialized setting. The experience is one of a non-purposive state, as one might say a sort of ticking over of the unintegrated personality. I referred to this as formlessness.
> . . . I am trying to refer to the essentials that make relaxation possible. In terms of free association this means that the patient on the couch or the child patient among the toys on the floor must be allowed to communicate a succession of ideas, thoughts, impulses, sensations that are not linked except in some way that is neurological or psychological and perhaps

beyond detection. That is to say: it is where there is purpose
or where there is anxiety or where there is lack of trust based
on the need for defence that the analyst will be able to recognize and to point out the connection (or several connections)
between the various components of free association material.

In the relaxation that belongs to trust and to acceptance of
the professional reliability of the therapeutic setting (be it analytic, psychotherapeutic, social work, architectural, etc.) there
is room for the idea of unrelated thought sequences which the
analyst will do well to accept as such, not assuming the existence of a significant thread.

["Playing: Creative Activity", pp. 54–55]

And then Winnicott introduces an unusual theme for psychoanalysis—the value of nonsense. He advocates that the analyst should
surrender to a formlessness and timelessness within the structure
of the analytic session. The implication is that through surrender-
ing to uncertainty, the patient will be facilitated to find something
relating to his own sense of creativity.

The contrast between these two related conditions can perhaps be illustrated if one thinks of a patient who is able to rest
after work but *not able to achieve the resting state out of which a
creative reaching-out can take place.* According to this theory,
free association that reveals a coherent theme is already affected by anxiety, and the cohesion of ideas is a defence
organization. Perhaps it is to be accepted that there are patients who at times need the therapist to note the nonsense
that belongs to the mental state of the individual at rest without the need even for the patient to communicate this
nonsense, that is to say, without the need for the patient to
organize nonsense. Organized nonsense is already a defence,
just as organized chaos is a denial of chaos. The therapist who
cannot take this communication becomes engaged in a futile
attempt to find some organization in the nonsense, as a result
of which the patient leaves the nonsense area because of
hopelessness about communicating nonsense. An opportunity
for rest has been missed because of the therapist's need to
find sense where nonsense is. The patient has been unable to
rest because of a failure of the environmental provision,
which undid the sense of trust. The therapist has, without
knowing it, abandoned the professional role, and has done so

by bending over backwards to be a clever analyst, and to see order in chaos.

["Playing: Creative Activity", pp. 55–56]

In order to illustrate his thesis, Winnicott relates a piece of clinical work over two long sessions with one of his patients. The patient eventually arrives at asking a question. This is where, after long silences, Winnicott interjects.

> She had asked a question, and I said that the answer to the question could take us to a long and interesting discussion, but it was the *question* that interested me. I said: "You had the idea to ask that question."
>
> After this she said the very words that I need in order to express my meaning. She said, slowly, with deep feeling: "Yes, I see, one could postulate the existence of a ME from the question, as from the searching."
>
> She had now made the essential interpretation in that the question arose out of what can only be called her creativity, creativity that was a coming together after relaxation, which is the opposite of integration.
>
> ["Playing: Creative Activity", pp. 63–64]

Winnicott's conclusions from this session provide a Cartesian flavour to his work: I question, therefore I am. The awareness of a sense of self has to come out of "desultory formlessness"—this is the third area, to which Winnicott refers in this paper as the "neutral zone". (*see* SELF: 11; TRANSITIONAL PHENOMENA: 5, 7)

7 Male and female elements

In "Creativity and Its Origins" (1971), Winnicott includes a paper he had presented in 1966 to the British Psycho-Analytical Society concerning "Male and Female Elements to be Found in Men and Women". This difficult and dense paper is instigated by Winnicott's clinical work at the time—something that is true of all his theoretical papers.

In a brief account, Winnicott describes that whilst listening to a male patient, it occurs to him that he is listening to a female. Winnicott shares his countertransference feeling with the patient.

What emerges is the analyst's discovery that although his male patient feels like a man in every way, at the early stages of his life his mother had seen him as a girl. This is what was being repeated in the transference relationship of the analysis, and why Winnicott (as the mother) heard a female. How does this relate to male and female elements?

Winnicott details this experience with his male patient and explains the effect it has on him. Now, as he writes, he is himself free-associating:

> When I gave myself time to think over what had happened I was puzzled. Here was no new theoretical concept, here was no new principle of technique. In fact, I and my patient had been over this ground before. Yet we had here something new, new in my own attitude and new in his capacity to make use of my interpretative work. I decided to surrender myself to whatever this might mean in myself, and the result is to be found in this paper that I am presenting.

> *DISSOCIATION*

> The first thing I noticed was that I had never before fully accepted the complete dissociation between the man (or woman) and the aspect of the personality that has the opposite sex. In the case of this man patient the dissociation was nearly complete.

> ["Creativity and Its Origins", pp. 75–76]

The "split-off female element" in Winnicott's patient was traced back to the mother's conviction (presumably because of her desire) that when she looked at her baby boy, she saw a baby girl. (Her first baby had been a boy.) Although this does not happen to each person, it did nevertheless push Winnicott to reflect and rethink something that Freud had introduced as the "bisexuality" of each person.

> . . . I found myself with a new edge to an old weapon, and I wondered how this would or could affect the work I was doing with other patients, both men and women, or boys and girls. I decided, therefore, to study this type of dissociation, leaving aside but not forgetting all the other types of splitting.

> ["Creativity and Its Origins", p. 76]

The difficulty in this paper is that the clinical material refers to a dissociated gender identity in one of Winnicott's patients, which initiates his thinking on the male and female elements in both men and women. Although these notions do overlap, there is a difference between gender identity and the existence of male and female elements in each person. The issue of gender identity is a huge area of research that has developed since Winnicott's writing—the male and female elements he wishes to explore are metapsychological, although rooted in the reality of the mother–infant relationship in the early weeks.

The main thesis of Winnicott's comments on male and female elements is that the sense of self depends on a marriage of both these elements emerging at the appropriate developmental phase.

8   Pure female element

The female element is placed at the beginning of life, when mother and infant are merged and do not *feel* one but *are* one (*see* BEING: 1). For a sense of self to be even possible, an establishment of being-one has to have occurred:

> . . . no sense of self emerges except on the basis of this relating in the sense of BEING. This sense of being is something that antedates the idea of being-at-one-with, because there has not yet been anything else except identity. Two separate persons can *feel* at one, but here at the place that I am examining the baby and the object *are* one. The term primary identification has perhaps been used for just this that I am describing and I am trying to show how vitally important this first experience is for the initiation of all subsequent experiences of identification.
>
> ["Creativity and Its Origins", p. 80]

For Winnicott, the female element is rooted in the experience of merger with the mother. This primary identification, where the infant experiences absolutely no difference between himself and mother, is the precursor to and foundation of any further development.

In this way Winnicott places the female element at the centre of the environment–individual set-up and at the same place as the location of culture and creativity.

Winnicott sees the female element as rooted in *being* between mother and infant who are merged and unintegrated. From this root of primary identification grows the process of identification which leads to differentiation between Me and Not-me.

> Projective and introjective identifications both stem from this place where each is the same as the other.
>
> In the growth of the human baby, as the ego begins to organize, this that I am calling the object-relating of the pure female element establishes what is perhaps the simplest of all experience, the experience of BEING. Here one finds a true continuity of generations, being which is passed on from one generation to another, via the female element of men and women and of male and female infants. I think this has been said before, but always in terms of women and girls, which confuses the issue. It is a matter of the female elements in both males and females.
>
> ["Creativity and Its Origins", p. 80]

9   Pure male element

The male element comes into play as the infant struggles to distinguish between Me and Not-me; it is part of the process of separation and relates to the stage of concern, when there is a precarious bringing-together of two mothers: the environment–mother and the object–mother. (see CONCERN: 3)

> By contrast, the object-relating of the male element to the object presupposes separateness. As soon as there is the ego organization available, the baby allows the object the quality of being not-me or separate, and experiences id satisfactions that include anger relative to frustration.
>
> ["Creativity and Its Origins", p. 80]

So the pure male element denotes the capacity for differentiation, based on separateness and ego development.

Creative living is associated with a bringing-together of male and female elements with the ability to both *be* and *do*, and this has to appear in a sequence:

> After being—doing and being done to. But first, being.
> ["Creativity and Its Origins", p. 85]

Winnicott implies that the dissociation of the male or the female elements prevents the individual from living creatively, although this is to be distinguished from gender identity.

Winnicott's thoughts regarding male and female elements certainly resemble Jung's ideas on male and female aspects of the personality (anima and animus) and the marriage of opposites in relation to the self. There are also parallels between Jung's transcendent function and Winnicott's theory of creative living. However, it is Winnicott's use of these concepts in the context of the mother–infant relationship that distinguishes his theory from Jung's.

REFERENCES

1951 Transitional Objects and Transitional Phenomena [W6]
1953 Review of *Psychoanalytic Studies of the Personality* [W19]
1967 The Location of Cultural Experience [W10]
1968 Communication between Infant and Mother, and Mother and Infant, Compared and Contrasted [W16]
1970 Living Creatively [W14]
1971 Creativity and Its Origins [W10]
1971 Playing: Creative Activity and the Search for the Self [W10]

Dependence

For Winnicott, the reality of the infant's dependence on his environment is one of the major determining features for his emotional development. He postulates three stages of dependency: "absolute dependence", "relative dependence", and "towards independence". The infant's successful negotiation of the first two stages of dependency relies on a good-enough environmental provision from the very beginning. It is the establishment of these stages that will facilitate the stage of maturity—named "towards independence".

1   A journey through dependency

Winnicott's statements on the sequential stages of dependence can be studied in his work during the 1960s, particularly in three papers that are to be found in the second volume of his theoretical papers, *The Maturational Processes and the Facilitating Environment* (W9): "The Theory of the Parent–Infant Relationship" (1960), "Providing for the Child in Health and Crisis" (1962), and "From

Dependence towards Independence in the Development of the Individual" (1963).

Essentially, Winnicott views the individual's emotional development as journeying from absolute dependence (often referred to as "double dependence" during his papers of the 1950s) to independence. The last stages of this journey he names "Towards Independence", implying that no one ever achieves full independence. The stages are dynamically related in the individual's internal world, so that although adult life is characterized by interdependency with responsibility, there will be times, such as illness, when the adult is thrown back to a state of absolute dependency.

In "The Theory of the Parent–Infant Relationship", the three stages of dependency are briefly defined:

Dependence

In the holding phase the infant is maximally dependent. One can classify dependence thus:

(i)   Absolute Dependence.   In this state the infant has no means of knowing about the maternal care, which is largely a matter of prophylaxis. He cannot gain control over what is well and what is badly done, but is only in a position to gain profit or to suffer disturbance.

(ii) Relative Dependence.   Here the infant can become aware of the need for the details of maternal care, and can to a growing extent relate them to personal impulse, and then later, in a psychoanalytic treatment, can reproduce them in the transference.

(iii) Towards Independence.   The infant develops means for doing without actual care. This is accomplished through the accumulation of memories of care, the projection of personal needs and the introjection of care details, with the development of confidence in the environment. Here must be added the element of intellectual understanding with its tremendous implications.

["Theory of Parent–Infant Relationship", p. 46]

Two years later, in "Providing for the Child In Health and Crisis", Winnicott breaks down the stages to degrees of dependence related to needs and provision. Here his emphasis on the environmental provision becomes very clear. The earlier the failure of the environment, the more disastrous the outcome for the individual's mental health. If the infant's needs are met during the early precarious stages of development, he will be in a strong position to survive an environmental failure later on.

5. We discuss providing for the child—and for the child in the adult. The mature adult is in fact taking part in the providing. In other words, childhood is a progression from dependence to independence. We need to examine the changing needs of the child as dependence changes over into independence. This leads us to a study of the very early needs of small children and of infants, and to the extremes of dependence. We can think of the degrees of dependence as a series:

   (a) Extreme dependence. Here conditions must be good enough, otherwise the infant cannot start the development that is born with him.
       Environmental failure: Mental defect non-organic; childhood schizophrenia; liability to mental-hospital disorder at a later date.

   (b) Dependence: Here conditions that fail do in fact traumatize, but there is already a person there to be traumatized.
       Environmental failure: Liability to affective disorders; antisocial tendency.

   (c) Dependence–independence mixtures. Here the child is making experiments in independence, but needs to be able to re-experience dependence.
       Environmental failure: Pathological dependence.

   (d) Independence–dependence. This is the same, but with the accent on independence.
       Environmental failure: Defiance; outbreaks of violence.

   (e) Independence. Implying an internalized environment: an ability on the part of the child to look after himself or herself.
       Environmental failure: Not necessarily harmful.

   (f) Social sense. Here it is implied that the individual can identify with adults and with a social group, or with society, without too great a loss of personal impulse and originality, and without too much loss of the destructive and aggressive impulses that have, presumably, found satisfactory expression in displaced forms. Environmental failure: Partly the responsibility of the individual, himself or herself, a parent, or a parent-figure in society.

["Providing for the Child", pp. 66–67]

Winnicott tends not to specify the stages in terms of an age. However, it can be seen across his work that absolute dependence and varying degrees of it will exist in the infant from birth to anything to between six weeks and three to four months; relative dependence subsequently follows, up to between 18 months and 2 years of age. The stage of "towards independence" will start once the baby/toddler has achieved the tasks of these earlier stages.

2   The fact of dependence

Winnicott often refers to the "fact" of dependence at the beginning of life.

It is valuable to recognize the *fact* of dependence. Dependence is real. That babies and children cannot manage on their own is so obvious that the simple facts of dependence are easily lost.

It can be said that the story of the growing child is a story of absolute dependence moving steadily through lessening degrees of dependence, and groping towards independence.

["Dependence in Child Care", 1970, p. 83]

The fact of dependence of the infant's predicament at the beginning of life is the holding phase. So as to emphasize the environment's contribution to the infant's development, Winnicott points out that the infant's absolute dependence makes up one half of the theory of the parent–infant relationship.

One half of the theory of the parent–infant relationship concerns the infant, and is the theory of the infant's journey from absolute dependence, through relative dependence, to independence, and, in parallel, the infant's journey from the pleasure principle to the reality principle, and from autoerotism to object relationships. The other half of the theory of the parent–infant relationship concerns maternal care, that is to say the qualities and changes in the mother that meet the specific and developing needs of the infant towards whom she orientates.

["Theory of Parent–Infant Relationship", p. 42]

Winnicott uses the term "absolute dependence" specifically to describe the infant's predicament—he needs his mother's womb in which to develop, and when he is born he needs his mother to "perfectly adapt" to his needs. If she is in a state of primary maternal preoccupation (intense identification with her baby), then he is more likely to grow well, both physically and emotionally.

Winnicott draws attention to the paradox contained in the newborn infant's predicament:

> . . . in terms of psychology we have to say that the infant is at one and the same time dependent and independent. It is this paradox that we need to examine. There is all that is inherited, including the maturational processes, and perhaps patho-logical inherited trends, and these have a reality of their own, and no one can alter these; at the same time, the maturational processes depend for their evolution on the environmental provision.
>
> ["From Dependence towards Independence", p. 84]

He then makes a crucial point:

> We can say that the facilitating environment makes possible the steady progress of the maturational processes. But the environment does not make the child. At best it enables the child to realize potential.
>
> ["From Dependence towards Independence", pp. 84–85]

The parents do not know what the infant's inherited tendencies will be. It is their child's personal idiom that is what they will need to adapt and respond to. All they can do is provide the right environment (adaptation to needs), because they cannot make the baby into the baby of their fantasies.

The time during which the baby is absolutely dependent links with many other themes of Winnicott's—going-on-being or the continuity-of-being, reactions to impingement, primary maternal preoccupation, merging, objects that are subjectively perceived, communication, and holding. (*see* BEING: 1; CREATIVITY: 1; EGO: 2; ENVIRONMENT: 4; MOTHER: 11, 12; PLAYING: 9; SELF: 6)

From the infant's point of view, the main feature of absolute dependence is that he is absolutely *not* aware of his mother's care and his dependence on her. His mother is himself, and when he receives what he needs, he believes he has caused this because he is God (the necessary experience of omnipotence).

3   The fear of WOMAN

Misogyny was not a word used by Winnicott; however, he alludes to the roots of misogyny when, as early as 1950, he writes about the fear of WOMAN, in a paper entitled, "Some Thoughts on the Meaning of the Word 'Democracy'", published in 1950 in *Human Relations*:

> In psychoanalytical and allied work it is found that all individuals (men and women) have in reserve a certain fear of WOMAN. Some individuals have this fear to a greater extent than others, but it can be said to be universal. This is quite different from saying that an individual fears a particular woman. This fear of WOMAN is a powerful agent in society structure, and it is responsible for the fact that in very few societies does a woman hold the political reins. It is also responsible for the immense amount of cruelty to women, which can be found in customs that are accepted by almost all civilizations.
>
> The root of this fear of WOMAN is known. It is related to the fact that in the early history of every individual who develops well, and who is sane, and who has been able to find himself, there is a debt to a woman—the woman who was devoted to that individual as an infant, and whose devotion was absolutely essential for that individual's healthy development. The original dependence is not remembered, and therefore the debt is not acknowledged, except in so far as the fear of WOMAN represents the first stage of this acknowledgement.
>
> ["Meaning of Word 'Democracy'", p. 252]

Winnicott adds, in a footnote:

> It would be out of place to discuss this here in detail, but the
> idea can be reached best if approached gradually:
> (i)   Fear of the parents of very early childhood
> (ii) Fear of a combined figure, a woman with male potency
>   included in her powers (witch).
> (iii) Fear of the mother who had absolute power at the begin-
>   ning of the infant's existence to provide, or to fail to
>   provide, the essentials for the early establishment of the
>   self as an individual.
>
> ["Meaning of Word 'Democracy'", p. 252]

In the subsequent two paragraphs, Winicott makes a revolutionary (albeit contentious) statement—the beginnings of a psycho-
analytical understanding as to why there is a preponderance of
patriarchal societies.

> The foundation of the mental health of the individual is laid
> down at the very beginning when the mother is simply being
> devoted to her infant, and when the infant is doubly depend-
> ent because totally unaware of dependence. There is no
> relation to the father which has such a quality, and for this
> reason a man who in a political sense is at the top can be
> appreciated by the group much more objectively than a
> woman can be if she is in a similar position.
>   Women often claim that if women were in charge of affairs,
> there would be no wars. There are reasons why this may be
> doubted as a final statement of truth, but, even if the claim
> were justified, it would still not follow that men or women
> would ever tolerate the general principle of women generally
> at the highest point of political power. (The Crown, by being
> outside or beyond politics, is not affected by these considera-
> tions.)
>
> ["Meaning of Word 'Democracy'", pp. 252–253]

In the following two paragraphs, Winnicott extends this idea to
apply to reasons behind dictatorship and groups of people who
require a dominating leader:

> . . . one can consider the psychology of the dictator, who is at
> the opposite pole to anything that the word "democracy" can

mean. *One of the roots of the need to be a dictator can be a compulsion to deal with this fear of woman by encompassing her and acting for her.* The dictator's curious habit of demanding not only absolute obedience and absolute dependence but also "love", can be derived from this source.

Moreover, the tendency of groups of people to accept or even seek *actual* domination is derived from a fear of domination by *fantasy woman*. This fear leads them to seek, and even welcome, domination by a known human being, especially one who has taken on himself the burden of personifying and therefore limiting the magical qualities of the all-powerful woman of fantasy, to whom is owed the great debt. The dictator can be overthrown, and must eventually die; but the woman figure of primitive unconscious fantasy has no limits to her existence or power.

["Meaning of Word 'Democracy'", p. 253]

Across Winnicott's writings there are few places that plug in so explicitly to politics, although there is always the potential for the application of his theories in this way. The fear of WOMAN is Winnicott's contribution to an understanding of the treatment of women in the majority of societies. Although potentially important, it remains one of the theories that he never elaborates.

In 1957, in a postscript to Winnicott's collection of broadcasts, entitled "The Mother's Contribution to Society", he stresses the importance of each individual acknowledging the fact of dependence, and how this acknowledgement will lessen fear.

Once again, let me emphasize, the result of such recognition when it comes will not be gratitude or even praise. The result will be a lessening in ourselves of a fear. If our society delays making full acknowledgement of this dependence, which is a historical fact in the initial stage of development of every individual, there must remain a block both to progress and to regression, a block that is based on fear. If there is no true recognition of the mother's part, then there must remain a vague fear of dependence. This fear will sometimes take the form of a fear of WOMAN, or a fear of a woman, and at other times will take less easily recognized forms, always including the fear of domination.

["Mother's Contribution to Society", p. 125]

Again he refers to the dictator's need to dominate and people's need to be dominated—a consequence of not acknowledging the fact of dependence.

> Unfortunately, the fear of domination does not lead groups of people to avoid being dominated; on the contrary, it draws them towards a specific or chosen domination. Indeed, were the psychology of the dictator studied, one would expect to find that, amongst other things, he in his own personal struggle is trying to control the woman whose domination he unconsciously fears, trying to control her by encompassing her, acting for her, and in turn demanding total subjection and "love".
>
> Many students of social history have thought that fear of WOMAN is a powerful cause of the seemingly illogical behaviour of human beings in groups, but this fear is seldom traced to its root. Traced to its root in the history of each individual, this fear of WOMAN turns out to be a fear of recognizing the fact of dependence.
>
> ["Mother's Contribution to Society", p. 125]

Some years later, in 1964, in a paper he presented to the Progressive League, Winnicott briefly developed these themes by designating the term "WOMAN" to mean "the unacknowledged mother of the first stages of the life of every man and woman" ("This Feminism", 1964, p. 192).

This leads on to Winnicott's personal way of differentiating between men and women. In every woman there are three women:

> ... we may find a new way of stating the difference between the sexes. Women have it in them to deal with their relation to WOMAN by identification with her. For every woman, there are always three women: (1) girl baby; (2) mother; (3) mother's mother.
>
> In myth the three generations of woman constantly appear, or three women with three separate functions. Whether a woman has babies or not, she is in this infinite series; she is baby, mother and grandmother, she is mother, girl baby and baby's baby ... while man starts off with a tremendous urge to be one. One is one and all alone, and ever more shall be so.
>
> Man cannot do this that woman can do, this being merged in with the race, without violating the whole of his nature.

> ... The awkward fact remains, for men and women, that each was once dependent on woman, and somehow a hatred of this has to be transformed into a kind of gratitude if full maturity of the personality is to be reached.
>
> ["This Feminism", pp. 192–193]

Men envy women the risk they take in childbirth, postulates Winnicott, which leads men to seek dangerous sports, where they are compelled to take risks. But, he points out enigmatically, "when a man dies he is dead, whereas women always were and always will be" ("This Feminism", p. 193).

4   Relative dependence

The phase where the infant starts to distinguish between Me and Not-me involves five important, overlapping features, all to do with the process of weaning, that occur in both the mother and the infant in relation to each other.

Winnicott estimates that this phase normally lasts from around 6 months to 2 years, and he indicates that the aim in weaning is "to use the baby's developing ability to get rid of things and to let the loss of the breast be not just simply a chance affair".

The five main features of the stage of relative dependence are:

• mother's gradual failing and de-adaptation in response to the infant's development;

• the infant's beginning of an intellectual understanding;

• mother's reliable steady presentation of the world to baby, which depends on her capacity *to be herself* (object-presenting);

• the infant's growing awareness of his dependency;

• the infant's ability to identify.

5   De-adaptation and failing

The mother begins to emerge from her state of primary maternal preoccupation and remembers who she is in terms of being an independent individual in the world. She is recovering, both physically and emotionally, from the last important stages of pregnancy, giving birth, and being merged in identification with her infant's absolute dependence on her.

The infant requires his mother to de-adapt, which is part and parcel of her remembering herself. This "failure" on the mother's part introduces the "reality principle" to the child and is part of the disillusioning process, related to weaning (*see* MOTHER: 11). By "failing" in this way, the mother, unknowingly, allows the infant to feel and experience his needs. This "failure" contributes to his developing sense of self—a self that is Me and separate from mother.

If, however, the mother cannot "fail" (we could say, instead, to let-go-and-allow her-baby-to-grow), then the infant's drive to self-realization is impeded.

> . . . the infant who has begun to become separate from the mother has no means of gaining control of all the good things that are going on. The creative gesture, the cry, the protest, all the little signs that are supposed to produce what the mother does, all these things are missing, because the mother has already met the need just as if the infant were still merged with her and she with the infant. In this way the mother, by being a seemingly good mother, does something worse than castrate the infant. The latter is left with two alternatives: either being in a permanent state of regression and of being merged with the mother, or else staging a total rejection of the mother, even of the seemingly good mother.
>
> We see therefore that in infancy and in the management of infants there is a very subtle distinction between the mother's understanding of her infant's need based on empathy, and her change over to an understanding based on something in the infant or small child that indicates need. This is particularly difficult for mothers because of the fact that children vacillate between one state and the other; one minute they are merged with their mothers, and require empathy, while the next they are separated from her, and then if she knows their needs in advance she is dangerous, a witch.
>
> ["Theory of Parent–Infant Relationship", pp. 51–52]

It is worth clarifying Winnicott's use of the word "failure". Failure with a small "f" is associated with de-adaptation. This is healthy because it is a necessary aspect of the infant's development—

necessary, because it facilitates (unconsciously and *en passant*) the process of disillusionment through the mother/woman being herself (continuing to develop and live her life).

The mother who cannot do this for herself and who clings to her baby beyond the appropriate age prevents her infant from reaching the stage of concern and the ability to use transitional space. (*see* CONCERN: 7; TRANSITIONAL PHENOMENA: 3)

On the other hand, the mother who really lets her infant down and causes a sudden break in the infant's continuity-of-being constitutes a failure with a capital "F". The aetiology of the antisocial tendency arises from this sort of environmental failure. (*see* ANTISO-CIAL TENDENCY: 2, 3)

One of the crucial components during this time of relative dependence, then, is that the infant lets the mother know what he needs. This "signal" from infant to mother can also be applied to the patient–analyst relationship.

> . . . At the end of merging, when the child has become separate from the environment, an important feature is that the infant has to give a signal. We find this subtlety appearing clearly in the transference in our analytic work. It is very important when the patient is regressed to earliest infancy and to a state of merging, that the analyst shall *not* know the answers except in so far as the patient gives the clues.
>
> ["Theory of Parent–Infant Relationship", p. 50]

Winnicott explores dependency in the therapeutic relationship in his 1963 paper, "Dependence in Infant-Care, in Child-Care, and in the Psychoanalytic Setting". This paper links up with his 1954 paper, "Metapsychological and Clinical Aspects of Regression within the Psychoanalytical Set-Up", in that it refers to the aspects of infant care that relate to the analytic relationship. Both papers refer to the phases of dependence that patients may develop in the therapeutic relationship.

In the 1963 paper Winnicott describes the importance of the analyst's mistakes within the transference relationship. If the mistakes are made too early they may cause a repeated trauma for the patient, but at the right time in the therapeutic relationship they will contribute to the necessary disillusionment phases parallel to the mother's de-adaptation and "failure".

6   *The beginning of an intellectual understanding*

The dawn of intelligence in the infant derives from the holding
phase of absolute dependence, and it develops into the infant's
ability to understand intellectually by the time of relative dependence. Winnicott provides an example:

> Think of an infant expecting a feed. The time comes when the
> infant can wait a few minutes because noises in the kitchen
> indicate that food is about to appear. Instead of simply being
> excited by the noises, the infant uses the news item in order to
> be able to wait.
>
> ["From Dependence towards Independence", p. 87]

This example of how the infant is able to wait also illustrates how
the mother may take advantage of her infant's ability to think.
Through the phase of absolute dependence, she had to think for the
infant in her capacity as ego auxiliary. During this phase of relative
dependence, she can now allow the infant to start thinking for
himself. This developing capacity in the infant releases the mother
from her primary maternal preoccupation, as she is able to recover
her own sense of self and separate from her infant:

> It could be said that at the beginning the mother must adapt
> almost exactly to the infant's needs in order that the infant
> personality shall develop without distortion. She is able to fail
> in her adaptation, however, and to fail increasingly, and this
> is because the infant's mind and the infant's intellectual pro-
> cesses are able to account for and so to allow for failures of
> adaptation. In this way the mind is allied to the mother and
> takes over part of her function. In the care of an infant the
> mother is dependent on the infant's intellectual processes,
> and it is these that enable her gradually to re-acquire a life of
> her own.
>
> ["The First Year of Life:
> Modern Views of Emotional Development", p. 7]

There are inherent dangers in depending on the infant's intellect
at this stage of development; the infant who is forced into a position of releasing his mother and has to use his intelligence too
much may develop an intellectual split-off false self. (*see* SELF: 8)

The infant's ability to think will depend on how the world is presented to him by mother:

> Naturally infants vary very much in their capacity to use intellectual understanding early, and often the understanding they might have had is delayed by the existence of a muddle in the way reality is presented. There is an idea for emphasis here, for the whole procedure of infant care has as its main characteristic a steady presentation of the world to the infant. This is something that cannot be done by thought, nor can it be managed mechanically. It can only be done by continuous management by a human being who is consistently herself. There is no question of perfection here. Perfection belongs to machines; what the infant needs is just what he usually gets, the care and attention of someone who is going on being herself. This of course applies to fathers too.
>
> ["From Dependence towards Independence", pp. 87–88]

Mother's ability to object-present is one of her crucial functions. (*see* MOTHER: 8)

Winnicott then distinguishes between parents who "act" the part and parents who are able to parent *and* be themselves, introducing the idea of the true and false parents.

> A special point needs to be made of this "being herself" because one should separate out the person from the man or woman, mother or nurse, who is *acting* the part, perhaps acting it quite well at times, and perhaps acting it well because of having learned how to care for infants from books or in a class. But this acting is not good enough. The infant can only find an unmuddled presentation of external reality by being cared for by a human being who is devoted to the infant and to the infant-care task. The mother will grow up out of this state of easy devotion, and soon she will be back to the office desk, or to writing novels, or to a social life along with her husband, but for the time being she is in it up to the neck.
>
> ["From Dependence towards Independence", p. 88]

The word "failure" is re-introduced at this juncture of the paper. Winnicott points out that "being herself" means "being human", and human beings make mistakes and fail. Paradoxically, Winnicott stresses, it is the mother's failures that will communicate to the infant her true reliability:

> As development proceeds, and the baby has acquired an inside and an outside, then the environmental reliability becomes a belief, an introject based on the experience of reliability (human, not mechanically perfect).
>
> Is it not true that the mother has communicated with the baby? She has said: "I am reliable—not because I am a machine, but because I know what you are needing; and I care, and I want to provide what you need. This is what I call love at this stage of your development."
>
> But this kind of communication is silent. The baby does not hear or register the communication, only the effects of the reliability; this is registered in terms of on-going development. The baby does not know about the communication except from the effects of *failure* of reliability. This is where the difference comes in between mechanical perfection and human love. Human beings fail and fail; and in the course of ordinary care a mother is all the time mending her failures. These relative failures with immediate remedy undoubtedly add up eventually to a communication, so that the baby comes to know about success. Successful adaptation thus gives a sense of security, a feeling of having been loved.
>
> ["Communication between Infant and Mother, and Mother and Infant, Compared and Contrasted", 1968, pp. 97–98]

These human failures will only make sense to the infant because of the "immediate remedy"—it is the *"failures mended"* that contribute to the infant's sense of well-being:

> It is the innumerable failures followed by the sort of care that mends that build up into a communication of love, of the fact that there is a human being there who cares. Where failure is not mended within the requisite time, second, minutes, hours, then we use the term deprivation. A deprived child, after knowing about failures mended, comes to experience failure unmended. It is then the lifework of the child to provoke conditions in which failures mended once more give the pattern to life.
>
> ["Communication between Infant and Mother", p. 98]

Failures mended also needs to occur in the analytic relationship in relation to the analyst's mistakes.

7 Awareness—towards independence

Absolute dependency is characterized by the infant's lack of awareness of his dependence on his mother. During the stage of relative dependence, the baby begins to become aware of his dependence. This awareness leads on to the feeling of anxiety in the infant when he is separated from his mother; the demonstration of anxiety indicates that the infant knows about his mother's care and protection:

> The next stage beyond that at which the infant in some way feels a need for the mother is one in which the infant begins to *know in his mind* that mother is necessary.
>
> Gradually the need for the actual mother (in health) becomes fierce and truly terrible, so that mothers do really hate to leave their children, and they sacrifice a great deal rather than cause distress and indeed produce hatred and disillusionment during this phase of special need. This phase could be said to last from (roughly) six months to two years.
>
> ["From Dependence towards Independence", p. 88]

The infant's demonstration of his anxiety when separated from his mother also shows that he is beginning to distinguish between Me and Not-me.

Identity is also part of this process, and the infant who is able to identify with his mother, and see her as separate from himself, has reached a crucial stage of development, which Winnicott described as "unit status". The infant is now a person in his own right ("Theory of Parent–Infant Relationship", p. 44).

> I wish to mention a form of development that especially affects the infant's capacity for making complex identifications. This has to do with the stage at which the integrating tendencies of the infant bring about a state in which the infant is a unit, a whole person, with an inside and an outside, and a person living in the body, and more or less bounded by the skin. Once outside means "not-ME" then inside means ME,

and there is now a place in which to store things. In the child's fantasy the personal psychic reality is located inside. If it is located outside there are good reasons.

Now the infant's growth takes the form of a continuous interchange between inner and outer reality, each being enriched by the other.

["From Dependence towards Independence", pp. 90–91]

It is this "continuous interchange between inner and outer reality" that makes "perception almost synonymous with creation". This is the frame of unit status.

The child is now not only a potential creator of the world, but also the child becomes able to populate the world with samples of his or her own inner life. So gradually the child is able to "cover" almost any external event, and perception is almost synonymous with creation.

["From Dependence towards Independence", p. 91]

This links up with Winnicott's concept of creative apperception, relating to subjective objects and the necessity of illusion in creative living. (*see* BEING: 3; COMMUNICATION: 9; CREATIVITY: 2; MOTHER: 4)

In "The Theory of the Parent–Infant Relationship", Winnicott describes the stage of "towards independence" thus:

. . . The infant develops means for doing without actual care. This is accomplished through the accumulation of memories of care, the projection of personal needs and the introjection of care details, with the development of confidence in the environment. Here must be added the element of intellectual understanding with its tremendous implications.

["Theory of Parent–Infant Relationship", p. 46]

Winnicott means that the first two stages of dependency have been negotiated well enough, so that the young child/toddler has now established a strong internal world based on his experiences. This stage heralds development for the rest of his life.

The young child's growing independence is juxtaposed with continuing to be dependent. This necessary contradiction is at its most intense during adolescence:

Parents are very much needed in the management of their own adolescent children who are exploring one social circle after another, because of their ability to see better than their children can when this progression from the limited social circle towards the unlimited social circle is too rapid, perhaps because of dangerous social elements in the immediate neighbourhood, or because of the defiance that belongs to puberty and to a rapid development in the sexual capacity. They are needed especially because of the instinct tensions and patterns that reappear and which were first laid down at the toddler age.

["From Dependence towards Independence", p. 92]

Winnicott's work highlights the infant's struggle during the first two stages of dependency, because emotional development from then on is based and elaborated on this beginning. Being an adult does not mean that emotional maturity has been reached. Adult life begins when the individual has

... found a niche in society through work, and ... settled in some pattern that is a compromise between copying the parents and defiantly establishing a personal identity.

["From Dependence towards Independence", p. 92]

REFERENCES

1950 Some Thoughts on the Meaning of the Word "Democracy" [W14]

1957 The Mother's Contribution to Society [W14]

1958 The First Year of Life: Modern Views of Emotional Development [W8]

1960 The Theory of the Parent–Infant Relationship [W9]

1962 Providing for the Child in Health and in Crisis [W9]

1963 From Dependence towards Independence in the Development of the Individual [W9]

1964 This Feminism [W14]

1968 Communication between Infant and Mother, and Mother and Infant, Compared and Contrasted [W16]

1970 Dependence in Child Care [W16]

Depression

W innicott's view of depression covers a wide spectrum, with, at one end, depression as a sign of achievement and a normal part of emotional development, and, at the other end, a pathological and affective disorder associated with a blockage in emotional development.

The way depression as a mood is negotiated in each individual depends on what occurs between mother and infant, particularly during the time of weaning, when the infant is beginning the journey of differentiating between Me and Not-me.

1   Depression and its value

Throughout Winnicott's work, his use of the word "depression" emerges in many contexts, with varying emphases. Essentially, he designates the word "depression" to indicate a mood or state of mind. However, he can very easily appear to be using the term in contradictory ways. For example, in his 1954 paper, "The Depressive Position in Normal Emotional Development", he states very clearly that the term "depressive position" is misleading, because "depressive" implies that healthy development involves a "mood illness", which, he states, is *not* part of normal development (*see* CONCERN: 2). Yet in 1958, in his paper "The Family Affected by Depressive Illness in One or Both Parents", Winnicott implies that depression *is* normal and something experienced by "valuable" people (by using the term "valuable", he implies the value of depression).

By 1963, in a paper entitled "The Value of Depression", Winnicott seems to be almost celebrating depression as a sign of health, creating individuals who are responsible members of society. It is in this paper that he distinguishes between purities and impurities of the depressed mood.

The apparent contradiction occurs because Winnicott is referring to a mood that affects each person differently. The individual who has reached "unit status" will be able to experience a depression that is valuable and healing; the individual who has not reached "unit status" will either mobilize defences against feeling the pain of depression or become stuck.

Winnicott was critical of Klein's term "depressive position" because it implied illness whilst describing an aspect of emotional health. Yet he himself designated a similarly laden psychiatric term, "depression", to refer to both emotional health and pathology.

In an attempt to distinguish qualitatively between the different depressions in Winnicott's work, it may be useful to delineate (artificially) three main areas:

1. *Depression as a capacity that develops as a normal part of the maturational processes.* This "normal" sort of depression is an achievement and signifies the successful negotiation of weaning, the sense of loss, the sense of guilt/capacity for concern, working through disillusionment. It leads the individual from object-relating to object-usage, which indicates the object has survived (*see* AGGRESSION: 9, 10). There is no cure needed for the depression of the first kind. The mood has to be tolerated by others. The only prescription is to wait.

2. *Depression as an affective disorder which emerges as a result of the lack of opportunity to contribute-in (see CONCERN: 7).* This sort of depression is the result of a blockage in development due to

failure of the early environment. It is an indication that the object has not survived and the subject has not reached object usage.

3. *Defences that are mobilized in order to avoid the pain of depression,* such as the manic defence, hypomania, and psychosis.

2   Healthy depression

Winnicott sees that the capacity to feel depressed is a sign of health. This sort of "depression" is more akin to sadness linked with a sense of loss and a sense of guilt. To be aware of loss and guilt leads the individual to take responsibility and motivates a wish to contribute-in. It is a sign that the individual has achieved "unit status" and a capacity for concern (*see* CONCERN: 5, 6). In 1958, Winnicott provides a scale.

> . . . at one end of the scale there is melancholia, at the other end there is depression, a condition which is common to all inte-grated human beings. When Keats said of the world: "Where but to think is to be full of sorrow and leaden-eyed despair", he did not mean that he was of no value or even that he was in an ill state of mind. Here was someone who took the risk of feeling things deeply and of taking responsibility. At the one extreme, therefore, are the melancholiacs, who take responsi-bility for all the ills of the world, especially those which are quite obviously nothing to do with them, and at the other extreme are the truly responsible people of the world, those who accept the fact of their own hate, nastiness, cruelty, things which coexist with their capacity to love and to construct. Sometimes their sense of their own awfulness gets them down.
>   If we look at depression in this way we can see that it is the really valuable people in the world who get depressed. . . .
>   ["The Family Affected by Depressive Illness", 1958, pp. 51–52]

When Winnicott writes of "people who get depressed", he is not referring to breakdown or hospitalization but, rather, to "people who feel sad". The sadness is the result of the capacity to recog-nize one's own awfulness, which usually leads to taking responsibility.

This responsibility was referred to, *en passant*, in a paper Winnicott gave in 1963 to the Association of Psychiatric Social Workers, entitled "The Value of Depression". He pointed out that people involved in working with depressed patients, like analysts and psychiatric social workers, were at some level treating their own depression. This, he said, was an example of the constructive and valuable aspect of depression.

In this same paper, Winnicott associates unit status and ego strength with depression (*see* EGO: 3):

> The development and establishment of ego strength is the important or basic feature indicating health. Naturally the term "ego strength" comes to mean more and more as the child matures, and at first the ego has strength only because of the ego support given by the adapting mother, who for a while was able to identify closely with her own infant.
>
> There comes a stage at which the child has become a unit, becomes able to feel: I AM, has an inside, is able to ride his or her instinctual storms, and also is able to contain the strains and stresses that arise in the personal inner psychic reality. *The child has become able to be depressed.* This is an achievement of emotional growth.
>
> ["Value of Depression", p. 73]

This could be misleading, because Winnicott does not mean that the child becomes pathologically depressed; rather, he is able to feel sad *and* concerned, linked with a healthy sense of guilt (*see* CONCERN: 3). Following on from the above, Winnicott clarifies his meaning of depression:

> Our view of depression, then, is closely bound up with our concept of ego strength and of self-establishment and of the discovery of a personal identity, and it is for this reason that we can discuss the idea that depression has value.
>
> ["Value of Depression", p. 73]

3   Weaning in relation to illusion and disillusion

The capacity to feel sad, therefore, is an aspect of the weaning stage in infancy which goes along with a disillusionment:

Just behind weaning is the wider subject of disillusionment.
Weaning implies successful feeding and disillusionment implies the successful provision of opportunity for illusion.

["Psychoses and Child Care", p. 221]

The subject of illusion/disillusionment relates to Freud's work on
the infant's transition from the pleasure principle to the reality
principle. Winnicott's observations of mothers and infants, in tan-
dem with his work as a psychoanalyst, led him to explore what he
described as the intermediate area of experience. (see TRANSITIONAL
PHENOMENA: 3)

The successful feeding and subsequent weaning, as referred to
above, depicts the infant who has experienced a sense of omnipotence during the phase of absolute dependence, when his mother
was able to adapt to his needs (see MOTHER: 8; PRIMARY MATERNAL
PREOCCUPATION: 4). Without this primary experience of omnipotence, Winnicott believes that it is not possible for the infant to
"develop a capacity to experience a relationship to external reality
or even to form a conception of reality" ("Transitional Objects and
Transitional Phenomena", 1951, p. 238).

A valuable, healthy depression, in Winnicott's work, is part of
the process an infant is undergoing when working through the
transition from being merged with mother to perceiving her as
separate and Not-me. The depression—or, more appropriately,
sadness—is the psychological working-through of the sense of loss
at the end of the time of merger—the pattern of mourning. This is
all part and parcel of the disillusionment process as the infant
realizes he is not, in fact, the centre of the universe. (see DEPEND-
ENCE: 5, 6; MOTHER: 8)

4   The depressed mood

Winnicott uses the metaphor of a fog or mist to describe the depressed mood:

> . . . a fog over the city represents the depressed mood. Every-
> thing is slowed down and brought towards a state of
> deadness. This state of relative deadness controls all, and in
> the case of the human individual blurs instincts and the ca-

pacity for relating to external objects. Gradually the fog gets thin in places or even begins to lift. The mood lessens in intensity and life begins again. . . .

Here consideration is being given not so much to anxiety and to anxiety content, as to ego structure and the internal economy of the individual. Depression coming on, continuing and lifting, indicates that the ego structure has held over a phase of crisis. This is a triumph of integration.

["Value of Depression", pp. 75–76]

Winnicott relates the depressed mood to a "new experience of destructiveness and of destructive ideas that go with loving. The new experiences necessitate internal reassessment, and it is this reassessment we see as depression" ("Value of Depression", p. 76).

This destruction emanates from innate "primary aggression", which seeks an object in order to realize the fact of reality (Not-me). The repeated destruction *in fantasy* creates the externality of the object, and the consequence is the ability to differentiate between Me and Not-me. (*see* AGGRESSION: 7, 8)

This "destruction" is particularly pertinent to the adolescent period described by Winnicott as the "doldrums" ("Adolescence: Struggling through the Doldrums", 1961).

The mood of depression is, therefore, associated with the preoccupation involved in what Winnicott describes as primary creativity: the creativity of creative living and/or the preoccupation of the creative artist. (*see* CREATIVITY: 4, 5, 6)

In his 1963 paper "The Value of Depression", Winnicott refers to the pathological end of the spectrum of depression as *impurities* of the depression mood. He sketches seven categories. In the first, he includes all *"the failures of ego organization* which indicate a tendency in the patient towards a more primitive type of illness, towards schizophrenia" ("Value of Depression", p. 77). This category certainly refers to the person who has not reached "unit status" and has not experienced a good-enough holding environment.

The other categories refer to the various defences used by individuals in order to avoid the working-through that the "purity" of the depression mood can achieve ("Value of Depression", pp. 78–79).

One of these defences is explored by Winnicott in his 1948 paper, "Reparation in Respect of Mother's Organized Defence against Depression", where he describes how the mother's depression is taken on by the child who subsequently is unable to differentiate between personal depression and mother's depression.

> Watching many of these cases continuously over periods of ten or even twenty years I have been able to see that the depression of the child can be the mother's depression in reflection. The child uses the mother's depression as an escape from his or her own; this provides a false restitution and reparation in relation to the mother, and this hampers the development of a personal restitution capacity because the restitution does not relate to the child's own guilt sense. . . .
>
> It will be seen that these children in extreme cases have a task which can never be accomplished. Their task is first to deal with mother's mood. If they succeed in the immediate task, they do no more than succeed in creating an atmosphere in which they can start on their own lives.
>
> ["Reparation in Respect of Mother's", pp. 92–93]

Winnicott points out that mother's or father's depression can too easily be used by the patient to avoid feeling personal depression, and that through analysis the patient can arrive at distinguishing between the parent's and his own depression.

5   Waiting, not curing

Winnicott warns against the tendency to "cheer up" the person who is depressed:

> We do not want to be jogged or jigged out of our mood, but a real friend to tolerate us, help us a little, and wait.
>
> ["Family Affected by Depressive Illness", p. 52]

> As a medical student I was taught that depression has within itself the germ of recovery. This is the one bright spot in psychopathology, and it links depression with the sense of guilt (a capacity for which is a sign of healthy development) and with the mourning process. Mourning too tends eventually to finish its job. The built-in tendency to recover links depression

also with the maturation process of the individual's infancy and childhood, a process which (in a facilitating environment) leads on to personal maturity, which is health.

["Value of Depression", p. 72]

The healthy individual who is feeling depressed is in the process of working something out and working through the loss, as in bereavement.

... depression is a healing mechanism; it covers the battle-ground as with a mist, allowing for a sorting out at a reduced rate, giving time for all possible defences to be brought into play, and for a working through, so that eventually there can be a spontaneous recovery. Clinically, depression (of this sort) tends to lift. . . .

["Depressive Position", p. 275]

And on behalf of depressed adolescents, Winnicott makes a plea:

... if the adolescent is to get through this development stage by natural process, then there must be expected a phenomenon which could be called adolescent doldrums. Society needs to include this as a permanent feature and to tolerate it, to react actively to it, in fact to come to meet it, *but not to cure it.*

["Adolescence", pp. 85–86]

As depression contains a healthy element, the best help "is accept-ance of the depression not an urge to cure it" ("The Family Affected by Depressive Illness", p. 60).

By the 1960s, Winnicott stresses the value of waiting more and more in his psychoanalytic work. The analyst's waiting, which can be the most containing and holding aspect of the analysis, implies faith that the patient will work through the difficulties and arrive at the place he needs to be, in his own time.

REFERENCES

1948 Reparation in Respect of Mother's Organized Defence against Depression   [W6]
1951 Transitional Objects and Transitional Phenomena   [W6]
1952 Psychoses and Child Care   [W6]

Ego

Winnicott, when he is being specific, makes a distinction between the "ego" and the "self"; when he is not being specific, he uses the terms almost synonymously.
Generally, in Winnicott's work the use of the word "ego" refers to an aspect of the true and/or false "self" as well as the psyche–soma. It is this aspect that serves to integrate self-experience.

1   Psychoanalytic terminology

The technical language of psychoanalysis in English is problematic due to the medicalized translation of Freud's work by Strachey (Bettelheim, 1983). The use of the word "ego" has a complex history.

It has already been pointed out that Winnicott tends to use the major psychoanalytic terms without strict reference to their original meaning (Phillips, 1988); the word "ego" is no exception.

In *Human Nature* (W18), Winnicott makes it clear that he is familiar with Freud's topographical and structural theories. How-

ever, throughout Winnicott's work—and particularly in the last
decade of his writing—his notion of the "ego" can be seen to be
distinct from Freud's.

The most definitive statement on specifying the role and function of the ego in emotional development can be found in
Winnicott's 1962 paper, "Ego Integration in Child Development".

Here the description of the ego is twofold—it is a "part of the
personality that tends under suitable conditions, to become integrated into a unit", which suggests that at the beginning the ego
exists as potential. The realization of the potential relies on an
intact brain, which is capable of organizing experience because
"with no electronic apparatus there can be no experience, and
therefore no ego". However, the ability to organize experience also
depends on suitable conditions—that is, good-enough mothering.

In Freud's theory the ego emerges from the id. Winnicott, like
Klein, believes there is an ego, however undeveloped, at the very
beginning.

> In the very early stages of the development of a human child,
> therefore, ego-functioning needs to be taken as a concept that
> is inseparable from that of the existence of the infant as a
> person. What instinctual life there may be apart from ego-
> functioning can be ignored, because the infant is not yet an
> entity having experiences. There is no id before ego.
>
> ["Ego Integration in Child Development", p. 56]

For Winnicott, the ego is responsible for gathering in information
(external and internal experiences) and organizing it. However,
this is only possible *if* the mother is good enough, because at the
very beginning she *is* the baby's ego. During the infant's phase of
absolute dependence, the mother's state of primary maternal preoccupation enables her to be the necessary ego-support for her
infant, through her adaptation to his needs. The strength of this
ego-support depends entirely on the mother's ability to adapt. (*see*
PRIMARY MATERNAL PREOCCUPATION: 4)

The term "ego-relatedness", used mostly in the 1950s, refers to
the merger between mother and infant at the beginning. By the
1960s, Winnicott refers to the same phenomenon as "object-relating". It is the time when the infant is not aware of what he needs,

and he depends on the environment, his mother, to know. She, through her intense identification with him, has to be his ego in order to protect and support him. (*see* ALONE: 1; DEPENDENCE: 2; HOLDING: 4)

With the aid of this strong ego-support at the beginning, the infant is enabled to develop and grow. The foundation of mental health begins here.

From this basis, the infant is set up to negotiate the next stages of development, which journey through the dependency stages and arrive towards a state of health and maturity. This is a continual dynamic occurring in each individual at each stage of life. (*see* DEPENDENCE)

2   Integration

From the matrix of the good-enough mother–infant relationship, the ego is able to develop. It is the function of the ego, in Winnicott's schema, to integrate experiences into the personality.

> Ego development is characterized by various trends:
>
> (1) The main trend in the maturational process can be gathered into the various meanings of the word *integration.* Integration in time becomes added to (what might be called) integration in space.
>
> ["Ego Integration in Child Development", p. 59]

Winnicott then refers to the ego that is based in the body and the ego that initiates object-relating:

> (2) The ego is based on a body ego, but it is only when all goes well that the person of the baby starts to be linked with the body and the body-functions, with the skin as the limiting membrane. I have used the term *personalisation* to describe this process. . . .
>
> ["Ego Integration in Child Development", p. 59]

The handling the baby receives from the mother and others—all the multitude of aspects of bodily care—contributes to the infant's sense of himself as a person. By using the term "personalization", Winnicott highlights the converse of "depersonalization"—the psyche–soma split in the patient who has not experienced good-enough handling. (*see* HOLDING: 2)

> (3) The ego *initiates object-relating*. With good-enough mother-ing at the beginning the baby is not subjected to instinctual gratifications except in so far as there is ego-participation. In this respect it is not so much a question of giving the baby satisfaction as of letting the baby find and come to terms with the object (breast, bottle, milk, etc.)
>
> ["Ego Integration in Child Development", pp. 59–60]

Winnicott refers here to the infant whose mother will respond to his need, rather than provide him with what he needs before he has made the signal. In this way the infant feels that he is responsible for receiving what he needs.

> It must be understood that when reference is made to the mother's adaptive capacity this has only a little to do with her ability to satisfy the infant's oral drives, as by giving a satis-factory feed. What is being discussed here runs parallel with such a consideration as this. It is indeed possible to gratify an oral drive and by so doing to *violate* the infant's ego-function, or that which will later on be jealously guarded as the self, the core of the personality. A feeding satisfaction can be a seduc-tion and can be traumatic if it comes to a baby without coverage by ego-functioning.
>
> ["Ego Integration in Child Development", p. 57]

This aspect of infant feeding is often referred to by Winnicott; as early as 1945, in a paper entitled "Primitive Emotional Develop-ment", he describes a male patient of his whose "chief fear was of satisfaction". In a footnote, he adds:

> I will just mention another reason why an infant is not satis-fied with satisfaction. He feels fobbed off. He intended, one might say, to make a cannibalistic attack and he has been put off by an opiate, the feed. At best he can postpone the attack.
>
> ["Primitive Emotional Development", p. 154]

To be not satisfied with satisfaction is one of Winnicott's impor-tant paradoxes and is associated with a mother who cannot survive her infant's need to be ruthless. (*see* AGGRESSION: 3, 8; ENVI-RONMENT: 7; MOTHER: 11)

This sort of "fobbing off", then, would lead to an ego distortion, because it deters integration.

The ability to integrate grows out of the very early stages of life:

(1) *Integration from what?*

It is useful to think of the material out of which integration emerges in terms of motor and sensory elements, the stuff of primary narcissism. This would acquire a tendency towards a sense of existing. Other language can be used to describe this obscure part of the maturational process, but the rudiments of an imaginative elaboration of pure body-functioning must be postulated if it is to be claimed that this new human being has started to be, and has started to gather experience that can be called personal.

["Ego Integration in Child Development", p. 60]

3   Ego-coverage

Winnicott uses the term "ego-coverage" to refer to the mother's specific task of protecting her infant from primitive agonies, which he also calls unthinkable anxieties and psychotic anxieties.

The first ego organization comes from the experience of threats of annihilation which do not lead to annihilation and from which, repeatedly, there is *recovery*. Out of such experiences confidence in recovery begins to be something which leads to an ego and to an ego capacity for coping with frustration.

It will, I hope, be felt that this thesis contributes to the subject of the infant's recognition of the mother as a frustrating mother. This is true later on but not at this early stage.

["Primary Maternal Preoccupation", 1956, p. 304]

With the appropriate ego-coverage, the going-on-being of the infant will result in what Winnicott, in his 1962 paper, "Ego Integration in Child Development", calls a "unit self", which the infant harnesses to integrate his experience, to form a personality, and to become himself.

(2) *Integration with what?*

... it cannot be over-emphasised that what happens at this very early stage depends on the ego-coverage given by the mother of the infant–mother coupling.

It can be said that good-enough ego-coverage by the mother (in respect of the unthinkable anxieties) enables the new human person to build up a personality on the pattern of a continuity of going-on-being.

["Ego Integration in Child Development", p. 60]

Winnicott finishes this 1962 paper by defining the process of integration, and he replaces the term "ego" with "I".

Integration is closely linked with the environmental function of holding. The achievement of integration is the unit. First comes "I" which includes "everything else is not me". Then comes "I am, I exist, I gather experiences and enrich myself and have an introjective and projective interaction with the NOT-ME, the actual world of shared reality". Add to this: "I am seen or understood to exist by someone"; and further, add to this: "I get back (as a face seen in a mirror) the evidence I need that I have been recognized as a being".

In favourable circumstances the skin becomes the boundary between the me and the not-me. In other words, the psyche has come to live in the soma and an individual psycho-somatic life has been initiated.

["Ego Integration in Child Development", p. 61]

This is also the description of "unit-status"—a term occasionally used by Winnicott to denote the achievement in the baby of differentiating between Me and Not-me. During the 1960s, Winnicott also refers to the unit self.

Overall, it could be helpful and more accurate to say that when Winnicott uses the word "ego", he is in fact defining *an aspect of the self that serves the specific function of integration*. It may be useful to bear this in mind when coming across the variety of hyphenated "egos" that Winnicott creates throughout his work. It also implies that, in Winnicott's theory of the true and false self, the healthy "ego" serves both the true and false self and is therefore part of or an aspect of the true and false self. (*see* SELF: 1)

4   Unintegration and disintegration

Winnicott uses the word "unintegration" to describe the "quiet states" of the infant.

The opposite of integration would seem to be disintegration. This is only partly true. The opposite, initially, requires a word like unintegration. Relaxation for an infant means not feeling a need to integrate, the mother's ego-supportive function being taken for granted.

["Ego Integration in Child Development", p. 61]

The infant and adult who are able to relax and become unintegrated know existentially the experience of trust and the sense of feeling safe. This is an experience that leads on to the ability to enjoy cultural pursuits. Unintegration is associated with being and creativity. The ability to unintegrate, therefore, also constitutes a developmental achievement.

Disintegration, conversely, is a defence.

The term disintegration is used to describe a sophisticated *defence*, a defence that is an active production of chaos in defence against unintegration in the absence of maternal ego-support, that is, against the unthinkable or archaic anxiety that results from failure of holding in the stage of absolute dependence. The chaos of disintegration may be as "bad" as the unreliability of the environment, but it has the advantage of being produced by the baby and therefore of being non-environmental. It is within the area of the baby's omnipotence. In terms of psychoanalysis, it is analysable, whereas the unthinkable anxieties are not.

["Ego Integration in Child Development", p. 61]

Disintegration always implies that a degree of integration has taken place; consequently, the analyst will be able to interpret in the transference and facilitate the patient's integration.

The patient who has experienced unthinkable anxieties and primitive agonies is not able to use the analytic setting in the same way as the person who has not experienced their intensity. The analyst must adapt to needs and wait until the patient is able to use the interpretation. (*see* REGRESSION: 3)

REFERENCES

1945 Primitive Emotional Development   [W6]
1956 Primary Maternal Preoccupation   [W6]
1962 Ego Integration in Child Development   [W9]

Environment

W innicott's theory of emotional development lays an emphasis on the environment and its responsibility for the emotional health of the infant.

The first environment for the infant is mother, and at the beginning they are merged together in an environment–individual set-up.

The environment cannot be held totally responsible for what becomes of the infant in terms of his mental health; it can only provide a spectrum of available experience: at the good end it is facilitating, at the other it is damaging.

The facilitating environment enables the individual to take the opportunity to grow and will usually lead to health, whereas the environment that fails, particularly in the beginning, is more likely to lead to mental instability and ill health.

1   The impact of the environment on human development

Psychoanalytic literature makes reference to the mother's role in relation to her infant, but, in the main, until around 1950, the

154

theoretical thrust had been very much on the individual and his inner world. The impact of the environment on the mental health of the individual had not really been accorded the importance it has since held in analytic theory. Winnicott's contribution on this front is not negligible.

In 1942, Winnicott found himself jumping up in a meeting and saying, "There's no such thing as a baby!" It was, for him, a moment of true discovery, which he relates ten years later, in his paper, "Anxiety Associated with Insecurity", presented to the British Psycho-Analytical Society in 1952. The individual was from then on no longer a unit, but an environment–individual set-up—the nursing couple.

> . . . if you show me a baby you certainly show me also some-one caring for the baby, or at least a pram with someone's eyes and ears glued to it. One sees a nursing couple . . . before object relationships the state of affairs is this: that the unit is not the individual, the unit is the environment–individual set-up. The centre of gravity of the being does not start off in the individual. It is in the total set-up.
>
> ["Anxiety Associated with Insecurity", p. 99]

In other words, there is no such thing as an individual—only an individual in relation to an external world. Winnicott is trying to show that a one-body relationship does not *precede* a two-body relationship but, rather, *follows* it.

> We sometimes loosely assume that before the two-body object relationship there is a one-body object relationship, but this is wrong, and obviously wrong if we look closely. The capacity for a one-body relationship *follows* that of a two-body relation-ship, through the introjection of the object.
>
> ["Anxiety Associated with Insecurity", p. 99]

This is a theme Winnicott develops six years later, in 1958, in "The Capacity to be Alone", where he states that the capacity to be alone is paradoxically based on the experience of being alone in the presence of another—namely, the environment–mother. (*see* ALONE: 1, 2)

2   The analytic setting—a holding environment

In 1954, in his paper "Metapsychological and Clinical Aspects of Regression within the Psycho-Analytical Set-Up", Winnicott comments on how Freud came intuitively to choose a setting for his psycho-neurotic patients. This setting mirrors that of the early environment, and Freud created it because he unconsciously knew about the good-enough early environment.

> Freud takes for granted the early mothering situation and my contention is that *it turned up in his provision of a setting for his work*, almost without his being aware of what he was doing. Freud was able to analyze himself as an independent and whole person, and he interested himself in the anxieties that belong to interpersonal relationships.
>
> ["Metapsychological and Clinical Aspects", p. 284]

In this paper, Winnicott starts to separate the techniques of psychoanalysis into interpretation and the setting. It is the setting which, by the end of the 1950s, becomes the holding environment.

There are two crucial aspects concerning Winnicott's observations at this time in psychoanalytic development. First, through his extensive work with mothers and infants Winnicott had by now discovered the difference between a good environment and one that is not good. Second, he observed that this essential first good environment is duplicated in the Freudian setting, which, of course, includes the personality of the analyst. Therefore, the patient who has been damaged by an early environmental failure, may have a chance to heal in the highly specialized Freudian setting (*see* HOLDING: 4; REGRESSION: 2). And it is the psychotic patient who needs the stability and reliability of the holding environment in a more literal way. (*see* HATE: 5)

> Now I wish to make clear in what way I artificially divide Freud's work into two parts. First, there is the technique of psychoanalysis as it has gradually developed, and which students learn. The material presented by the patient is to be *understood* and to be *interpreted*. And second, there is the *setting* in which this work is carried through.
>
> ["Metapsychological and Clinical Aspects", p. 285]

Winnicott enumerates 12 aspects of the necessary setting. Unlike Freud, Winnicott does not take the setting for granted; rather, he illustrates and defines each crucial aspect of the holding environment:

1. At a stated time daily, five or six times a week, Freud put himself at the service of the patient. (This time was arranged to suit the convenience of both the analyst and the patient).

2. The analyst would be reliably there, on time, alive, breathing.

3. For the limited period of time prearranged (about an hour) the analyst would keep awake and become preoccupied with the patient.

4. The analyst expressed love by the positive interest taken, and hate in the strict start and finish and in the matter of fees. Love and hate were honestly expressed, that is to say not denied by the analyst.

5. The aim of the analysis would be to get into touch with the process of the patient, to understand the material presented, to communicate this understanding in words. Resistance implied suffering and could be allayed by interpretation.

6. The analyst's method was one of objective observation.

7. This work was to be done in a room, not a passage, a room that was quiet and not liable to sudden unpredictable sounds, yet not dead quiet and not free from ordinary house noises. This room would be lit properly, but not by a light staring in the face, and not by a variable light. The room would certainly not be dark and it would be comfortably warm. The patient would be lying on a couch, that is to say, comfortable, if able to be comfortable, and probably a rug and some water would be available.

8. The analyst (as is well known) keeps moral judgement out of the relationship, has no wish to intrude with details of the analyst's personal life and ideas, and the analyst does not wish to take sides in the persecutory systems even when these appear in the form of real shared situations, local, political, etc. Naturally if there is a war or an earthquake or if the king dies the analyst is not unaware.

9. In the analytic situation the analyst is much more reliable than people are in ordinary life; on the whole punctual,

free from temper tantrums, free from compulsive falling in love, etc.

10. There is a very clear distinction in the analysis between fact and fantasy, so that the analyst is not hurt by an aggressive dream.

11. An absence of the talion reaction can be counted on.

12. The analyst survives.

["Metapsychological and Clinical Aspects", pp. 285–286]

Winnicott stresses that the analyst's conduct is what really matters within the physical and temporal environment. Although he is not specific, it is the transference and countertransference that are major aspects of this specialized environment. In addition, this environment functions along the same lines as ordinary parenting.

> There is rich material here for study, and it will be noted that there is a very marked similarity between all these things and the ordinary task of parents, especially that of the mother with her infant or with the father playing a mother role, and in some respects with the task of the mother at the very beginning.
>
> ["Metapsychological and Clinical Aspects", p. 286]

3   Psychosis—an environmental deficiency disease

Winnicott places the aetiology of psychosis in the environment–individual set-up. Therefore, if the mother is not able to go into the state of primary maternal preoccupation, she lets the baby down. This "dropping", as opposed to holding, means that later on she is faced with making up for failing her infant at the most crucial time:

> In practice the result is that such women, having produced a child, but having missed the boat at the earliest stage, are faced with the task of making up for what has been missed. They have a long period in which they must closely adapt to their growing child's needs, and it is not certain that they can succeed in mending the early distortion. Instead of taking for granted the good effect of an early and temporary preoccupation they are caught up in the child's need for therapy, that is

to say, for a prolonged period of adaptation to need, or spoiling. They do therapy instead of being parents. . . . This work of the mother (or of society) proves a great strain because it does not come naturally. The task in hand properly belongs to an earlier date, in this case to the time when the infant was only beginning to exist as an individual.

["Primary Maternal Preoccupation", 1956, p. 303]

The sense of feeling real, on which Winnicott lays such stress, is unavailable to the infant who has not had the good fortune of experiencing ordinary devotion:

. . . without the initial good-enough environmental provision, this self (that can afford to die) never develops. The feeling of real is absent and if there is not too much chaos the ultimate feeling is of futility. The inherent difficulties of life cannot be reached, let alone the satisfactions.

["Primary Maternal Preoccupation", pp. 304–305]

The mother who is not in the state of primary maternal preoccupation is unable to empathize with her infant, and therefore she cannot offer the necessary ego-support. The infant is left to his own devices.

. . . the fate of the baby who misses good-enough care in the early stage before the baby has separated off the "not-me" from the "me". This is a complex subject because of all the degrees and varieties of maternal failure. It is profitable, first, to refer to:

(1) distortions of the ego-organization that lay down the basis for schizoid characteristics, and

(2) the specific defence of self-holding, or the development of a caretaker self and the organization of an aspect of the personality that is false (false in that what is showing is a derivative not of the individual but of the mothering aspect of the infant–mother coupling) This is a defence whose success may provide a new threat to the core of the self though it is designed to hide and protect this core of the self.

["Ego Integration in Child Development", 1962, p. 58]

This second distortion is explored by Winnicott in his 1960 paper, "Ego Distortion in Terms of True and False Self" (*see* SELF: 6, 9).

Environmental failure brings about various possible outcomes of mental ill health:

> The consequences of a defective ego support by the mother can be very severely crippling, and include the following:

> A. *INFANTILE SCHIZOPHRENIA OR AUTISM*

> This well-known clinical grouping contains disorder second-ary to physical brain lesions or deficiency, and also includes some degree of every kind of failure of the earliest matura-tional details. In a proportion of cases there is no evidence of neurological defect or disease.

> B. *LATENT SCHIZOPHRENIA*

> There are many clinical varieties of latent schizophrenia in children who pass for normal, or who may even show special brilliance of intellect or precocious performance. The illness shows in the brittleness of the "success". Strain and stress at later stages of development may trigger off an illness.

> C. [*FALSE-SELF DEFENCE*]

> The use of defences, especially that of a successful false self, enable many children to seem to give good promise, but eventually a breakdown reveals the fact of the true self's ab-sence from the scene.

> D. *SCHIZOID PERSONALITY*

> Commonly there develops personality disorder which de-pends on the fact that a schizoid element is hidden in a personality that is otherwise sane. Serious schizoid elements become socialized in so far as they can hide in a pattern of schizoid disorder that is accepted in a person's local culture.

> ["Ego Integration", pp. 58–59]

The aetiology of the above is located at the very beginning of the mother–infant relationship:

> These degrees and kinds of personality defects can be related, in investigations of individual cases, to various kinds and de-grees of failure of holding, handling and object-presenting at the earliest stage.

> ["Ego Integration", p. 59]

Winnicott contends that the ramifications of failure at this early stage lead on to a fear of WOMAN, linked with the fear of dependence. (*see* DEPENDENCE: 3)

> . . . a recognition of absolute dependence on the mother and of her capacity for primary maternal preoccupation . . . is something which belongs to *extreme sophistication*, and to a stage not always reached by adults. The general failure of recognition of absolute dependence at the start contributes to the fear of WOMAN that is the lot of both men and women.
> ["Primary Maternal Preoccupation", p. 304]

4 Psychotic anxiety

The above-stated forms of psychosis are, for Winnicott, psychological organizations that have to be gone through in order to protect the core self against unthinkable anxieties or primitive agonies. They are described thus:

1. Going to pieces.
2. Falling for ever.
3. Having no relation to the body.
4. Having no orientation.

["Ego Integration", p. 58]

And one that he added six years later, in 1968:

> [5.] Complete isolation because of there being no means of communication.
> [Communication between Infant and Mother,
> and Mother and Infant, Compared and Contrated, p. 99]

These anxieties are "unthinkable" because this kind of anxiety could not be thought about and came about through shock and trauma (reaction to impingement). For Winnicott, the primitive agonies constitute *impingement*. The result in the infant of too much impingement is that the sense of self is annihilated. This is the opposite of being; it is the trauma of *annihilation*, which violated the very core of the self. (*see* COMMUNICATION: 10)

> Anxiety in these early stages of the parent–infant relationship relates to the threat of annihilation, and it is necessary to explain what is meant by this term.

In this place which is characterized by the essential existence of a holding environment, the "inherited potential" is
becoming itself a "continuity of being". The alternative to being is reacting, and reacting interrupts being and annihilates.
Being and annihilation are the two alternatives. The holding
environment therefore has as its main function the reduction
to a minimum of impingements to which the infant must react
with resultant annihilation of personal being.

["The Theory of the Parent–Infant Relationship", 1960, p. 47]

Annihilation occurs because of a threat to the isolation of the
core self. The mother's ego-support is required to protect the infant's core self; without ego-support, the infant is forced to
maintain the protection himself—that is, to develop psychotic defences.

Another phenomenon that needs consideration at this phase
is the hiding of the core of the personality. Let us examine the
concept of a central or true self. The central self could be said
to be the inherited potential which is experiencing a continuity of being, and acquiring in its own way and at its own
speed a personal psychic reality and a personal body-scheme.
It seems necessary to allow for the concept of the isolation of
this central self as a characteristic of health. Any threat to this
isolation of the true self constitutes a major anxiety at this
early stage, and defences of earliest infancy appear in relation
to failures on the part of the mother (or in maternal care) to
ward off impingements which might disturb this isolation.

["Theory of Parent–Infant Relationship", p. 46]

Later on, Winnicott adds to the list of primitive agonies the kind
of defences that may be mobilized in the infant or individual who
has suffered a break in the continuity of being:

. . . it is possible to make a list of primitive agonies (anxiety is
not a strong enough word here).
Here are a few:

1. A return to an unintegrated state. (Defence: disintegration)
2. Falling for ever. (Defence: disintegration)
3. Loss of psycho-somatic collusion, failure of indwelling.
   (Defence: depersonalization)

4. Loss of sense of real. (Defence: exploitation of primary narcissism)
5. Loss of capacity to relate to objects. (Defence: autistic states, relating only to self-phenomena).

["Fear of Breakdown", 1963, p. 90]

Thus Winnicott saw psychotic illness as a *defence against primitive agony*.

It is my intention to show here that what we see clinically is always a defence organisation, even in the autism of childhood schizophrenia. The underlying agony is unthinkable.

It is wrong to think of psychotic illness as a breakdown, it is a defence organization relative to a primitive agony, and it is usually successful (except when the facilitating environment has been not deficient but tantalising, perhaps the worst thing that can happen to a human baby).

["Fear of Breakdown", p. 90]

5   Impingement

By "impingement", Winnicott means that which interrupts the infant's continuity of being. The nature of an impingement essentially comes from the environment; however, impingement can be either traumatic (as described above) or strengthening. If the infant is properly protected at the beginning—if he has good-enough ego-support from the environment—then he will gradually learn to meet the impingement, which will result in a strengthening of his self-awareness. However, if the impingement is too early or too intense, the result will be traumatic, and the infant can do nothing but *react*. It is the *reactions* to impingement happening over a period of time that cause damage to the personality and result in fragmentation:

If reacting that is disruptive of going-on-being recurs persistently it sets going a pattern of fragmentation of being. The infant whose pattern is one of fragmentation of the line of continuity of being has a developmental task that is, almost from the beginning, loaded in the direction of psychopathology. Thus there must be a very early factor (dating from the first days or hours of life) in the aetiology of restlessness, hyperkinesis, and inattentiveness (later called inability to concentrate).

["Ego Integration", pp. 60–61]

Winnicott's thesis of impingement relates to states of readiness and being prepared. It links with the capacity to allow things to take their course. For example, birth is the first major environmental impingement, which, if normal, will not in and of itself harm the infant:

Before birth, and especially if there is delay, there can quite easily be repeated experiences for an infant in which, for the time being, the stress is on environment rather than on self, and it is likely that the unborn infant becomes more and more caught up in this sort of intercourse with the environment as the time for birth arrives. Thus, in the natural processes *the birth experience is an exaggerated sample of something already known to the infant.* For the time being, during birth, the infant is a reactor and the important thing is the environment; and then after birth there is a return to a state of affairs in which the important thing is the infant. ... In health the infant is prepared before birth for some environmental impingement, and already has had the experience of a natural return from reacting to a state of not having to react, which is the only state in which the self can begin.

["Birth Memories, Birth Trauma, and Anxiety", 1947, p. 183]

If a pattern of reacting is set up, there is less opportunity for the sense of self to develop. (*see* SELF: 1, 2)

6   *Fear of breakdown*

Published posthumously in 1974, but thought to have been written in 1963, Winnicott's paper, "The Fear of Breakdown", explores one of the outcomes of an environment that had failed the individual in the early stages:

Fear of breakdown is a feature of significance in some of our patients, but not in others. From this observation, if it be a

correct one, the conclusion can be drawn that fear of breakdown is related to the individual's past experience, and to
environmental vagaries.

["Fear of Breakdown", p. 87]

Winnicott's thesis in this paper is that the patient's fear of
breakdown in the future is based on a breakdown that occurred *in
the past*.

If the fear of breakdown emerges as a symptom during the
course of analysis, it is a sign of progress. The patient becomes
dependent on the analysis, which facilitates a sense of trust. This,
in turn, leads on to the patient feeling safe enough to experience
the original trauma (primitive agony) in the context of the analysis
and transference. The "breakdown" then refers to the breakdown
of the defences, originally set up (as above) to ward off unthinkable anxieties. The patient is allowing himself, therefore, to be
more open to his sensibilities.

> . . . in the more psychotic phenomena that we are examining
> it is a breakdown of the establishment of the unit self that is
> indicated. The ego organises defences against breakdown of
> the ego-organization, and it is the ego-organization that is
> threatened. But the ego cannot organise against environment
> failure in so far as dependence is a living fact.
>
> ["Fear of Breakdown", p. 88]

By saying that a defence is successful, Winnicott means that the
suffering of the individual is, so to speak, kept at bay. In a 1967
paper, "The Concept of Clinical Regression Compared with That
of Defence Organization", the "keeping at bay" is referred to by
Winnicott as an *organization towards invulnerability*, as in schizophrenia and autism.

> What we observe in children and in infants who become ill in
> a way that forces us to use the word "schizophrenia", although
> this word originally applied to adolescents and adults, what
> we see very clearly is an *organization towards invulnerability*.
> Differences must be expected according to the stage of the
> emotional development of the adult or child or baby who
> becomes ill. What is common to all cases is this, that the baby,
> child, adolescent or adult *must never again experience* the un-
> thinkable anxiety that is at the root of schizoid illness.

The autistic child who has travelled almost all the way to mental defect is not suffering any longer; invulnerability has almost been reached. Suffering belongs to the parents. The organization towards invulnerability has been successful, and it is this that shows clinically along with regressive features that are not in fact essential to the picture.

["Concept of Clinical Regression", pp. 197–198]

This "invulnerability" is reminiscent of Winnicott's question, posed in 1963: "How to be isolated without being insulated?" (*see* COMMUNICATION: 10).

Based on the discovery that "the fear of breakdown is *the fear of a breakdown that has already been experienced*", Winnicott recommends that the patient be told:

There are moments, according to my experience, when a patient needs to be told that the breakdown, a fear of which destroys his or her life, *has already been*. It is a fact that is carried round hidden away in the unconscious. ... In this special context the unconscious means that the ego integration is not able to encompass something. The ego is too immature to gather all the phenomena into the area of personal omnipotence.

["Fear of Breakdown", pp. 90–91]

In other words, the reaction to the impingement from the environment was a shock and a trauma to the infant's psyche because the infant was not ready to receive it and could not therefore *think* about it—that is, gather it in as an experience and integrate it. It happened, but it was not experienced in the sense of being processed. Winnicott poses a question:

It must be asked here: why does the patient go on being worried by this that belongs to the past? The answer must be that the original experience of primitive agony cannot get into the past tense unless the ego can first gather it into its own present time experience and into omnipotent control now (assuming the auxiliary ego-supporting function of the mother [analyst]).

In other words the patient must go on looking for the past detail which is *not yet experienced*. This search takes the form of a looking for this detail in the future.

> Unless the therapist can work successfully on the basis that this detail is already a fact, the patient must go on fearing to find what is being compulsively looked for in the future.
>
> ["Fear of Breakdown", p. 91]

Winnicott suggests that both therapist and patient need to be aware that what has happened in early life to the patient, in terms of environmental failure, must occur in the therapeutic relationship, where there is the hope that it can be experienced *for the first time.*

> The purpose of this paper is to draw attention to the possibility that the breakdown has already happened, near the beginning of the individual's life. The patient needs to "remember" this but it is not possible to remember something that has not yet happened, and this thing of the past has not happened yet because the patient was not there for it to happen to. The only way to "remember" in this case is for the patient to experience this past thing for the first time in the present, that is to say, in the transference. This past and future thing then becomes a matter of the here and now, and becomes experienced by the patient for the first time. This is the equivalent of remembering, and this outcome is the equivalent of the lifting of repression. . . .
>
> ["Fear of Breakdown", p. 92]

This thesis also applies to the fear of death and the fear of emptiness—the death and the emptiness have occurred in early life, through environmental failure.

Winnicott's recommendations to the therapist here are similar to those to the therapist working with the deprived child, adolescent, or adult. The therapist must help the child go back to the moment before the deprivation had occurred. (*see* ANTISOCIAL TENDENCY: 5)

7   "We are poor indeed if we are only sane"

It is clear from Winnicott's papers that, although he did distinguish between health and non-health, he stated very early on in his work that psychosis is something to which any of us could be susceptible:

It is sometimes assumed that in health the individual is always integrated, as well as living in his own body, and able to feel that the world is real. There is, however, much sanity that has a symptomatic quality, being charged with fear or denial of madness, fear or denial of the innate capacity of every human being to become unintegrated, depersonalized, and to feel that the world is unreal. Sufficient lack of sleep produces these conditions in anyone.

["Primitive Emotional Development", 1945, p. 150]

And to this he added one of his more famous footnotes:

Through artistic expression we can hope to keep in touch with our primitive selves whence the most intense feelings and even fearfully acute sensations derive, and we are poor indeed if we are only sane.

["Primitive Emotional Development", p. 150]

Perhaps this is what Winnicott means when, in 1960, he writes that "healthy people can play about with psychosis":

Psychosis is much more down to earth and concerned with the elements of human personality and existence than is psychoneurosis, and (to quote myself!) we are poor indeed if we are only sane.

["The Effect of Psychosis on Family Life, 1960, p. 61]

In the last year of his life, in "Creativity and Its Origins", he added:

It is important for us that we find clinically *no sharp line* between health and the schizoid state or even between health and full-blown schizophrenia. While we recognize the hereditary factor in schizophrenia and while we are willing to see the contributions made in individual cases by physical disorders we look with suspicion on any theory of schizophrenia that divorces the subject from the problems of ordinary living and the universals of individual development in a given environment. We do see the vital importance of the environmental provision especially at the very beginning of the individual's infantile life, and for this reason we make a special study of the facilitating environment in human terms, and in terms of human growth in so far as dependence has meaning.

["Creativity and Its Origins", pp. 66–67]

This is a recognition of the human condition (*see* DEPENDENCE: 2).

8   *Father—the indestructible environment*

Although in Winnicott's work the role of the father is not always specifically referred to, it does, in terms of the environment, contribute to the strength of the family as a "going concern". In a paper, "What about Father?", written in 1945 and consequently rather dated in terms of men and women's roles of today but nevertheless still pertinent as a concept, Winnicott sees the value of the father in three main areas: the relationship between the parents, father's support of mother in her authority, and being himself "that which distinguishes him from other men":

> A child is very sensitive indeed to the relationship between the parents, and if all goes well off-stage, so to speak, the child is the first to appreciate the fact, and tends to show this appreciation by finding life easier, and by being more contented and more easy to manage. I suppose this is what an infant or a child would mean by "social security".
>
> The sexual union of father and mother provides a fact, a hard fact around which the child may build a fantasy; a rock to which he can cling and against which he can kick; and furthermore it provides part of the natural foundation for a personal solution to the problem of a triangular relationship.
>
> ["What about Father?", pp. 114–115]

Supporting the mother and being himself, as well as loving and *enjoying* the relationship with the mother, are all factors that contribute to the good-enough environment. Later on, Winnicott specifies that the strength of such an environment for the growing child is that it could not be destroyed by his hate and aggression. And it is the *survival* of the environment that enables the infant to feel safe and move from object-relating to object-usage. (*see* AGGRESSION: 10)

Much later, in 1967, Winnicott emphasizes the importance of the indestructible environment in relation to father and society.

> The child ... finds that it is safe to have aggressive feelings and to be aggressive, because of the framework of the family representing society in a localized form. The mother's confidence in her husband or in the support that she will get, if she calls out, from local society, perhaps from the policeman,

makes it possible for the child to explore crudely destructive
activities which relate to movement in general, and also more
specifically destruction that has to do with the fantasy that
accumulated round the hate. In this way (because of environmental security, mother supported by father, etc.) the child
becomes able to do a very complex thing, that is to say, integrate all his destructive impulses in with the loving ones. . . .
In order to achieve this in his development, the child *absolutely requires an environment that is indestructible in essential
respects*: certainly carpets get dirtied and the walls have to be
re-papered and an occasional window gets broken, but somehow the home sticks together, and behind all this is the
confidence that the child has in the relationship between the
parents; the family is a going concern.

["Delinquency as a Sign of Hope", 1967, p. 94]

Themes surrounding the "survival of the object" are ubiquitous
in Winnicott's work, although only in 1968, in "The Use of an
Object", is he able to clarify his theory of destruction and survival
and the importance of the father's function. (*see* AGGRESSION: 10, 11)

One of the major debates between the Independent Group in
the British Psycho-Analytical Society and the Kleinian group is the
extent to which the environment contributes to the mental health
of the individual. In 1962, whilst valuing Melanie Klein's contribution in terms of the infant's inner world, Winnicott voices his
criticisms over what he felt to be her dismissal of the role of the
environment:

I suggest that Melanie Klein could not develop her argument
of the analyst's "good breast" without going into the matter of
the quality of the analyst's work, that is to say, the capacity
of the analyst to adapt to the needs of the patient. Linked with
this is the mother's capacity to make adaptation at the very
beginning to the newborn infant's ego-needs (including id-
needs). Klein's argument took her to a point at which she
must either deal with *the dependence of the infant on the mother*
(patient on analyst) or else deliberately ignore the variable
external factor of the mother (analyst) and dig right back in
terms of *primitive mechanisms that are personal to the infant.* By
choosing the latter course Klein involved herself in an implicit
denial of the environmental infancy itself, which is a time of

dependence. In this way she was forced into a premature arrival at the inheritance factor.

["The Beginnings of a Formulation of an Appreciation and Criticism of Klein's Envy Statement", 1962, p. 448]

REFERENCES

1945 What about Father? [W7]

1945 Primitive Emotional Development [W6]

1949 Birth Memories, Birth Trauma, and Anxiety [W6]

1952 Anxiety Associated with Insecurity [W6]

1954 Metapsychological and Clinical Aspects of Regression [W6]

1956 Primary Maternal Preoccupation [W6]

1960 The Effect of Psychosis on Family Life [W8]

1960 The Theory of the Parent–Infant Relationship [W9]

1962 The Beginnings of a Formulation of an Appreciation and Criticism of Klein's Envy Statement [W19]

1962 Ego Integration in Child Development [W9]

1963 The Fear of Breakdown [W19]

1967 The Concept of Clinical Regression Compared with Defence Organization [W19]

1967 Delinquency as a Sign of Hope [W14]

1968 Communication between Infant and Mother, and Mother and Infant, Compared and Contrasted [W16]

1971 Creativity and Its Origins [W10]

Hate

n Winnicott's thesis of hate, a parallel is drawn between the mother's hatred of her newborn infant and the analyst's hatred of the regressed, needy, and psychotic patient.

The ability to hate, alongside loving, means that ambivalence has been reached. This, for Winnicott, is a developmental achievement and arrives in the infant at the time of relative dependence and the stage of concern.

1   *"Hate in the countertransference"*

In Winnicott's work, the word "hate" is closely associated with what has become one of his most famous papers, "Hate in the Countertransference", which he presented to the British Psycho-Analytical Society in 1947. It should be remembered that in the 1940s, when this paper was written, the treatment of psychiatric patients was very different from that of today, particularly in terms of the availability of medication for the seriously disturbed patient. Nevertheless, the thesis of hate, and all that it entails as set out in this paper, remains the same throughout Winnicott's entire work.

This paper focuses on the emotional strain the analyst is put under when working with the psychotic patient. The implication throughout is that the psychotic/borderline patient demands as much emotional input as does the newborn infant.

Winnicott never accepts Klein's theory that hate is innate in the infant and a manifestation of the death instinct. For him the ability to hate—the awareness of hate as distinct from love—indicates that the infant has reached a stage of emotional development. The struggle for the infant when arriving at the capacity to distinguish his feelings was to "store" the hate for appropriate use.

Before 1949, "countertransference" as a concept had not developed in the theory of psychoanalysis beyond being seen as the analyst's problem. Paula Heimann's seminal paper, simply entitled "On Countertransference", was first presented in 1950 and updated ten years later. Although the whole of Winnicott's work on the technique of psychoanalysis is linked with what is now considered the analyst's countertransference (emotional response to the patient's transference), Winnicott rarely uses it as a term, and in this paper he refers to it in the sense of an abnormality or a sign of the analyst needing more analysis. In this respect, Winnicott's use of the term "countertransference" fitted in with the way most analysts viewed it in 1947.

Separating patients into two categories, psychotic and neurotic, Winnicott points out that work with the psychotic is far more "irksome" than work with the neurotic, and therefore what he has to say about working with the psychotic patient in a psychoanalytic relationship should also be of value to the psychiatrist.

> To help the general psychiatrist the psychoanalyst must not only study for him the primitive stages of the emotional development of the ill individual, but also must study the nature of the emotional burden which the psychiatrist bears in doing his work. What we as analysts call the countertransference needs to be understood by the psychiatrist too. However much he loves his patients he cannot avoid hating them and fearing them, and the better he knows this the less

will hate and fear be the motives determining what he does to
his patients.

["Hate in the Countertransference", pp. 194–195]

This thesis would naturally apply to the team working within the
psychiatric setting. Winnicott warns that the psychotic patient is
able to stir up feelings in others that are difficult to resist and may
often lead to acting out in the carer. He is referring to the intensity
of the projections from the psychotic patient, and he sets out three
components of countertransference:

1. Abnormality in countertransference feelings, and set relationships and identifications that are under repression in
   the analyst. The comment on this is that the analyst needs
   more analysis. . . .

2. The identifications and tendencies belonging to an analyst's personal experiences and personal development
   which provide the positive setting for his analytic work
   and make his work different in quality from that of any
   other analyst.

The above links specifically with the analyst's personal idiom:

3. From these two I distinguish the truly objective countertransference, or if this is difficult, the analyst's love and
   hate in reaction to the actual personality and behaviour of
   the patient, based on objective observation.

["Hate in the Countertransference", p. 195]

Winnicott suggests that it is vital for the analyst to work out
whether personal inner feelings relate to that which the patient is
stirring up (projecting) or to (what could be seen as) the analyst's
transference to the patient. Of course, both sets of feelings *do* belong to the analyst.

> I suggest that if an analyst is to analyse psychotics or anti-
> socials he must be able to be so thoroughly aware of the
> countertransference that he can sort out and study his *objective*
> reactions to the patient. These will include hate.

["Hate in the Countertransference", p. 195]

To further aid analysts' awareness, Winnicott reminds them that
each type of patient will only be capable of seeing the analyst as he

feels himself to be. The obsessional, therefore, "will tend to be thinking of the analyst as doing his work in a futile obsessional way", the hypomanic "who cannot feel guilt in a deep way or a sense of concern or responsibility, is unable to see the analyst's work as an attempt on the part of the analyst to make reparation in respect of his own (the analyst's) guilt feelings", and the neurotic will see the analyst as "ambivalent towards the patient, and to expect the analyst to show a splitting of love and hate; this patient, when in luck, gets the love, because someone else is getting the analyst's hate". And so the psychotic patient is not able to imagine the analyst as feeling any different from himself, and he is in a state of "coincident love–hate" ("Hate in the Countertransference", p. 195).

By "coincident love–hate", Winnicott means that the psychotic patient is not able to tell the difference between love and hate and therefore fears that "should the analyst show love, he will surely at the same time kill the patient" ("Hate in the Counter-transference", p. 195).

The "coincident love–hate" in the psychotic patient "implies that there was an environmental failure at the time of the first object-finding instinctual impulses" ("Hate in the Countertransference", p. 196). Winnicott refers to psychosis as an "environmental deficiency disease". The environment was not facilitating, and the primitive love impulse in the infant had not been met. The consequence of this kind of failure forces the infant to make use of psychotic defences. (*see* ENVIRONMENT: 3)

2   *The analyst's hate*

The analyst working with the psychotic must be prepared to receive the full power of the projections from the patient. These projections will need to be contained by the analyst and "stored", and to achieve this, the analyst must be analysed and able to analyse the hate existing inside.

> If the analyst is going to have crude feelings imputed to him he is best forewarned and so forearmed, for he must tolerate being placed in that position. Above all he must not deny hate that really exists in himself. Hate *that is justified* in the present

setting has to be sorted out and kept in storage and available for eventual interpretation.

["Hate in the Countertransference", p. 196]

Winnicott stresses the importance of analysis for the analyst and indicates that many analysts may choose to work with psychotics (described by him as "research cases") as a way of reaching "further than the point to which his own analyst could get him" ("Hate in the Countertransference", p. 196). In other words, the analyst should be open enough to be moved on emotionally by the patient, just as parents are moved on by their babies and children.

In working with the neurotic, hate in the analyst could stay more repressed and "latent"; Winnicott provides a list as to why hate is more contained with the less regressed patient.

> Analysis is my chosen job, the way I feel I will best deal with my own guilt, the way I can express myself in a constructive way.
>
> I get paid, or I am training to gain a place in society by psychoanalytic work.
>
> I am discovering things.
>
> I get immediate rewards through identification with the patient, who is making progress, and I can see still greater rewards some way ahead, after the end of the treatment.
>
> Moreover, as an analyst I have ways of expressing hate. Hate is expressed by the existence of the end of the "hour".
>
> I think this is true even when there is no difficulty whatever, and when the patient is pleased to go. In many analyses these things can be taken for granted, so that they are scarcely mentioned, and the analytic work is done through verbal interpretation of the patient's emerging unconscious transference. The analyst takes over the role of one or other of the helpful figures of the patient's childhood. He cashes in on the success of those who did the dirty work when the patient was an infant.
>
> These things are part of the description of ordinary psychoanalytic work, which is mostly concerned with patients whose symptoms have a neurotic quality.
>
> ["Hate in the Countertransference", pp. 196–197]

However, the strain put on the analyst by the psychotic has altogether a different quality.

3   *The analyst's healing dreams*

Winnicott's dreams instigated by his work with his patients are seen by him as healing, in as much as they bring him to a new stage of his personal emotional development. What he learns from the dream described in his paper of 1947 is that his patient

> ... was requiring of me that I should have no relation to her body at all, not even an imaginative one; there was no body that she recognized as hers and if she existed at all she could only feel herself to be a mind. .... What she needed of me was that I should have only a mind speaking to her mind.
>
> ["Hate in the Countertransference", p. 198]

Winnicott's dream is useful to illustrate (a) the use the patient makes of her analyst, causing him (unconsciously) to experience in his body what she felt like and was unable to integrate herself, and (b) the components of countertransference—that is, the analyst's unconscious response after a session where he *reacted* to the impingement she caused.

The dissociation of body from mind in Winnicott's dream helps him to understand the difference between castration anxiety (neurotic) and psychotic anxiety linked with annihilation and falling forever.

> At the culmination of my difficulties on the evening before the dream I had become irritated and had said that what she was needing of me was little better than hair-splitting. This had a disastrous effect and it took many weeks for the analysis to recover from my lapse. The essential thing, however, was that I should understand my own anxiety and this was represented in the dream by the absence of the right side of my body. .... This right side of my body was the side related to this particular patient and was therefore affected by her need to deny absolutely even an imaginative relationship of our bodies. This denial was producing in me this psychotic type of anxiety, much less tolerable than ordinary castration anxiety. ....
>
> ["Hate in the Countertransference", p. 198]

It perhaps won't go without notice that what Winnicott says to his patient has some significance—she *did* indeed need him to split hairs in order to realize the split in herself. Winnicott explains how important it had been to have the dream, and what the dream enables him to do:

> Whatever other interpretations might be made in respect of this dream the result of my having dreamed it and remembered it was that I was able to take up this analysis again and even to heal the harm done to it by my irritability which had its origin in a reactive anxiety of a quality that was appropriate to my contact with a patient with no body.
>
> ["Hate in the Countertransference", p. 198]

Here Winnicott reveals his sense of guilt in relation to this patient. It is reminiscent of his 1963 paper, "Dependence in Infant-Care, in Child-Care, and in the Psychoanalytic Setting", where he explores the analyst's mistakes as a necessary component of the analysis, and where he realizes one of his mistakes with a new patient occurring too soon in the therapeutic relationship (*see* DEPENDENCE: 5; REGRESSION: 7). However, here, in 1947, Winnicott was still clear that the patient must not know of the enormous burden the analyst has to endure:

> The analyst must be prepared to bear strain without expecting the patient to know anything about what he is doing, perhaps over a long period of time. To do this he must be easily aware of his own fear and hate.
>
> ["Hate in the Countertransference", p. 198]

And then, out of the blue but hinting at what is to come by the end of the paper, Winnicott says of the analyst in this predicament:

> He is in the position of the mother of an infant unborn or newly born.
>
> ["Hate in the Countertransference", p. 198]

4   *The necessary environment*

For the patient who has not had a good-enough start, the analyst "has to be the first in the patient's life to supply certain environmental essentials" ("Hate in the Countertransference", p. 198). This means that the setting, which is taken for granted by most patients, must be thought about more literally by the analyst, who has to provide something that has never before been provided. Winnicott illustrates his point:

> I asked a colleague whether he does analysis in the dark, and he said: "Why, no! Surely our job is to provide an ordinary environment: and the dark would be extraordinary". He was surprised at my question. He was orientated towards analysis of neurotics. But this provision and maintenance of an ordinary environment can be in itself a vitally important thing in the analysis of a psychotic, in fact it can be, at times, even more important than the verbal interpretations which also have to be given.
>
> ["Hate in the Countertransference", p. 199]

In fact, Winnicott accords this ever greater importance, and in his papers of the 1960s he increasingly stresses that the analyst needs to wait for the patient to arrive at his own interpretations:

> For the neurotic the couch and warmth and comfort can be *symbolical* of the mother's love; for the psychotic it would be more true to say that these things *are* the analyst's physical expression of love. The couch *is* the analyst's lap or womb, and the warmth *is* the live warmth of the analyst's body.
>
> ["Hate in the Countertransference", p. 199]

Therefore, in Winnicott's theory, the analytic setting provides a literal holding without the use of touch. (see COMMUNICATION: 3; REGRESSION: 1)

5   *The patient's need to be hated before being loved*

A huge and crucial part of the environment that needs to be offered to the patient is the analyst's emotional availability—specifically, hate:

> I want to add that in certain stages of certain analyses the analyst's hate is actually sought by the patient, and what is then needed is hate that is objective. If the patient seeks objective or justified hate he must be able to reach it, else he cannot feel he can reach objective love.
>
> ["Hate in the Countertransference", p. 199]

And from Winnicott's personal experience of working with children evacuated during the war, as well as his consultations with families over the years, he recognizes how crucial it is for the new environment to tolerate the hate caused by the deprived child, who is really demonstrating his unconscious hope. (*see* ANTISOCIAL TENDENCY: 5)

> It is perhaps relevant here to cite the case of the child of the broken home, or the child without parents. Such a child spends his time unconsciously looking for his parents. It is notoriously inadequate to take such a child into one's home and to love him. What happens is that after a while a child so adopted gains hope, and then he starts to test out the environment he has found, and to seek proof of his guardian's ability to hate objectively. It seems that he can believe in being loved only after reaching being hated.
>
> ["Hate in the Countertransference", p. 199]

Winnicott illustrates this with his personal experience of looking after a deprived child during the Second World War.

The crucial theoretical point in this section of the paper is that the mother hates the baby first.

> Out of all the complexity of the problem of hate and its roots I want to rescue one thing, because I believe it has an importance for the analyst of psychotic patients. I suggest that the mother hates the baby before the baby hates the mother, and before that baby can know his mother hates him.
>
> ["Hate in the Countertransference", p. 200]

The mother hates the baby first, in Winnicott's thesis, because the baby is not yet able to hate. His need for his mother is ruthless, and it is this ruthlessness that arouses her hate. The implied theory is that the psychotic is also not yet aware of his hate and comes to analysis with his ruthless need for the analyst. Developmentally, this phenomenon occurs in the holding phase, when the baby is absolutely dependent. This is the time of merger, when the infant is unable to relate to whole objects and is therefore unaware of the other as Not-me.

> However early integration may be achieved—perhaps integration occurs earliest at the height of excitement or rage—there is a theoretical earlier stage in which whatever

the infant does that hurts is not done in hate. I have used the term "ruthless love" in describing this stage. . . . As the infant becomes able to feel to be a whole person, so does the word hate develop meaning as a description of a certain group of his feelings.

["Hate in the Countertransference", p. 201]

6 Why mother hates her infant

As a way of providing even more evidence for the analyst's need to hate the psychotic patient first, Winnicott lists 17 reasons why a mother hates her infant from the start:

The mother hates her infant from the word go. I believe Freud thought it possible that a mother may in certain circumstances have only love for her boy baby; but we may doubt this. We know about a mother's love and we appreciate its reality and power. Let me give some of the reasons why a mother hates her baby, even a boy:

The baby is not her own (mental) conception.

The baby is not the one of childhood play, father's child, brother's child, etc.

The baby is not magically produced.

The baby is an interference with her private life, a challenge to preoccupation.

To a greater or lesser extent a mother feels that her own mother demands a baby, so that her baby is produced to placate her mother.

The baby hurts her nipples even by suckling, which is at first a chewing activity.

He is ruthless, treats her as scum, an unpaid servant, a slave.

She has to love him, excretions and all, at any rate at the beginning, till he has doubts about himself.

He tries to hurt her, periodically bites her, all in love.

He shows disillusionment about her.

His excited love is cupboard love, so that having got what he wants he throws her away like orange peel.

The baby at first must dominate, he must be protected from coincidences, life must unfold at the baby's rate and all this needs his mother's continuous and detailed study. For instance, she must not be anxious when holding him, etc.

At first he does not know at all what she does or what she sacrifices for him. Especially he cannot allow for her hate.

He is suspicious, refuses her good food, and makes her doubt herself, but eats well with his aunt.

After an awful morning with him she goes out, and he smiles at a stranger, who says: "Isn't he sweet?"

If she fails him at the start she knows he will pay her out for ever.

He excites her but frustrates—she mustn't eat him or trade in sex with him.

["Hate in the Countertransference", p. 201]

This list could also apply to the psychotic patient in relation to the analyst.

I think that in the analysis of psychotics, and in the ultimate stages of the analysis, even of a normal person, the analyst must find himself in a position comparable to that of the mother of a newborn baby. When deeply regressed the patient cannot identify with the analyst or appreciate his point of view any more than the foetus or newly born infant can sympathize with the mother.

["Hate in the Countertransference", p. 202]

Nine years after this paper was written, in his paper, "Primary Maternal Preoccupation", Winnicott describes the mother just before giving birth and for a few weeks afterwards as being in a state of merger with her new-born infant. Although the theory of hate has not been linked with primary maternal preoccupation by Winnicott, the same themes are present in terms of what the analyst has to be able to tolerate from the regressed patient. It is the toleration of a ruthless love, and it is this ruthlessness that will instigate hate (see PRIMARY MATERNAL PREOCCUPATION: 4; REGRESSION: 12). These themes are also related to absolute dependence, the fear of woman, and depression. (see DEPENDENCE: 1, 3; DEPRESSION)

REFERENCE

1947   Hate in the Countertransference   [W6]

Holding

1   *Boundaries and structure*
2   *The holding function*
3   *Personalization*
4   *Management*

A II the details of maternal care just before birth and immediately afterwards go towards making up the holding environment. This includes the mother's primary maternal preoccupation, which enables her to provide the infant with the necessary ego-support.

The psychological and physical holding an infant needs throughout his development continues to be important, and the holding environment never loses its importance for everyone.

1   Boundaries and structure

Although Winnicott recognized the importance of holding right from the beginning of his work, he did not use the word "holding" until the mid-1950s. During the Second World War, while he was working with Clare Britton, who eventually became his wife, they had both seen the great need for a holding environment in terms of the management and treatment of the antisocial child. (*see* ANTISOCIAL TENDENCY: 1)

183

By the 1950s, Winnicott's use of the good-enough mother–infant paradigm as a way of understanding what could be provided in the analytic relationship had become the foundation of his theory of holding, and his focus was on the psychological holding-the-baby-in-mind in combination with the physical feeding, bathing, and dressing:

> ... the infant is held by the mother, and only understands love that is expressed in physical terms, that is to say, by live, human holding. Here is absolute dependence, and environmental failure at this very early stage cannot be defended against, except by a hold-up of the developmental process, and by infantile psychosis ... we are more concerned with the mother *holding* the baby than with the mother *feeding* the baby.
>
> ["Group Influences and the Maladjusted Child", 1955, pp. 147–148]

It is *because of* the good-enough holding that the infant is more likely to develop the capacity to integrate experience and develop a sense of "I AM" (Me).

> No doubt the instinctual experiences contribute richly to the integration process, but there is also all the time the good-enough environment, someone holding the infant, and adapting well enough to changing needs. That someone cannot function except through the sort of love that is appropriate at this stage, love that carries a capacity for identification with the infant, and a feeling that adaptation to need is worth while. We say that the mother is devoted to her infant, temporarily but truly. . . .
>
> I suggest that this I AM moment is a raw moment; the new individual feels infinitely exposed. Only if someone has her arms round the infant at this time can the I AM moment be endured, or rather, perhaps, risked.
>
> ["Group Influences", p. 148]

This is the time of absolute dependence, to which Winnicott refers as the "holding phase". Generally speaking he believed that it is best if there is one main carer at the beginning of the baby's life, and in optimum circumstances this person should be the biological mother. However, Winnicott's contention throughout his work is that an adoptive mother who is able to go into a state of primary maternal preoccupation will also be able to offer the necessary ingredients of the holding environment. (*see* MOTHER: 5).

Winnicott's view of the good-enough holding environment begins with the mother–infant relationship within the family and grows outwards to other groups in society. In the preface to his collection of papers, *The Family and Individual Development* (W8), he emphasizes this point:

> The family has a clearly defined position at the place where the developing child meets the forces that operate in society. The prototype of this interaction is to be found in the original infant–mother relationship in which, in an extremely complex way, the world represented by the mother is helping or hindering the inherited tendency of the infant to grow. It is this idea that is developed in the course of this collection of papers. . . .
>
> [Preface to *The Family and Individual Development*, 1965, p. vii]

In 1960, Winnicott's definitive statement on holding appears in his paper, "The Theory of the Parent–Infant Relationship". The holding environment necessarily includes the father.

> Satisfactory parental care can be classified roughly into three overlapping stages:
> a. Holding.
> b. Mother and infant living together. Here the father's function (of dealing with the environment for the mother) is not known.
> c. Father, mother, and infant, all three living together.
>
> ["Parent–Infant Relationship", p. 44]

"Living together" refers to the infant's ability to separate Me from Not-me and to see mother and father as separate, whole people. This can occur only as *a consequence* of a successful holding by the parents and leads to an appreciation of reality and "to a three-dimensional or space relationship with time gradually added" ("Parent–Infant Relationship", p. 44).

It is Winnicott's contention in his theory of holding that good-enough holding by the environment is responsible for the initiation of certain developmental processes.

2   *The holding function*

The parents must provide their infant with an environment that is suited to his needs. It is of no use to the child if they offer him something that they themselves think he needs. This attitude may force the child to become compliant, because under pressure from the parent the child may say he likes something when he does not. Winnicott means that the parents must always take the infant's integrity into account when providing for their child and respect him as a separate human being, which necessarily includes the right to be different.

Winnicott enumerates the necessary characteristics of the environmental provision.

> It meets physiological needs. Here physiology and psychology have not yet become distinct, or are only in the process of doing so; and
>
> It is reliable. But the environmental provision is not mechanically reliable. It is reliable in a way that implies the mother's empathy.
>
> Holding:
>
> > Protects from physiological insult.
> >
> > Takes account of the infant's skin sensitivity—touch, temperature, auditory sensitivity, visual sensitivity, sensitivity to falling (action of gravity) and of the infant's lack of knowledge of the existence of anything other than the self.
> >
> > It includes the whole routine of care throughout the day and night, and it is not the same with any two infants because it is part of the infant, and no two infants are alike.
> >
> > Also it follows the minute day-to-day changes belonging to the infant's growth and development, both physical and psychological.
>
> ["Parent–Infant Relationship", pp. 48–49]

Winnicott stresses that the quality of maternal care at the very beginning of life is responsible for the mental health of the individual in terms of freedom from psychosis.

Transposed to the therapeutic relationship, it is the setting in analysis that provides the necessary holding environment for the patient (*see* ENVIRONMENT: 2). (The analytic setting = a holding environment.)

3   *Personalization*

Part and parcel of holding is what Winnicott refers to as *handling*—the way the mother handles her infant in all the day-to-day details of maternal care. Here is included a mother's *enjoyment* of her baby, which is an expression of her love. (*see* MOTHER: 9)

Good-enough handling results in the infant's "psyche indwelling in the soma"; Winnicott refers to this as "personalization". This means that the infant comes to feel, as a consequence of loving handling, that his body is himself or/and that his sense of self is centred inside his body. (*see* PSYCHE–SOMA: 1)

Winnicott uses the term "personalization" to accentuate the opposite of "depersonalization"—the condition in which the individual experiences a mind–body split and does not feel himself inside his body:

> Being loved at the beginning means being accepted . . . the child has a blueprint for normality which is largely a matter of the shape and functioning of his or her own body. . . .
>
> Almost every child has been accepted in the last stages before birth, but love is shown in terms of the physical care which is usually adequate when it is a matter of the fetus in the womb. In these terms, the basis for what I call personalisation, or an absence of a special liability to depersonalisation, starts even before the child's birth, and is certainly very much a matter of significance once the child has to be held by people whose emotional involvement needs to be taken into account, as well as their physiological response. The beginning of that part of the baby's development which I am calling personalisation, or which can be described as an indwelling of the psyche in the soma, is to be found in the mother's ability to join up her emotional involvement, which originally is physical and physiological.
>
> ["On the Basis for Self in Body", 1970, p. 264]

In the analytic situation, it is the analyst's attention—in combination with the physicality of the environment, the couch, the warmth, the colour of the room, and so on—that mirrors the mother's primary maternal preoccupation. Winnicott's concept of holding in the therapeutic setting does not include the analyst touching the patient. (*see* COMMUNICATION: 3; HATE:4; REGRESSION: 1)

4   *Management*

Winnicott often referred to holding as a form of management—
especially when he was addressing groups of professionals who
were involved in the daily care of people who could not care for
themselves. Management was also the term used for the care of
patients in a psychiatric setting, as well as in the analytic relationship. The degree of management depends on the pathology of the
patient in terms of how much holding is required:

> In treatment of schizoid persons the analyst needs to know all
> about the interpretations that might be made on the material
> presented, but he must be able to refrain from being side-
> tracked into doing this work that is inappropriate because the
> main need is for an unclever ego-support, or a holding. This
> "holding", like the task of the mother in infant-care, acknowl-
> edges tacitly the tendency of the patient to disintegrate, to
> cease to exist, to fall forever.
>
> ["Psychiatric Disorder in Terms of Infantile
> Maturational Processes", 1963, p. 241]

Winnicott stresses the importance of management as a holding
environment for the treatment of children and adolescents who
are demonstrating an antisocial tendency. However, he was
aware of how much holding the staff also required in order to
work with individuals who made such heavy emotional demands
on the carers. A paper written with Clare Britton in 1947, "Residential Management as Treatment for Difficult Children", details
all the aspects of residential care in relation to the crucial aspects
of a holding environment. Its conclusions are relevant to this
day.

In terms of the analytic relationship it is the setting, the analyst's attention, along with and including the interpretative work
that creates the holding environment that manages the patient's
psychological and physical needs. Only from this holding can a
potential space be realized (*see* TRANSITIONAL PHENOMENA: 7). (The
consequences of the failure of the holding environment are explored in ENVIRONMENT: 3, 4, 5, 6.)

REFERENCES

1955 Group Influences and the Maladjusted Child   [W8]

1960 The Theory of the Parent–Infant Relationship   [W9]

1963 Psychiatric Disorder in Terms of Infantile Maturational Processes   [W9]

1965 *The Family and Individual Development*   [W8]

1970 On the Basis for Self in Body   [W19]

Mother

The mother is pivotal in Winnicott's theory of emotional development. She is, for the baby, the first environment, biologically and psychologically. How the mother behaves and feels in relation to her infant will influence the infant's health—particularly around the time of pregnancy and just after birth—for the rest of his life.

The concept of mother as environment includes the woman mother is—that is, the woman she was before baby was born and will continue to become as she develops in her own right—as well as the father, siblings, the extended family, society, and the world at large.

The recognition of the details of good mothering are used as a paradigm for Winnicott in the therapeutic setting. The analyst's techniques in the consulting room symbolically mirror the techniques of good mothering.

1 Paediatrics and psychoanalysis

The unusual position in which Winnicott found himself—as a paediatrician whilst training in psychoanalysis—means that throughout his work as an analyst the mother–infant relationship is always
very present. Although he no longer continued his work as a paediatrician after the Second World War, he did carry on with his
work at Paddington Green, where he held what he describes as
"therapeutic consultations". Winnicott published a collection of the
details of these consultations, in which he was concerned with "the
application of psychoanalysis to child psychiatry", in his book,
Therapeutic Consultations in Child Psychiatry (W11). (*see* SPATULA
GAME; SQUIGGLE GAME)

In 1957, in the postscript to Winnicott's first collection of
broadcast talks—published under the title *The Child and the Family*
(W4) and re-published in 1964 under the extended title, *The Child,
the Family, and the Outside World* (W7)—Winnicott made it very
clear that he had a "driving propulsion" to speak to mothers in
particular, largely because the mother's contribution to society
was only just being recognized. This did not mean that he ignored
the father's role:

> . . . I can already see what a big part has been played in my
> work by the urge to find and to appreciate the ordinary good
> mother. Fathers, I know, are just as important, and indeed an
> interest in mothering includes an interest in fathers, and in the
> vital part they play in child care. But for me it has been to
> mothers that I have so deeply needed to speak.
>
> It seems to me that there is something missing in human
> society. Children grow up and become in their turn fathers
> and mothers, but, on the whole, they do not grow up to know
> and acknowledge just what their mothers did for them at the
> start. The reason is that the part the mother plays has only
> recently begun to be perceived.
>
> ["The Mother's Contribution to Society", 1957, p. 124]

Winnicott believed that if society were able to appreciate the
crucial nature of parenting, there would be less fear in society and
consequently less need for the kind of conflicts and destruction
that is caused essentially by the unacknowledged fear of dependence. (*see* DEPENDENCE: 2, 3)

Is not this contribution of the devoted mother unrecognised precisely because it is immense? If this contribution is accepted, it follows that every man or woman who is sane, every man or woman who has the feeling of being a person in the world, and for whom the world means something, every happy person, is in infinite debt to a woman. At the time when as an infant (male or female) this person knew nothing about dependence, there was absolute dependence.

Once again, let me emphasize, the result of such recognition when it comes will not be gratitude or even praise. The result will be a lessening in ourselves of a fear. If our society delays making full acknowledgement of this dependence, which is a historical fact in the initial stage of development of every individual, there must remain a block both to progress and to regression, a block that is based on fear. If there is not true recognition of the mother's part, then there must remain a vague fear of dependence. This fear will sometimes take the form of a fear of WOMAN, or a fear of a woman, and at other times will take less easily recognized forms, always including the fear of domination.

["Mother's Contribution to Society", p. 125]

Winnicott links the "fear of WOMAN" with the time of absolute dependence. (*see* DEPENDENCE: 3, 4)

2   The "natural" and "healthy" mother

Winnicott lays an emphasis on the "natural" mother and what she does "naturally". By "natural" Winnicott is referring to a mother who could first of all identify with her newborn baby (primary maternal preoccupation) and subsequently allow him to grow and become himself.

... true strength belongs to the individual's experience of the developmental process along *natural* lines. ... From my point of view the mental health of the individual is being laid down from the very beginning by the mother who provides what I have called a facilitating environment, that is to say one in which the infant's natural growth processes and interactions with the environment can evolve according to the inherited pattern of the individual. The mother is (without knowing it) laying down the foundations of mental health of the individual.

["Breast-feeding as Communication", 1968, pp. 24–25]

Winnicott's emphasis on the word "natural" really implies "normal". What would come naturally to a bad mother, for instance, would not be normal, and certainly would not be healthy. The "natural lines" to which Winnicott refers imply the allowance of the healthy maturational processes that occur within the facilitating environment. So the "natural" mother is the "healthy" mother. What does Winnicott mean by "health"?

In his paper, "The Concept of the Healthy Individual" (1967), Winnicott expounds on his thoughts on health; it covers virtually the whole of his theory of emotional development—the early mother–infant relationship, psychosomatic collusion, true and false self, culture, the value of "feeling real", and a new word, "psychomorphology", which Winnicott invented for use in this paper. Psychomorphology means that the inherited potential of the infant is as external as the environment is to begin with in terms of emotional development; the coming together of these two factors, inheritance and environment, contributes to the health or pathology of the individual. In brief,

> in terms of development . . . health means maturity according
> to the maturity that belongs to the age of the individual.
>
> "Concept of Healthy Individual", p. 22]

Winnicott's de-construction of the components of good-enough mothering includes all those aspects that lead to health in the individual. Consequently, it follows that the natural, healthy mother is the woman who has herself received good mothering.

3   The good-enough mother

Winnicott's use of the term "good-enough" relates to the mother's adaptation to her newborn infant's need. He uses this term from the early 1950s on as a way of distinguishing between his own and Kleinian terminology. In a letter written in 1952 to Roger Money-

Kyrle (a psychoanalyst and member of the Kleinian group), Winnicott clarifies what he means by good-enough.

> I am often thought to be talking about mother, actual people with babies, as if they were perfect or as if they were corresponding to "the good mother" which is part of the Kleinian jargon. Actually I always talk about "the good-enough mother" or "the not good-enough mother" because in point of fact we are talking about the actual woman, we know that the best she can do is to be good enough, and the word "enough" gradually (in favourable circumstances) widens in scope according to the infant's growing ability to deal with failure by understanding, toleration of frustration, etc. The "good mother" and "the bad mother" of the Kleinian jargon are internal objects and are nothing to do with real women. The best a real woman can do with an infant is to be sensitively good *enough* at the beginning so that illusion is made possible to the infant *at the start* that this good-enough mother is "the good breast".
>
> ["Letter to Roger Money-Kyrle", p. 38]

In the context of Winnicott's theory of emotional development, it is the mother's adaptation to the infant's needs that provides him with the experience of omnipotence, and this experience of omnipotence creates the illusion necessary for healthy development.

4   Good-enough illusion

In 1960, in his paper, "Ego Distortion in Terms of True and False Self", Winnicott elaborates on the link between his term "good-enough" and "illusion and omnipotence."

> . . . by one extreme the mother is *a good-enough mother* and by the other the mother is *not a good-enough mother*. The question will be asked: what is meant by the term "good-enough"?
>
> The good-enough mother meets the omnipotence of the infant and to some extent makes sense of it. She does this repeatedly. A True Self begins to have life, through the strength given to the infant's weak ego by the mother's implementation of the infant's omnipotent expressions.

The mother who is not good-enough is not able to imple-
ment the infant's omnipotence, and so she repeatedly fails to
meet the infant gesture; instead she substitutes her own gesture which is to be given sense by the compliance of the
infant. This compliance on the part of the infant is the earliest
stage of the False Self, and belongs to the mother's inability to
sense her infant's needs.

It is an essential part of my theory that the True Self does
not become a living reality except as a result of the mother's
repeated success in meeting the infant's spontaneous gesture
or sensory hallucination.

["Ego Distortion", p. 145]

In this respect, then, the good-enough mother is the same as the
"ordinary devoted mother", who is the mother, in health, in a
state of "primary maternal preoccupation".

5   Biology and mother's body

A simple conclusion to Winnicott's thesis of the healthy mother—
who naturally goes into a state of primary maternal preoccupation
during pregnancy and immediately afterwards—is that consequently the biological mother would be the best person to carry
out the task of mothering. However, Winnicott is not rigid about
this view:

We can now say why we think the baby's mother is the most
suitable person for the care of that baby; it is she who can
reach this special state of primary maternal preoccupation
without being ill. But an adoptive mother, or any woman who
can be ill in the sense of "primary maternal preoccupation",
may be in a position to adapt well enough, on account of
having some capacity for identification with the baby.

["Primary Maternal Preoccupation", 1956, p. 304]

The biological mother's identification with her infant is at the
centre of the "being ill . . . in the sense of primary maternal preoccupation". This state enables the mother to adapt to her infant's
needs, which optimally includes the ability to breast-feed. But
Winnicott does not see breast-feeding as an essential component
of primary maternal preoccupation.

Winnicott is also aware that women who are not able to achieve the "normal illness of primary maternal preoccupation", may still be good mothers, in the sense that they try hard to provide for the infant. However, their task in child care later on will be complicated because they will be forced to make up for the loss to the infant at the beginning:

> There are certainly many women who are good mothers in every other way and who are capable of a rich and fruitful life but who are not able to achieve this "normal illness" which enables them to adapt delicately and sensitively to the infant's needs at the very beginning; or they achieve it with one child and not another. Such women are not able to become preoccupied with their own infant to the exclusion of other interests, in the way that is normal and temporary. It may be supposed that there is a "flight to sanity" in some of these people. . . .
>
> In practice the result is that such women, having produced a child, but having missed the boat at the earliest stage, are faced with the task of making up for what has been missed. They have a long period in which they must closely adapt to their growing child's needs, and it is not certain that they can succeed in mending the early distortion.
>
> ["Primary Maternal Preoccupation", pp. 302–303]

There is also the woman who is psychotic and able to manage initially with her infant, but who may later not be able to read the infant's signs as he needs to become separate.

> At the other extreme is the mother who tends to be preoccupied in any case, and the baby now becomes her *pathological* preoccupation. This mother may have a special capacity for lending her own self to her infant, but what happens at the end? It is part of the normal process that the mother recovers her self-interest, and does so at the rate at which her infant can allow her to do so. The pathologically preoccupied not only goes on being identified with her baby too long, but also she changes suddenly from preoccupation with the infant to her former preoccupation.
>
> The normal mother's recovery from her preoccupation with her infant provides a kind of weaning. The first kind of ill mother cannot wean her infant because her infant has never had her, and so weaning has no meaning; the other

kind of ill mother cannot wean, or she tends to wean suddenly, and without regard for the gradually developing need
of the infant to be weaned.

> ["The Relationship of a Mother to Her Baby
> at the Beginning", 1960, pp. 15–16]

However, it is important to point out that Winnicott did not believe in a maternal instinct as such, and he felt that too much
emphasis on biology detracts from the emotional states between
mother and infant:

> ... when thinking of a *maternal instinct* we get bogged down
> in theory, and we get lost in a mix-up of human beings and
> animals. Most animals do in fact manage this early mothering
> pretty well, and at the early stages of the evolutionary pro-
> cess reflexes and simple instinctual responses sufficed. But
> somehow or other human mothers and babies have human
> qualities and these must be respected. They also have reflexes
> and crude instincts, but we cannot satisfactorily describe hu-
> man beings in terms of that which they share with animals.
>
> ["Relationship of Mother to Her Baby", p. 16]

It is also clear that whatever emphasis Winnicott placed on the
crucial nature of the mother's role in the care of her infant, he was
neither romantic nor sentimental about how much this would cost
her:

> The question is: can a mother defend herself successfully
> and keep her secrets without at the same time depriving the
> child of an essential element—the feeling that the mother is
> accessible? At the beginning the child was in possession, and
> between possession and independence there must surely be a
> half-way house of accessibility.
>
> ["What Irks?", 1960, p. 74]

By "possession", Winnicott means the very physical and emotional takeover that is primary maternal preoccupation.

> The onlooker can easily remember that it is only for a limited
> time that this mother is free-house to her children. She had
> her secrets once and she will have them again. And she will
> count herself lucky that for a while she was infinitely both-
> ered by the infinite claims of her own children.

For the mother who is right in it there is no past and no future. For her there is only the present experience of having no unexplored area, no North or South Pole but some intrepid explorer finds it, and warms it up; no Everest but a climber reaches to the summit and eats it. The bottom of her ocean is bathyscoped, and should she have one mystery, the back of the moon, then even this is reached, photographed, and reduced from mystery to scientifically proven fact. Nothing of her is sacred.

Who would be a mother?

["What Irks?", p. 74]

6   The woman becoming mother and the man becoming father

It is useful to look at the five pertinent areas that Winnicott covers when referring to the "beginning of the individual" within the context of the making of a family.

- the memories of the woman and man who are potential mother and father;
- the fantasies surrounding sexual intercourse;
- the parents' need for a baby;
- conception;
- the mother's true birth memories, enabling her to surrender in giving birth.

Winnicott, in line with Freud's theory of the unconscious, believed that there is a store of memories inside each individual. These memories cannot all be accessible in a cognitive way because so many of them are unconscious. For new parents, however, these memories will emerge in their dreaming and their emotional life associated with their planning for their first baby.

This orientation to the needs of the baby depends on many things, one of which is that the mother and the father do really carry round with them hidden memories of having been babies themselves, and of having been cared for in terms of reliability, of shielding from unpredictability, and of opportunity to get on with the highly individual matter of personal growth.

["The Building up of Trust", 1969, p. 133]

Memories and feelings in each human being relate to the past and contribute to what is made out of the present in terms of the parents' relationship to one another and in relation to other social groups. All this is part of the general atmosphere that emerges from the past and contributes to the evolving culture of the new family. Addressing mothers in 1969, Winnicott says:

The environment you provide is primarily yourself, your person, your nature, your distinguishing features that help you to know you are yourself. This includes of course all that you collect around yourself, your aroma, the atmosphere that goes with you, and it includes the man who will turn out to be the baby's father, and it may include other children if you have them, as well as grandparents and aunts and uncles. In other words, I am doing no more than describing the family as the baby gradually discovers it, including the features of the home that make your home not quite like any other home.

["Building up of Trust", p. 125]

Twelve years earlier, in a 1957 paper exploring both the integrating and disruptive factors in family life, Winnicott has taken the family milieu into account:

The existence of a family and the maintenance of a family atmosphere result from the relationship between the parents in the social setting in which they live. What the parents can "contribute in" to the family that they are building up depends a great deal on their general relationship to the wider circle around them, their immediate social setting. One can think of ever-widening circles, each social group depending for what it is like inside on its relationship to another outside social group. Of course the circles overlap. Many a family is a going concern, yet would not stand being uprooted and transplanted.

["Integrative and Disruptive Factors in Family Life", p. 41]

The quality of the parents' relationship with each other is a major component in the creation of an atmosphere.

7   *Fantasies surrounding sexual intercourse*

Winnicott points out that the force of sexual attraction between the man and woman in creating a family is important, and the "sexual satisfactions are an achievement of personal emotional growth; when such satisfactions belong to relationships that are personally and socially agreeable they represent a peak of mental health". But Winnicott is quick to add that sexual satisfaction in the relationship is desirable but not always possible:

> . . . although sex power is vitally important, complete satisfaction is not in itself an aim when the subject of the family is considered. It is worth noting that a large number of families exist and are counted good though they are built on a basis of not very powerful physical satisfactions on the part of the parents.
>
> ["Integrative and Disruptive Factors", pp. 41–42]

Aside from this, however, there is the difficulty of the aggressive drive involved in the sexual act, and how the couple deal with their fantasies of either damaging the other or being damaged by the other. Both men and women have these fears, which, Winnicott states, are mostly unconscious. However, particularly at the time around pregnancy and giving birth, these fantasies will emerge in terms of a heightened anxiety. (It was with this type of anxiety that Winnicott was concerned in constructing his theory of "the use of an object" ten years after this paper had been written.) (*see* AGGRESSION: 7, 8, 9, 10)

> The total sex fantasy, conscious and unconscious is almost infinitely variable, and has vital significance. It is important to understand, among other things, the sense of concern or guilt that arises out of the destructive elements (largely unconscious) that go along with the love impulse when this is expressed physically. It can be readily conceded that this sense of concern and guilt contributes a good deal to the need of each parent, and of the parents together, for a family. The very real anxieties in the father at the time of the mother's parturition reflect as clearly as anything else the anxieties that belong to the fantasy of sex and not just to the physical realities.
>
> ["Integrative and Disruptive Factors", p. 42]

The parents' anxieties, Winnicott points out, will potentially be relieved by the baby, for the happiness when a baby is born alive and well is intensified because the baby's aliveness alleviates the parents' anxieties that damage could have been caused:

> The growing family better than anything else *neutralizes the frightening ideas of harm done,* of bodies destroyed, of monsters generated. . . . Surely a great deal of the joy that the baby brings into the parents' lives is based on the fact that the baby is whole and human, and furthermore that the baby contains something that makes for living—that is to say, living apart from being kept alive; that the baby has an innate tendency towards breathing and moving and growing. The child *as a fact* deals, for the time being, with all the *fantasies* of good and bad, and the innate aliveness of each child gives the parents a great sense of relief as they gradually come to believe in it; relief from ideas that arise from their sense of guilt or unworthiness.
>
> ["Integrative and Disruptive Factors", p. 42]

However, the child's contribution to the evolution of the family, Winnicott believes, goes beyond the relief of the anxieties associated with sexual intercourse:

> It cannot be too strongly emphasized that the integration of the family derives from the integrative tendency of *each individual child.* Integration of the individual is not a thing that can be taken for granted. Personal integration is a matter of emotional growth. . . .
>
> Each individual child, by healthy emotional growth and by the development of his or her personality in a satisfactory way, promotes the family and the family atmosphere. The parents, in their efforts to build a family, benefit from the sum of the integrative tendencies of the individual children. It is not just simply a matter of the lovableness of the infant or the child; there is something more than that, for children are not always sweet. The infant and the small child and the older child flatter us *by expecting a degree of reliability and availability* to which we respond, partly I suppose because of our capacity to identify with them. This capacity to identify with the children again depends on our having made a good-enough growth in our own personality development when we were at

the same age. In this way, our own capacities are strengthened and are brought out, developed, by what is expected of
us from our children. In innumerable and very subtle ways,
as well as in obvious ways, infants and children produce a
family around them, perhaps by needing something, something which we give because of what we know about
expectation and fulfilment. We see what the children create
when playing at families, and we feel that we want to make
real the symbols of their creativeness.

["Integrative and Disruptive Factors", pp. 46–47]

In 1966, in response to a letter in *The Times* from Dr. Fisher—then
Archbishop of Canterbury—on the debate concerning the beginning of life and abortion legislation, Winnicott wrote a short
paper, "The Beginning of the Individual". Winnicott distinguishes
between "conceiving of" and "conception". The "conceiving of" is
related to the child's creative play and demonstrates a potential in
the little girl to become a mother.

If she has had a good-enough start, she will "conceive of" a
baby in her play—"It is part of the stuff of dreams and of many
occupations" ("Beginning of the Individual", pp. 51–52). Winnicott neither poses nor answers the question as to whether *every*
female child grows up with the fantasy of having a baby.

When the woman conceives in reality, she has already gone
some way in preparing herself for motherhood. As the pregnancy
continues, so the preparation becomes less of a fantasy and more
of a reality, although fantasy in terms of the imagined baby is
always a feature:

We notice in the expectant mother an increasing identification
with the infant. The infant links up with the idea of an "internal object" in the mother, an object imagined to be set up
inside and maintained there in spite of all the persecutory
elements that also have place there. The baby has other meanings for the mother in the unconscious fantasy, but the
predominant feature may be a willingness as well as an ability on the part of the mother to drain interest from her own
self on to the baby. I have referred to this aspect of a mother's
attitude as "primary maternal preoccupation".

["Relationship of Mother to Her Baby", p. 15]

As her interest drains from herself into the imagined baby, who is becoming a real baby, so the mother becomes more and more merged emotionally with her infant as her own true birth memories are evoked. The ultimate irony is that as mother and baby finally separate through the act of birth, they become one— the environment–individual set-up. The healthy mother has to surrender to giving birth in the same way she, as a baby, had to surrender to being born. Throughout the stages of labour, therefore, her infantile unconscious memories are re-evoked.

> Among features typical of the true birth memory is the feeling of being in the grips of something external, so that one is helpless. . . . There is a very clear relation here between what the baby experiences and what the mother experiences in being confined, as it is called. There comes a state in the labour in which, in health, a mother has to be able to resign herself to a process almost exactly comparable to the infant's experience at the same time.
>
>   ["Birth Memories, Birth Trauma and Anxiety", p. 184]

This last paragraph was written in 1949; in 1957 Winnicott added the footnote:

> I now call this special state of sensitivity in the mother "Primary Maternal Preoccupation".

8   The myriad functions
of the good-enough mother

Winnicott breaks down the mother's natural functions into three areas: holding, handling, and object presenting. All three areas are part and parcel of the early weeks, during the infant's time of absolute dependence. Holding and handling contribute to the infant living in his body, which Winnicott describes as "personalization" and "psychosomatic collusion". (*see* HOLDING: 3; PRIMARY MATERNAL PREOCCUPATION: 1, 2)

Winnicott refers to the time during which mother and infant are merged as "ego-relatedness" in the 1950s and as "object-relating" in the 1960s. The terms are synonymous and refer to the fact of dependence—that is, that the baby depends on the mother's ego-support, protection, and coverage. (*see* DEPENDENCE: 2)

The mother is aware of things that the baby is not able to be aware of yet. Because of her awareness, she will know that when the baby cries, he is crying for a reason. This is something he does not know at the beginning of his life—he simply finds himself crying. So mother offers her breast (or bottle), and (if he is crying through hunger) he sucks and feels relieved and no longer needs to cry.

> Imagine a baby who has never had a feed. Hunger turns up, and the baby is ready to conceive of something; out of need the baby is ready to create a source of satisfaction, but there is no previous experience to show the baby what there is to expect. If at this moment the mother places her breast where the baby is ready to expect something, and if plenty of time is allowed for the infant to feel round, with mouth and hands, and perhaps with a sense of smell, the baby "creates" just what is there to be found. The baby eventually gets the illusion that this real breast is exactly the thing that was created out of need, greed, and the first impulses of primitive loving. Sight, smell, and taste register somewhere, and after a while the baby may be creating something like the very breast that mother has to offer. A thousand times before weaning a baby may be given just this particular introduction to external reality by one woman, the mother. A thousand times the feeling has existed that what was wanted was created, and was found to be there. From this develops a belief that the world can contain what is wanted and needed, with the result that the baby has hope that there is a live relationship between inner reality and external reality, between innate primary creativity and the world at large which is shared by all.
> ["Further Thoughts on Babies as Persons", 1947, p. 90]

It is the mother's offering of her breast at the right time that gives the infant the feeling that this is just what he needs. If the infant who has just been born could speak, he would say, "I need something, but I don't know what it is because I've only just been born". In response, the mother who hears the cry of hunger says to herself, "I recognize that cry; it reminds me of a feeling I had when I was just born—I wonder how I can relieve the need. Let's try this."

This communication between mother and infant, resulting in the mother providing the infant with what he needs, leads the infant to the feeling that he "created" what came his way. Consequently, the infant feels like God—omnipotent. This feeling is crucial, Winnicott believes, in the early stages of life, because it helps the infant to learn to trust that it is in the real world that he can find what he needs. The paradox is that the sense of trust in the world comes about through the illusion of being God who created the world:

> The mother's adaptation to the infant's needs, when good enough, gives the infant the *illusion* that there is an external reality that corresponds to the infant's own capacity to create. In other words, there is an overlap between what the mother supplies and what the child might conceive of. To the observer, the child perceives what the mother actually presents, but this is not the whole truth. The infant perceives the breast only in so far as a breast could be created just there and then. There is no interchange between the mother and the infant. Psychologically the infant takes from the breast that is part of the infant, and the mother gives milk to an infant that is part of herself.
>
> ["Transitional Objects and Transitional Phenomena", 1953, p. 239]

Winnicott places great value on the necessity for illusion in the infant through the experience of omnipotence. Without this illusion, there is no capacity for trust. (*see* CREATIVITY: 2; TRANSITIONAL PHENOMENA: 3, 4)

The way in which the mother offers her breast—or whatever else it may be the infant requires—Winnicott terms "object-presenting" (*see* DEPENDENCE: 6).

In 1949, in one of Winnicott's BBC broadcasts, he compared the infant who is fed in an institutional setting with the infant who is fed by his own mother:

> When I see in what a delicate way a mother who is not anxious manages the same situation I am always astounded. You see her there, making the baby comfortable, and arranging a *setting* in which the feeding may happen, if all goes well. The setting is a part of a human relationship. If the mother is feeding by the breast we see how she lets the baby, even a

tiny one, have the hands free so that as she exposes her breast
the texture of the skin can be felt, and its warmth—moreover
the distance of her breast from the baby can be measured, for
the baby has only a little bit of the world in which to place
objects, the bit that can be reached by mouth, hands, and eyes.
The mother allows the baby's face to touch the breast. At the
beginning babies do not know about breasts being part of
mother. If the face touches the breast they do not know at the
beginning whether the nice feeling comes in the breast or in
the face. In fact babies play with their cheeks, and scratch
them, just as if they were breasts, and there is plenty of reason
why mothers allow for all the contact that a baby wants. No
doubt a baby's sensations in these respects are very acute, and
if they are acute we can be sure they are important.

["Close-up of Mother Feeding Baby", 1949, p. 46]

Here is an infant who has not yet worked out Me from Not-me.
He is in what Winnicott would describe as an "unintegrated
state". It is an illustration of the merger between mothers and
infants, in terms of mutuality. This is the picture of what Winnicott means by *being* and *the female element*, of both mother and
infant separately and together. (*see* CREATIVITY: 2, 3, 8; COMMUNICA-
TION: 2)

The baby first of all needs all these rather *quiet* experiences
which I am describing, and needs to feel held lovingly, that is,
in an alive way, yet without fuss, and anxiety, and tenseness.
This is the setting. Sooner or later there will be some kind of
contact between the mother's nipple and the baby's mouth.
It does not matter what exactly happens. The mother is there
in the situation and part of it, and she particularly likes the
intimacy of the relationship. She comes without preconceived
notions as to how the baby ought to behave.

["Close-up of Mother", p. 46]

And then comes the excitement, the turning away, and the "building up of an imagination":

This contact of the nipple with the baby's mouth gives the
baby ideas!—"perhaps there is something outside the mouth
worth going for". Saliva begins to flow; in fact, so much saliva
may flow that the baby may enjoy swallowing it, and for a

time hardly needs milk. Gradually the mother enables the baby to build up in imagination the very thing that she has to offer, and the baby begins to mouth the nipple, and to get to the root of it with the gums and bite it, and perhaps to suck.

And then there is a pause. The gums let go of the nipple, and the baby turns away from the scene of action. The idea of the breast fades.

Do you see how important this last bit is? The baby had an idea, and the breast with the nipple came, and a contact was made. Then the baby was finished with the idea and turned away, and the nipple disappeared. This is one of the most important ways in which the experience of the baby we are now describing differs from that of the one that we placed in the busy institution. How does the mother deal with the baby's turning away? This baby does not have a thing pushed back into the mouth in order that sucking movements shall be started up again. The mother understands what the baby is feeling, because she is alive and has an imagination. She waits. In the course of a few minutes, or less, the baby turns once more towards where she is all the time willing to place the nipple, and so a new contact is made, just at the right moment. These conditions are repeated time and again, and the baby drinks not from a thing that contains milk, but from a personal possession lent for the moment to a person who knows what to do with it.

The fact that the mother is able to make such delicate adaptation shows that she is a human being, and the baby is not long in appreciating this fact.

["Close-up of Mother", p. 47]

As these experiences are repeated, so the infant eventually arrives "at the extreme of omnipotence". This can only be achieved if the mother has the ability to provide the infant with the opportunity to first of all feel like God, which, in health, needs to lead on to the infant knowing what the real world is, and that he is not God.

. . . from these silent communications we can go over to the ways in which the mother makes real just what the baby is ready to look for, so that she gives the baby the idea of what it is that the baby is just ready for. The baby says (wordlessly of course): "I just feel like . . ." and just then the mother comes along and turns the baby over, or she comes with the feeding

apparatus and the baby becomes able to finish the sentence:
". . . a turn over, a breast, nipple, milk, etc. etc." We have to
say that the baby created the breast, but could not have done
so had not the mother come along with the breast just at that
moment. The communication to the baby is: "Come at the
world creatively, create the world; it is only what you create
that has meaning for you." Next comes: "the world is in your
control". From this initial *experience of omnipotence* the baby is
able to begin to experience frustration and even to arrive one
day at the other extreme from omnipotence, that is to say,
having a sense of being a mere speck in a universe, in a universe that was there before the baby was conceived of and
conceived by two parents who were enjoying each other. Is it
not from *being God* that human beings arrive at the humility
proper to human individuality?"

> ["Communication between Infant and Mother, and Mother
> and Infant, Compared and Contrasted", 1968, pp. 100–101]

9   Mother's reliable enjoyment

The mother's object-presenting depends on her consistency and
reliability. In one of his most important early papers, "Primitive
Emotional Development" (1945), Winnicott creates one of his
famous paradoxes: "Only on a basis of monotony can a mother
profitably add richness." It is this repetition of reliability that creates the holding environment. However, "monotonous" here does
not imply dullness. The mother's pleasure in her infant is a crucial
aspect of her ability to hold.

> . . . enjoy yourself! Enjoy being thought important. Enjoy let-
> ting other people look after the world while you are
> producing a new one of its members. Enjoy being turned-in
> and almost in love with yourself, the baby is so nearly part of
> you. Enjoy the way in which your man feels responsible for
> the welfare of you and your baby. Enjoy finding out new
> things about yourself. Enjoy having more right than you have
> ever had before to do just what you feel is good. Enjoy being
> annoyed with the baby when cries and yells prevent accept-
> ance of the milk that you long to be generous with. Enjoy all
> sorts of womanly feelings that you cannot even start to ex-

plain to a man. Particularly, I know you will enjoy the signs that gradually appear that the baby is a person, and that you are recognized as a person by the baby.

Enjoy all this for your own sake, but the pleasure which you can get out of the messy business of infant care happens to be vitally important from the baby's point of view. The baby does not want to be given the correct feed at the correct time, so much as to be fed by someone who loves feeding her own baby. The baby takes for granted all things like the softness of the clothes and having the bath water at just the right temperature. What cannot be taken for granted is the mother's pleasure that goes with the clothing and bathing of her own baby. If you are there enjoying it all, it is like the sun coming out, for the baby. The mother's pleasure has to be there or else the whole procedure is dead, useless, and mechanical.

["The Baby as a Going Concern", 1949, pp. 26–27]

The mother's enjoyment is also linked to her capacity to enjoy life in her own social interactions away from the infant, and gradually, as her primary maternal preoccupation fades, she will carry on as before, to some extent. This is also very important for the infant, as long as the separations from the mother are no longer than can be coped with. This coping will vary from infant to infant, but separation from mother comes about through the infant's dawning *awareness* of his personal need. (*see* CONCERN: 8; DEPENDENCE: 6, 7)

The reward at this stage of relative dependence is that the infant begins to be in some way *aware of dependence*. When the mother is away for a moment beyond the time-span of his (or her) capacity to believe in her survival, anxiety appears, and this is the first sign that the infant knows. Before this, if the mother is away the infant simply fails to benefit from her special ability to ward off impingements, and essential developments in ego structure fail to become well established.

The next stage beyond that at which the infant in some way feels a need for the mother is one in which the infant begins to *know in his mind* that mother is necessary.

Gradually the need for the actual mother (in health) becomes fierce and truly terrible, so that mothers do really hate to leave their children, and they sacrifice a great deal rather

than cause distress and indeed produce hatred and disillusionment during this phase of special need. This phase could
be said to last from (roughly) six months to two years.

["From Dependence towards Independence
in the Development of the Individual", 1963, p. 88]

Winnicott does stress that the best holding environment is one in
which one person—preferably the biological mother—is responsible for the infant, up to the age of about 2 years. By this time, the
child is equipped to deal with loss and different caring environ-
ments. However, the child is struggling with working out what is
real and what is not real. The mother's role is to accommodate this
struggle by introducing the world in "small doses", whilst all the
time appreciating the growing child's intense feelings worked out
in play. (*see* PLAYING: 3)

> For the little child, and how much more for the infant, life
> is just a series of terrifically intense experiences. You have
> noticed what happens when you interrupt play; in fact you
> like to give warning, so that if possible the child will be able
> to bring the play to some sort of an end and so tolerate your
> interference. A toy that an uncle gave your little boy is a bit of
> the real world, and yet if it is given in the right way at the
> right time and by the right person it has a meaning for the
> child which we ought to be able to understand and allow for.
> ["The World in Small Doses", 1949, p. 70]

The difference between a shared outer reality and a personal inner
reality are part of what the small child is working out. What
adults allow for is the play involved with the sharing of both the
real and the imagined.

> The world that we share with the child is also the child's own
> imaginative world, and so the child is able to experience it
> intensely. The reason for this is that we do not insist, when we
> are dealing with a child of that age, on an exact perception of
> the external world. A child's feet need not be all the time
> firmly planted on the earth. If a little girl wants to fly we do
> not just say "Children don't fly". Instead of that we pick her
> up and carry her round above our heads and put her on top of
> the cupboard, so that she feels she has flown like a bird to her
> nest.

Only too soon the child will find that flying cannot be done magically. Probably in dreams magical floating through the air may be retained to some extent, or at any rate there will be a dream about taking rather long steps. Some fairy story like the one about the Seven-League Boots, or the Magic Carpet, will be the grown-ups' contribution to this theme. At ten years or so the child will be practising long-jump and high-jump, trying to jump farther and higher than the others. That will be all that remains, except dreams, of the tremendously acute sensations associated with the idea of flying that came naturally at the age of three.

The point is that we don't clamp down reality on the little child, and we hope that we shall not have to clamp it down even when the child is five or six years old, because, if all goes well, by that age the child will have started a scientific interest in this thing that grown-ups call the real world. This real world has much to offer, as long as its acceptance does not mean a loss of the reality of the personal imaginative or inner world.

For the little child it is legitimate for the inner world to be outside as well as inside, and we therefore enter into the imaginative world of the child when we play the child's games and take part in other ways in the child's imaginative experiences.

["World in Small Doses", pp. 70–71]

Although it is clear from the above that Winnicott is referring to the adult's ability to interact with the child in imaginative play, it is equally important, when the time comes, for the adult to be very clear about what is and is not real:

Here is a little boy of three. He is happy, he plays all day long on his own or with other children, and he is able to sit up at table and eat like grown-up people. In the day-time he is getting quite good at knowing the difference between what we call real things and what we call the child's imagination. What is he like in the night? He sleeps, and no doubt dreams. Sometimes he wakes with a piercing yell. Mother jumps out of bed and goes in and turns on the light, and makes to take the child up in her arms. Is he pleased? On the contrary; he screams, "Go away, you witch! I want my mummy". His

> dream world has spread into what we call the actual world,
> and for twenty minutes or so the mother waits, unable to do
> anything, because for the child she is a witch. Suddenly he
> puts his arms round her neck and clings to her as if she had
> only just turned up, and before he is able to tell her about the
> broomstick he drops off to sleep, so that his mother is able to
> put him back in the cot and return to her own bed.
>
> ["World in Small Doses", p. 71]

The mother is able to wait and understand intuitively that the
child is between a waking and a dreaming life.

> In all sorts of ways your clear knowledge of what is real and
> what is not real helps the child, because the child is only
> gradually getting to the understanding that the world is not
> as imagined, and that imagination is not exactly like the
> world. Each needs the other. You know that first object your
> baby loves—a bit of blanket or a soft toy—for the infant this is
> almost part of the self, and if it is taken away or washed the
> result is disaster. As the baby becomes able to start throwing
> this and other things away (expecting them to be picked up
> and returned, of course) you know the time is coming when
> you can begin to be allowed by your infant to go away and
> return.
>
> ["World in Small Doses", p. 73]

10 *Mirror-role of mother*

In 1967, Winnicott elaborated his thoughts about the functions of
mother in his paper, "Mirror-Role of Mother and Family in Child
Development". His main thesis is that in order to look creatively
and see the world, the individual must first of all have internalized the experience of having been seen. This experience occurs
naturally in the early weeks of the mother–infant relationship, and
the "precursor of the mirror is the mother's face".

There is nothing new in what Winnicott writes about the infant seeing himself when he looks at his mother. What *is* new in
this paper is that the infant depends on his mother's facial re-
sponses when he looks into her face in order to establish his sense
of self.

What does the baby see when he or she looks at the mother's face. I am suggesting that, ordinarily, what the baby sees is himself or herself. In other words the mother is looking at the baby and *what she looks like is related to what she sees there*. All this is too easily taken for granted. I am asking that this which is naturally done well by mothers who are caring for their babies shall not be taken for granted. I can make my point by going straight over to the case of the baby whose mother reflects her own mood, or, worse still, the rigidity of her own defences. In such a case what does the baby see? First their own creative capacity begins to atrophy, and in some way or other they look around for other ways of getting something of themselves back from the environment. . . . The mother's face is not then a mirror. So perception takes the place of apperception, perception takes the place of that which might have been the beginning of a significant exchange with the world, a two-way process in which self-enrichment alternates with the discovery of meaning in the world of seen things.

["Mirror-Role of Mother", pp. 112–113]

"Apperception", the term Winnicott gave to the infant's subjective experience of merger with mother, thus involves relating to subjective objects (*see* BEING: 3). Consequently, apperception means seeing oneself through being seen by mother. "Perception" comes out of apperception and refers to the ability to see whole objects, which is the ability to differentiate between Me and Not-me. If perception has to occur prematurely through the mother's inability to respond to her infant's face, the infant finds ways round it, but at great cost to his sense of self. This kind of failure on the mother's part results in premature ego development for the infant.

Some babies, tantalized by this type of relative maternal failure, study the variable maternal visage in an attempt to predict the mother's mood, just exactly as we all study the weather. The baby quickly learns to make a forecast: "Just now it is safe to forget the mother's mood and to be spontaneous, but any minute the mother's face will become fixed or her mood will dominate, and my own personal needs must then be withdrawn otherwise my central self may suffer insult". . . . If the mother's face is unresponsive, then a mirror is a thing to be looked at but not to be looked into.

["Mirror-Role of Mother", p. 113]

Winnicott sees a sequence in the journey from apperception to perception:

> When I look I am seen, so I exist.
> I can now afford to look and see.
> I now look creatively and what I apperceive I also perceive.
> In fact I take care not to see what is not there to be seen (unless I am tired).
>
> ["Mirror-Role of Mother", p. 114]

The infant who "can now afford to look and see" is fortunate to have a mother who can also "afford to look and see" and start the process of getting to know her baby. The infant's spontaneous gesture (which Winnicott defines as the true self in action), if responded to in a positive way, encourages the infant to develop his sense of self (*see* SELF: 9). Winnicott transposes this interaction into the analytic frame:

> This glimpse of the baby's and child's seeing the self in the mother's face, and afterwards in a mirror, gives a way of looking at analysis and at the psychotherapeutic task. Psychotherapy is not making clever and apt interpretations; by and large it is a long-term giving the patient back what the patient brings. It is a complex derivative of the face that reflects what is there to be seen. I like to think of my work this way, and to think that if I do this well enough the patient will find his or her own self, and will be able to exist and to feel real. Feeling real is more than existing; it is finding a way to exist as oneself, and to relate to objects as oneself, and to have a self into which to retreat for relaxation.
>
> ["Mirror-Role of Mother", p. 117]

Winnicott stresses that this business of mirroring is easier said than done, but the "being seen" is what is crucial.

> But I would not like to give the impression that I think this task of reflecting what the patient brings is easy. It is not easy, and it is emotionally exhausting. But we get our rewards. Even when our patients do not get cured they are grateful to us for seeing them as they are, and this gives us a satisfaction of a deep kind.
>
> ["Mirror-Role of Mother", pp. 117–118]

11   *The value of the process of disillusionment*

As the mother starts to recover her sense of self and emerge from the state of primary maternal preoccupation, she "de-adapts" and "fails" (*see* DEPENDENCE: 5). This is all part and parcel of the infant's disillusionment, which must take place for healthy development to occur.

Throughout Winnicott's work, there is a great deal of stress on the importance of the early mother–infant relationship in terms of illusion. Because of this, the value he places on the disillusionment process is sometimes lost. However, he does often refer to the infant's very real need to be disillusioned and to feel the sense of disappointment. (*see* DEPRESSION: 3).

The baby is only able to go through the process of disillusionment when he has had sufficient experience of the illusion that he is God, creator of the world. He is disillusioned when he starts to wake up, as it were, from this illusion, to the realization that indeed he is not. If the illusion ends too quickly—that is, before the infant is ready to acknowledge this fact—he is likely to be traumatized.

As early as 1939, in a short piece entitled "Early Disillusion", Winnicott presented a patient of his who had been disillusioned too soon as a baby. Early disillusionment is traumatic.

However, part of the function of the healthy mother is to "traumatize" gradually:

> Thus there is a normal aspect to trauma. The mother is always "traumatising" within a framework of adaptation. In this way the infant passes from absolute to relative dependence. But the result is not as of trauma, because of the mother's ability to sense the baby's capacity, moment by moment, to employ new mental mechanisms. The infant's sense of the not-me depends on the fact of the mother's operation in this field of maternal care. The parents acting together, and then the functioning of the family unit, continue this process of the disillusioning of the child.
> ["The Concept of Trauma in Relation to the Development
> of the Individual within the Family", 1965, p. 146]

Another way of putting this, in Winnicott's language, is that the mother fails and then mends her failures, which paradoxically teaches the baby and growing child the meaning of her reliability:

> The baby does not know about the communication except
> from the effects of *failure* of reliability. This is where the dif-
> ference comes in between mechanical perfection and human
> love. Human beings fail and fail: and in the course of ordi-
> nary care a mother is all the time mending her failures.
> These relative failures with immediate remedy undoubtedly
> add up eventually to a communication, so that the baby
> comes to know about success. Successful adaptation thus
> gives a sense of security, a feeling of having been loved. As
> analysts we know about this because we are all the time fail-
> ing, and we expect and get anger. If we survive we get used.
> It is the innumerable failures followed by the sort of care that
> mends that build up into a communication of love, of the fact
> that there is a human being there who cares. Where failure
> is not mended within the requisite time, seconds, minutes,
> hours, then we use the term *deprivation*. A deprived child is
> one who, after knowing about failures mended, comes to ex-
> perience failure unmended. It is then the lifework of the child
> to provoke conditions in which failures mended once more
> give the pattern to life.
>
> ["Communication between Infant and Mother", p. 98]

Mended failures are, of course, distinct from what Winnicott refers to as "gross failures", which lead to primitive agonies and
unthinkable anxieties.

12   *The not-good-enough mother*

Mothers who cannot provide the environment the infant needs for
healthy development can be (artificially) divided into three types:

- the psychotic mother;
- the mother who cannot surrender to primary maternal preoccupation;
- the tantalizing mother.

The psychotic mother may well be able to cope with the small
infant's demands in the beginning, but she is not able to separate

from the infant as he needs to grow away from her gaze. (*see* ENVIRONMENT: 3)

The mother who does not naturally find herself in a state of primary maternal preoccupation—perhaps because she is too depressed or preoccupied with something else—may later on have to be a therapist for her child, who is likely to be seeking compensation for the earlier loss.

The tantalizing mother has, for Winnicott, the worst effect on her infant's mental health, as the erratic nature of the environment violates the very core of the sense of self. (*see* COMMUNICATION: 10; PSYCHE–SOMA: 3)

Techniques of good-enough mothering are continually transposed by Winnicott into the analytic setting, so that positive use can be made of the good-enough mother–family–infant paradigm. For the patient with very little good-enough experience in the past:

> the analyst has to be the first in the patient's life to supply certain environmental essentials. In the treatment of a patient of the latter kind all sorts of things in analytic technique become vitally important. . .
>
> ["Hate in the Countertransference", 1947, p. 198]

(*see* HATE: 4)

REFERENCES

1939 Early Disillusion   [W19]
1947 Hate in the Countertransference   [W6]
1949 Birth Memories, Birth Trauma and Anxiety   [W6]
1949 The Baby as a Going Concern   [W7]
1949 Close-up of Mother Feeding Baby   [W7]
1947 Further Thoughts on Babies as Persons   [W7]
1949 The World in Small Doses   [W7]
1952 Letter to Roger Money-Kyrle   [W17]
1953 Transitional Objects and Transitional Phenomena   [W6]
1956 Primary Maternal Preoccupation   [W6]
1957 Integrative and Disruptive Factors in Family Life   [W8]
1957 The Mother's Contribution to Society   [W14]
1960 Ego Distortion in Terms of True and False Self   [W9]

1960   The Relationship of a Mother to Her Baby at the Beginning
       [W8]
1960   What Irks?   [W20]
1963   From Dependence towards Independence in the Development
       of the Individual   [W6]
1965   The Concept of Trauma in Relation to the Development of the
       Individual within the Family   [W19]
1966   The Beginning of the Individual   [W16]
1967   The Concept of a Healthy Individual   [W14]
1968   Breast-Feeding as Communication   [W16]
1968   Communication between Infant and Mother, and Mother and
       Infant, Compared and Contrasted   [W16]
1969   The Building up of Trust   [W20]
1971   Mirror-Role of Mother and Family in Child Development
       [W10]

Playing

The ability to play is an achievement in Winnicott's theory of emotional development. In playing, the infant/child/adult bridges the inner world with the outer world within and through the transitional space. For Winnicott, the quality of play in the third area—transitional phenomena—is synonymous with creative living and constitutes the matrix of self-experience throughout life. Transposed to the analytic relationship, playing is the ultimate achievement of psychotherapy, because only through playing can the self be discovered and strengthened.

1   The evolution of a theory for playing

Winnicott's close observation of infants and children meant that he was acutely aware of the role of play in human relationships. He first became aware of the significance and function of playing in the 1930s, and in the last decade of his life he stressed the value of play, particularly in relation to psychotherapy and the search for and discovery of self.

In his paper, "Playing: A Theoretical Statement" (1971), written in the last two years of his life, Winnicott himself reflects on his evolving thoughts on playing:

> As I look back over the papers that mark the development of my own thought and understanding I can see that my present interest in play in the relationship of trust that may develop between the baby and the mother was always a feature of my consultative technique, as the following example from my first book shows. And further, ten years later, I was to elaborate it in my paper "The Observation of Infants in a Set Situation".
>
> ["Playing: A Theoretical Statement", p. 48]

As he acknowledges, the theory of playing in Winnicott's work begins "as a feature of his consultative technique"—initially, the Spatula Game, which functions as a diagnostic tool (*see* SPATULA GAME). Later on, Winnicott invented the Squiggle Game for older children—another diagnostic tool for his therapeutic consultations. (*see* SQUIGGLE GAME)

The evolution of the Spatula and Squiggle games contributed to Winnicott's understanding of the crucial nature of the transitional object for the developing infant, as can be seen in his 1951 paper, "Transitional Objects and Transitional Phenomena" (*see* TRANSITIONAL PHENOMENA: 4). By the 1960s, Winnicott's prime preoccupation had become the role and function of playing in terms of creative living and the discovery of the self. (*see* CREATIVITY: 6; SELF: 11)

2   *The quality of play as a signifier*

Winnicott evaluated the quality of play as signifying the infant's development and sense of being. As early as 1936, in his paper "Appetite and Emotional Disorder", a scale of playing is postulated:

> In classification of a series of cases one can use a scale: at the normal end of the scale there is play, which is a simple and enjoyable dramatization of inner world life: at the abnormal

end of the scale there is play which contains a denial of the inner world, the play being in that case always compulsive, excited, anxiety driven, and more sense-exploiting than happy.

["Appetite and Emotional Disorder", p. 47]

Ten years later, in a paper written for parents—"What Do We Mean by a Normal Child?" (1946)—Winnicott advises that what may appear as abnormal behaviour may, in fact, be normal in some children at certain times. An enjoyment of playing is the hallmark of the growing child's health.

Instead of going on trying to explain why life is normally difficult I will end with a friendly hint. Put a lot of store on a child's ability to play. If a child is playing there is room for a symptom or two, and if a child is able to enjoy play, both alone and with other children, there is no very serious trouble afoot. If in this play is employed a rich imagination, and if, also, pleasure is got from games that depend on exact perception or external reality, then you can be fairly happy, even if the child in question is wetting the bed, stammering, displaying temper tantrums, or repeatedly suffering from bilious attacks or depression. The playing shows that this child is capable, given reasonably good and stable surroundings, of developing a personal way of life, and eventually of becoming a whole human being, wanted as such, and welcomed by the world at large.

["What Do We Mean?", p. 130]

The "employment of a rich imagination whilst playing" means that the child is making use of the third area, which is a sign of health.

Winnicott, more concerned with the playing child or adult than with the content of play, emphasizes the way the individual uses play to process self-experience and, at the same time, to communicate.

For him, language is simply an amplification and extension of playing and communicating, and the capacity to play is as relevant to the adult as it is to the child. (see COMMUNICATION: 1)

The therapist is reaching for the child's communication and knows that the child does not usually possess the command of language that can convey the infinite subtleties that are to be found in play by those who seek. . . .

Whatever I say about children playing really applies to adults as well, only the matter is more difficult to describe when the patient's material appears mainly in terms of verbal communication. I suggest that we must expect to find playing just as evident in the analyses of adults as it is in the case of our work with children. It manifests itself, for instance, in the choice of words, in the inflections of the voice, and indeed in the sense of humour.

["Playing: A Theoretical Statement", pp. 39–40]

In a short paper written for parents in 1942, "Why Children Play", Winnicott outlines some functions of play for the child. In this very short and simple paper, Winnicott covers all the key concerns that he will continue to develop until 1970: aggression, anxiety, self-experiencing, friendship, and integration.

3   Aggression

In 1942, the precursor of Winnicott's theme—survival of the object—of his 1968 paper, "The Use of an Object and Relating through Identifications", is already apparent. Play involves the enactment of aggressive feelings in relation to the environment— an environment that must "tolerate". It is this word, "tolerate", that, by 1968, becomes "survive" (*see* AGGRESSION: 10):

It is commonly said that children "work off hate and aggression" in play, as if aggression were some bad substance that could be got rid of. This is partly true, because pent-up resentment and the results of angry experience can feel to a child like bad stuff inside himself. But it is more important to state this same thing by saying that the child values finding that hate or aggressive urges can be expressed in a known environment, without the return of hate and violence from the environment to the child. A good environment, the child would feel, should be able to tolerate aggressive feelings if they are expressed in more or less acceptable form. It must be accepted that aggression is there, in the child's make-up, and the child feels dishonest if what is there is hidden and denied.

["Why Children Play", p. 143]

And in the 1971 paper—"Playing: A Theoretical Statement"—Winnicott returns to a series of consultations with a mother and her baby about which he had written in his first book, in 1931. He does not make it absolutely clear which point he wishes to illustrate by looking back at this case, but the implication is that taking the infant on his knee and allowing her to bite his knuckle, "so severely that the skin was nearly torn", led to her being able to start playing. The turning-point seems to be the moment the baby was able to bite Winnicott's knuckle "without showing guilt feelings", which illustrates (a) the baby's need to express her aggression and allow her "ruthless self" free reign, and (b) Winnicott's survival of her primary aggression.

> At one consultation I had the child on my knee observing her. She made a furtive attempt to bite my knuckle three times so severely that the skin was nearly torn. She then played at throwing spatulas on the floor incessantly for fifteen minutes. All the time she cried as if really unhappy. Two days later I had her on my knee for half an hour. She had had four convulsions in the previous two days. At first she cried as usual. She again bit my knuckle very severely, this time without showing guilt feelings, and then played the game of biting and throwing away spatulas; *while on my knee she became able to enjoy play.* After a while she began to finger her toes, and so I had her shoes and socks removed. The result of this was a period of experimentation which absorbed her whole interest. It looked as if she was discovering and proving over and over again, to her great satisfaction, that whereas spatulas can be put to the mouth, thrown away and lost, toes cannot be pulled off.
>
> ["Playing: A Theoretical Statement", p. 49]

This infant's ability to play, whilst on Winnicott's lap, contains the aspect of self-discovery in relation to the external world that is the working out of Me and Not-me.

4   Anxiety

The mastering of anxiety is another feature of playing:

> Anxiety is always a factor in a child's play, and often it is a
> major factor. Threat of excess of anxiety leads to compulsive
> play, or to repetitive play, or to an exaggerated seeking for the
> pleasures that belong to play; and if anxiety is too great, play
> breaks down into pure exploitation of sensual gratification.
>   . . . in so far as children play for pleasure they can be asked
> to give it up, whereas, in so far as play deals with anxiety, we
> cannot keep children from it without causing distress, actual
> anxiety, or new defences against anxiety (such as masturba-
> tion or day-dreaming).
>
> ["Why Children Play", p. 144]

Here again, the environment is implicated. If the child's playing is
in the service of dealing with anxiety, then its interruption has to
be carried out with sensitivity on the part of the adult.

The theme of playing in relation to anxiety is not really elaborated in Winnicott's work, perhaps because his focus is on the
healthy, creative process of playing.

5   Self-experiencing and friendship

Playing incorporates an enrichment of experience in living, and
Winnicott believes that it is only through playing that child and
adult are able to discover the self.

> The child gains experience in play. Play is a big part of his
> life. External as well as internal experiences can be rich for the
> adult, but for the child the riches are to be found chiefly in
> play and fantasy. Just as the personalities of adults develop
> through their experience in living, so those of children de-
> velop through their own play, and through the play
> inventions of other children and of adults. By enriching them-
> selves children gradually enlarge their capacity to see the
> richness of the externally real world. Play is the continuous
> evidence of creativity, which means aliveness.
>
> ["Why Children Play", p. 144]

Creativity, aliveness, and the sense of feeling real are the hall-marks of the healthy individual and—as concepts—of Winnicott's work.

It is only through playing that friendships can emerge, and Winnicott points out that playing with others is essential for a relationship to become a friendship. Within the context of friend-ship, the other is able to be different and separate.

> It is largely through play, in which the other children are fitted into preconceived roles, that a child begins to allow these others to have independent existence. Just as some adults make friends and enemies easily at work whereas other may sit in a boarding-house for years and do no more than wonder why no one seems to want them, so do children make friends and enemies during play, while they do not easily make friends apart from play. Play provides an organi-zation for the initiation of emotional relationships, and so enables social contacts to develop.
>
> ["Why Children Play", pp. 144–145]

6   Playing and the unconscious

Just as Freud saw dreaming as the "royal road to the uncon-scious", so Winnicott saw playing as the "gateway to the unconscious":

> The repressed unconscious must be kept hidden, but the rest of the unconscious is something that each individual wants to get to know, and play, like dreams, serves the function of self-revelation.
>
> ["Why Children Play", p. 146]

In 1968, Winnicott added four comments to this 1942 paper about the playing child and adult.

1. Playing is essentially creative.
2. Playing is always exciting because it deals with the exist-ence of a precarious borderline between the subjective and that which can be objectively perceived.

3. Playing takes place in the potential space between the baby and the mother-figure. This potential space belongs to the change that has to be taken into consideration when the baby who is merged in with the mother feels the mother to be separated off.

4. Playing develops in this potential space according to the opportunity that the baby has to experience separation without separation, this being possible because the state of being merged in with the mother is replaced by the mother's adaptation to the baby's needs. In other words, the initiation of playing is associated with the life experience of the baby who has come to trust the mother-figure.

["Why Children Play", p. 146]

7   *Playing in relation to a developmental sequence*

By 1968, Winnicott locates play in the context of relationships. The developmental sequence of relationships changes the nature of play.

It is possible to describe a sequence of relationships related to the developmental process and to look and see where playing belongs.

A. Baby and object are merged in with one another. Baby's view of the object is subjective and the mother is oriented towards the making actual of what the baby is ready to find.

["Playing: A Theoretical Statement", p. 47]

This links with the time of absolute dependence, primary maternal preoccupation, and mother's role of object-presenting. (*see* DEPENDENCE: 2; MOTHER: 8; PRIMARY MATERNAL PREOCCUPATION: 2)

B. The object is repudiated, re-accepted, and perceived objectively. This complex process is highly dependent on there being a mother or mother-figure prepared to participate and to give back what is handed out.

This means that the mother (or part of mother) is in a "to and fro" between being that which the baby had a capacity to find and (alternatively) being herself waiting to be found.

If the mother can play this part over a length of time without admitting impediment (so to speak) then the baby has
some *experience* of magical control, that is, experience of that
which is called "omnipotence" in the description of intrapsychic processes.

["Playing: A Theoretical Statement", p. 47]

All the aspects of Winnicott's thinking related to the facilitating
environment and holding are relevant here, and they overlap with
the capacity to be alone and the stage of concern. (*see* ALONE: 1;
BEING: 3; CONCERN: 5; ENVIRONMENT: 1; HOLDING: 3)

This leads to the baby being able to trust in his environment
and consequently the people around him.

In the state of confidence that grows up when a mother can do
this difficult thing well (not if she is unable to do it), the baby
begins to enjoy experiences based on a "marriage" of the omnipotence of intrapsychic processes with the baby's control of
the actual. Confidence in the mother makes an intermediate
playground here, where the idea of magic originates, since the
baby does to some extent *experience* omnipotence. . . . I call
this a playground because play starts here. The playground is
a potential space between mother and the baby or joining
mother and baby.

["Playing: A Theoretical Statement", p. 47]

At this point, Winnicott introduces the component of "precariousness" involved in play.

Play is immensely exciting. It is exciting *not primarily because
the instincts are involved,* be it understood! The thing about
playing is always the precariousness of the interplay of
personal psychic reality and the experience of control of
actual objects. This is the precariousness of magic itself, magic
that arises in intimacy, in a relationship that is being found
to be reliable. To be reliable the relationship is necessarily
motivated by the mother's love, or her love–hate, or her object-
relating, not by reaction-formations.

["Playing: A Theoretical Statement", p. 47]

This magic is inspired by the infant's experience of his mother's
empathy through her communication and mutuality—a sense that
"mother knows best". (*see* COMMUNICATION: 2; MOTHER: 3, 4)

C. The next stage is being alone in the presence of someone.
The child is now playing on the basis of the assumption
that the person who loves and who is therefore reliable is
available and continues to be available when remembered
after being forgotten. This person is felt to reflect back
what happens in the playing.

["Playing: A Theoretical Statement", pp. 47–48]

The ability to be alone is based on the paradox of the experience
of being alone in the presence of another—usually mother. (*see*
ALONE: 1, 2)

D. The child is now getting ready for the next stage, which is to
allow and to enjoy an overlap of two play areas. First,
surely, it is the mother who plays with the baby, but she is
rather careful to fit in with the baby's play activities. Sooner
or later, however, she introduces her own playing, and she
finds that babies vary according to their capacity to like or
dislike the introduction of ideas that are not their own.

Thus the way is paved for a playing together in a relationship.

["Playing: A Theoretical Statement", p. 48]

8   *Playing and psychotherapy*

For Winnicott, psychotherapy involves two people playing together—two people able to use the potential space.

Psychotherapy takes place in the overlap of two areas of
playing, that of the patient and that of the therapist. Psychotherapy
has to do with two people playing together. The corollary of this is
that where playing is not possible then the work done by the thera-
pist is directed towards bringing the patient from a state of not
being able to play into a state of being able to play.

["Playing: A Theoretical Statement", p. 38]

In this way, Winnicott places a new emphasis on the therapeutic
relationship in psychoanalysis, which radically, albeit quietly,
alters the Freudian brief. Whereas Freudian interpretation placed
an emphasis on the analyst *knowing* something of the patient's

unconscious, Winnicott considers *playing* and the ability to play to be more important. In fact, for him psychoanalysis was a "highly specialized form of playing":

> ... *it is play that is the universal*, and that belongs to health: playing facilitates growth and therefore health; playing leads into group relationships; playing can be a form of communication in psychotherapy; and, lastly, psychoanalysis has been developed as a highly specialized form of playing in the service of communication with oneself and others.
>
> The natural thing is playing, and the highly sophisticated twentieth-century phenomenon is psychoanalysis. It must be of value to the analyst to be constantly reminded not only of what is owed to Freud but also of what we owe to the natural and universal thing called playing.
>
> ["Playing: A Theoretical Statement", p. 41]

Winnicott indicates to the child therapist that the play-space is more important than the interpretation, precisely because it allows for the child's creativity rather than the analyst's cleverness in making the interpretation.

> It is my purpose here simply to give a reminder that children's playing has everything in it, although the psychotherapist works on the material, the content of playing. Naturally, in a set or professional hour a more precise constellation presents than would present in a timeless experience on the floor at home; but it helps us to understand our work if we know that the basis of what we do is the patient's playing, a creative experience taking up space and time, and intensely real for the patient.
>
> Also, this observation helps us to understand how it is that psychotherapy of a deep-going kind may be done without interpretative work. A good example of this is the work of Axline (1947) of New York. Her work on psychotherapy is of great importance to us. I appreciate Axline's work in a special way because it joins up with the point that I make in reporting what I call "therapeutic consultations", that the significant moment is that at which *the child surprises himself or herself*. It is not the moment of my clever interpretation that is significant.
>
> ["Playing: A Theoretical Statement", pp. 50–51]

The analyst's task is to create the space within which the child or the patient is able to discover something for himself. Winnicott implies that the danger is that the analyst's interpretations may lead to the patient's development of a false self, which is the consequence of a pseudo-analysis. (*see* SELF: 7, 10)

> Interpretation outside the ripeness of the material is indoctrination and produces compliance. A corollary is that resistance arises out of interpretation given outside the area of the overlap of the patient's and the analyst's playing together. Interpretation when the patient has no capacity to play is simply not useful, or causes confusion. When there is mutual playing, then interpretation according to accepted psychoanalytic principles can carry the therapeutic work forward. *This playing has to be spontaneous, and not compliant or acquiescent,* if psychotherapy is to be done.
>
> ["Playing: A Theoretical Statement", p. 51]

The spontaneous gesture comes from the true self, and the individual who is able to be spontaneous is, therefore, living creatively. These themes and playing as creative activity are explored in great detail in Winnicott's book, *Playing and Reality* (W10), especially in Chapter 4, "Playing: Creative Activity and the Search for the Self". (*see* CREATIVITY: 6; SELF: 11)

REFERENCES

1936   Appetite and Emotional Disorder   [W6]
1942   Why Children Play   [W7]
1946   What Do We Mean by a Normal Child?   [W7]
1971   Playing: A Theoretical Statement   [W10]

Primary maternal preoccupation

The healthy pregnant woman becomes mentally "ill" just before giving birth and for a few weeks after birth. This unique state is called by Winnicott "primary maternal preoccupation".
The psychological and physical health of the baby, according to this thesis, depends on whether the mother is able to go into and come out of this special state of being.

1   Ordinary devotion

The collection of unpublished talks, published posthumously in 1986 and entitled *Babies and Their Mothers* (W16), brings together Winnicott's presentations specifically about the time of the infant's very beginning—namely, the time of absolute dependence, when, in health, the mother is in a state of primary maternal preoccupation. Most of these papers come from Winnicott's lectures during the 1960s to various groups in Britain and around the world. One of these papers—"The Ordinary Devoted Mother"—is

based on a talk given to the London branch of the Nursery School
Association in 1966. But the term "the ordinary devoted mother"
came about as early as 1949, as Winnicott explains:

> I was walking, in the summer of 1949, to have drinks with the
> B.B.C. producer, Miss Isa Benzie . . . and she was telling me
> that I could give a series of nine talks on any subject that
> might please me. She was, of course, on the lookout for a
> catchphrase, but I did not know this. I told her that I had no
> interest whatever in trying to tell people what to do. To start
> with, I didn't know. But I would like to talk to mothers about
> the thing that they do well, and that they do well simply
> because each mother is devoted to the task in hand, namely
> the care of one infant, or perhaps twins. I said that ordinarily
> this just happens, and it is the exception when a baby has to
> do without being cared for at the start by a specialist. Isa
> Benzie picked up the clue in a matter of twenty yards, and she
> said: "Splendid! The Ordinary Devoted Mother". So that was
> that.
>
> ["Ordinary Devoted Mother", pp. 3–4]

Later on in the same paper, Winnicott himself refers to a mother
functioning on the "level" of "ordinary devoted mother", and explains why the words "ordinary" and "devoted" are useful to
describe the psychological preparation that occurs in women just
before birth.

> I suggest . . . that *ordinarily* the woman enters into a phase, a
> phase from which she *ordinarily* recovers in the weeks and
> months after the baby's birth, in which to a large extent she is
> the baby and the baby is her. After all, she was a baby once,
> and she has in her the memories of being a baby; she also has
> memories of being cared for, and these memories either help
> or hinder her in her own experiences as a mother.
>
> ["Ordinary Devoted Mother", p. 6]

It is through these unconscious memories that the mother becomes preoccupied and "devoted", because of her intense identification with her infant. (*see* MOTHER: 6, 7)

In 1956 Winnicott wrote his definitive theoretical paper on this
subject, entitled, "Primary Maternal Preoccupation".

From the introduction to this paper it can be seen that Winnicott is prompted to make this statement to emphasize his disagreement with both Anna Freud and Margaret Mahler. It is clear that Winnicott feels that not enough attention is paid to the state of mind the mother *ordinarily* finds herself in before and after pregnancy.

> It is my thesis that in the earliest phase we are dealing with a very special state of the mother, a psychological condition which deserves a name, such as *Primary Maternal Preoccupation*. I suggest that sufficient tribute has not been paid in our literature, or perhaps anywhere, to a very special psychiatric condition of the mother, of which I would say the following things:
>
>> It gradually develops and becomes a state of heightened sensitivity during, and especially towards the end of the pregnancy.
>>
>> It lasts for a few weeks after the birth of the child.
>>
>> It is not easily remembered by mothers once they have recovered from it.
>>
>> I would go further and say that the memory mothers have of this state tends to become repressed.
>
> ["Primary Maternal Preoccupation", p. 302]

This state is likened to an illness, which occurs in healthy women and indeed *must* occur to facilitate the infant's health.

> This organized state . . . could be compared with a withdrawn state, or a dissociated state, or a fugue, or even with a disturbance at a deeper level such as a schizoid episode in which some aspect of the personality takes over temporarily. I would like to find a good name for this condition and to put it forward as something to be taken into account in all references to the earliest phase of infant life. I do not believe that it is possible to understand the functioning of the mother at the very beginning of the infant's life without seeing that she must be able to reach this state of heightened sensitivity, almost an illness, and to recover from it. (I bring in the word "illness" because a woman must be healthy in order both to develop this state and to recover from it as the infant releases her.)
>
> ["Primary Maternal Preoccupation", p. 302]

2   Going-on-being

The healthy infant establishes a sense of self and a sense of "going-on-being". This can occur only in the appropriate setting—the one the mother who is in a state of primary maternal preoccupation is able to provide. (*see* BEING: 3, 4, 5; ENVIRONMENT: 1; SELF: 5)

> The mother who develops this state that I have called "primary maternal preoccupation" provides a setting for the infant's constitution to begin to make itself evident, for the developmental tendencies to start to unfold, and for the infant to experience spontaneous movement and become the owner of the sensations that are appropriate to this early phase of life. . . .
>
> A sufficiency of going on being is only possible at the beginning if the mother is in this state that (I suggest) is a very real thing when the healthy mother is near the end of her pregnancy, and over a period of a few weeks following the baby's birth.
>
> ["Primary Maternal Preoccupation", p. 304]

The early experiences set the stage for all the aspects of later development. (*see* MOTHER: 8, 9, 10)

3   Meeting needs

Meeting the infant's needs is not possible without the mother's unconditional love, which amounts to her entire empathy with her infant's predicament.

> Only if a mother is sensitized in the way I am describing can she feel herself into her infant's place, and so meet the infant's needs. These are at first body needs, and they gradually become ego needs as a psychology emerges out of the imaginative elaboration of physical experience.
>
> There comes into existence an ego-relatedness between mother and baby, from which the mother recovers, and out of which the infant may eventually build the idea of a person in the mother. From this angle the recognition of the mother as a person comes in a positive way, normally, and not out of the experience of the mother as the symbol of frustration.
>
> ["Primary Maternal Preoccupation", p. 303]

Primary maternal preoccupation is the early specialized environment. The mother in this state is healthy and good enough and able to offer a facilitating environment in which her infant may be able to *be* and to *grow*.

> According to this thesis a good enough environmental provision in the earliest phase enables the infant to begin to exist, to have experience, to build a personal ego, to ride instincts, and to meet with all the difficulties inherent in life. All this feels real to the infant who becomes able to have a self that can eventually even afford to sacrifice spontaneity, even to die.
>
> ["Primary Maternal Preoccupation", p. 304]

The main point that Winnicott wishes to get across with his thesis of primary maternal preoccupation is that infant and mother are psychologically merged from the beginning of the infant's life. It is a time, therefore, when there are no object relations yet, but only ego-support from mother to infant and ego-relatedness (later termed object-relating) from infant to mother. (*see* BEING: 4; EGO: 4)

The consequences of the failures that may occur at this time are explored in many other areas of Winnicott's work. (*see* ENVIRONMENT: 3; PSYCHE–SOMA: 3; REGRESSION: 1, 3)

REFERENCES

1956 Primary Maternal Preoccupation   [W6]
1966 The Ordinary Devoted Mother   [W16]

Psyche–soma

The integration of mind and body is described by Winnicott as a psychosomatic collusion; he also refers to the "psyche in-dwelling in the soma".

The psyche-indwelling-in-the-soma describes the successful out-come of the process of "personalization" that occurs as a result of the mother's "handling" of her infant during the holding phase. This is the time of absolute dependence, when the (healthy) mother is in a state of primary maternal preoccupation.

In Winnicott's work, the use of the word "psyche" is described as the "imaginative elaboration of somatic parts, feelings, and functions" and is often synonymous with "fantasy", "inner reality", and "self".

If the mother has not been able to provide good-enough handling during the holding phase, then her baby may never feel at one within his body, and a mind–body split therefore occurs.

Psychosomatic illness is a symptom of something having gone wrong in the individual's early emotional development.

1   Mind and psyche–soma

Winnicott's original contribution to the nature of psychosomatics began with his 1949 paper, "Mind and Its Relation to the Psyche–Soma" which was partly inspired by a comment by Ernest Jones in a 1946 paper, in which he writes, "I do not think that the mind really exists as an entity". Winnicott agrees but adds that in his clinical practice he notices that there are patients who feel that their mind *is* localized somewhere, as if it were a separate entity.

> This quotation . . . stimulated me to try to sort out my own ideas on this vast and difficult subject. The body scheme with its temporal and spatial aspects provides a valuable statement of the individual's diagram of himself, and in it I believe there is no obvious place for the mind. Yet in clinical practice we do meet with the mind as an entity localized somewhere by the patient. . . .
>
> ["Mind and Its Relation", p. 243]

Winnicott then designates the word "mind" to describe an intellectual functioning that is akin to a dissociation in the individual who feels that his mind as an entity is not part of his sense of self. Later on in his work, Winnicott refers to this phenomenon as the "split-off intellect" (*see* SELF: 7). It is this split in the personality that Winnicott addresses when he writes about psychosomatic illnesses.

In this 1949 paper, Winnicott criticizes doctors who insist on only seeing the physical component of the patient and do not see that psychosomatic disorders are "half-way between the mental and the physical".

> These physical doctors are completely at sea in their theory; curiously enough they seem to be leaving out the importance of the physical body, of which the brain is an integral part.
>
> ["Mind and Its Relation", p. 244]

For Winnicott, in healthy development, psyche and soma are not distinguishable as far as the infant and developing child are concerned. The healthy individual takes it for granted that his sense of self is part and parcel of his body.

> Here is a body, and the psyche and the soma are not to be distinguished except according to the direction from which

one is looking. One can look at the developing body or at the developing psyche. I suppose the word psyche here means the *imaginative elaboration of somatic parts, feelings, and functions,* that is, of physical aliveness. We know that this imaginative elaboration is dependent on the existence and the healthy functioning of the brain, especially certain parts of it. The psyche is not, however, felt by the individual to be localized in the brain, or indeed to be localized anywhere.

Gradually the psyche and the soma aspects of the growing person become involved in a process of mutual interrelation. This interrelating of the psyche with the soma constitutes an early phase of individual development.

["Mind and Its Relation", p. 244]

This "interrelating between psyche and soma" constitutes the centre from which the developing sense of self may grow.

At a later stage the live body, with its limits, and with an inside and an outside, is *felt by the individual* to form the core for the imaginative self.

["Mind and Its Relation", p. 244]

Consequently, the core of the self that emerges out of the early mother–infant relationship implies the notion of a body–mind integration. (*see* BEING: 2, 3; SELF: 3, 5)

Let us assume that health in the early development of the individual entails *continuity of being.* The early psyche–soma proceeds along a certain line of development provided its *continuity of being is not disturbed;* in other words, for the healthy development of the early psyche–soma there is a need for a *perfect* environment. At first the need is absolute.

["Mind and Its Relation", p. 245]

Winnicott is referring to the mother's complete identity with her infant, which is precisely that which provides the perfect environment. This means that she is able to hold, handle, and care for her infant with concern, protection, and all the components of love, and if this goes well enough in the early stages it provides the infant with the sense of being and self lodged in his own body. (*see* HOLDING: 3; PRIMARY MATERNAL PREOCCUPATION: 2)

2   *Alive neglect*

As the mother comes out of the state of primary maternal preoccu-pation, she begins to de-adapt and fail her infant, through her own process of recovery and remembering herself. This necessary process marks the beginning of disillusionment for the infant. It is at this point of emotional development, between illusion and dis-illusion, between absolute and relative dependence, that the infant's intellectual understanding develops.

> The need for a good environment, which is absolute at first, rapidly becomes relative. *The ordinary good mother is good enough.* If she is *good enough* the infant becomes able to allow for her deficiencies by mental activity. This applies to meeting not only instinctual impulses but also all the most primitive types of ego need, even including the need for negative care or an alive neglect. The mental activity of the infant turns a *good-enough* environment into a perfect environment, that is to say, turns relative failure of adaptation into adaptive success. What releases the mother from her need to be near-perfect is the infant's understanding. . . .
>
> The mind, then, has as one of its roots a variable function-ing of the psyche–soma, one concerned with the threat to continuity of being that follows any failure of (active) envi-ronmental adaptation. It follows that mind development is very much influenced by factors not specifically personal to the individual, including chance events.
>
> ["Mind and Its Relation", p. 246]

The infant's ability to use his intellectual apparatus to think and to understand depends for its effective functioning on the early environment and the presence of illusion. As the mother fails (she is a human being so will always fail), the infant has to compen-sate for her inconsistencies and does so by employing his mental capacities to fill the gap through working things out. In this way disillusionment contributes to the infant's development of intellect in a positive way (*see* DEPENDENCE: 5; DEPRESSION: 3; MOTHER: 11). However, there are dangers inherent in this stage of the baby's development.

3   *The tantalizing mother*

The worst environment, for Winnicott, is the erratic one—when
the infant is forced to compensate intellectually too much and too
often for the inconsistencies of a mother who is sometimes good
and sometimes bad. This leads to the defence of intellectualization.

> Certain kinds of failure on the part of the mother, especially
> erratic behaviour, produce over-activity of the mental func-
> tioning. Here, in the overgrowth of the mental function
> reactive to erratic mothering, we see that there can develop an
> opposition between the mind and the psyche–soma, since in
> reaction to this abnormal environmental state the thinking of
> the individual begins to take over and organize the caring for
> the psyche–soma, whereas in health it is the function of the
> environment to do this. In health the mind does not usurp the
> environment's function, but makes possible an understanding
> and eventually a making use of its relative failure.
>
> ["Mind and Its Relation", p. 246]

Through the "usurping" of the environment's function by the
"mind" the infant/child uses his own intellect to "mother" himself. Later, in his 1960 paper, "Ego Distortion in Terms of True and
False Self", Winnicott sees this activity of intellectualization as the
intellectual false self. (*see* SELF: 7, 8)

> ... one might ask what happens if the strain that is put on
> mental functioning organized in defence against a tantalizing
> early environment is greater and greater? One would expect
> confusional states, and (in the extreme) mental defect of the
> kind that is not dependent on brain-tissue deficiency. As a
> more common result of the lesser degrees of tantalizing infant
> care in the earliest stages we find *mental functioning becoming a
> thing in itself*, practically replacing the good mother and mak-
> ing her unnecessary. Clinically, this can go along with
> dependence on the actual mother and a false personal growth
> on a compliance basis. This is a most uncomfortable state of
> affairs, especially because the psyche of the individual gets
> "seduced" away into this mind from the ultimate relationship
> which the psyche originally had with the soma. The result is a
> mind-psyche, which is pathological.
>
> ["Mind and Its Relation", pp. 246–247]

Here Winnicott describes the individual who has to place his sense of self in his mind, which subsequently takes over the function of the mother–environment. The danger of this defence is that the individual's identity is not founded in the body, causing the person to feel increasingly empty and futile inside. (*see* SELF: 6, 7)

4   Cataloguing reactions

The mind–psyche is equivalent to the split-off intellect that is associated with schizoid defences; as Winnicott gleaned from his clinical practice, it is often located physically by the patient in the head:

> There cannot of course be a direct partnership between the mind-psyche and the body of the individual. But the *mind-psyche* is localized by the individual, and is placed either inside the head or outside it in some special relation to the head, and this provides an important source for headache as a symptom.
>
> ["Mind and Its Relation", p. 247]

Winnicott believed that some of these difficulties related to the mind–body split may be a consequence of a traumatic birth. In and of itself, Winnicott believes, birth is *not* necessarily traumatic, although some births may be.

> Typically at birth there is apt to be an excessive disturbance of continuity because of reactions to impingements, and the mental activity which I am describing at the moment is that which is concerned with exact memorizing during the birth process. In my psychoanalytic work I sometimes meet with regressions fully under control and yet going back to prenatal life. Patients regressed in an ordered way go over the birth process again and again, and I have been astonished by the convincing proof that I have had that an infant during the birth process not only memorizes every reaction disturbing the continuity of being, but also appears to memorize these in the correct order. . . . Mental functioning of the type that I am describing, which might be called memorizing or cataloguing, can be extremely active and accurate at the time of a baby's

birth. . . . I want to make clear my point that *this type of mental functioning is an encumbrance to the psyche–soma*, or to the individual human being's continuity of being which constitutes the self . . . this cataloguing type of mental functioning acts like a foreign body if it is associated with environmental adaptive failure that is beyond understanding or prediction.

["Mind and Its Relation", p. 248]

By "cataloguing", Winnicott is referring to an unconscious memory of a reaction to trauma, based on his belief that we remember everything that has happened to us, bodily and emotionally. If the experience of birth is too sudden, for example, it will be traumatic. It will be stored unconsciously, but it cannot be processed. This is what Winnicott means by cataloguing. The memory is there somewhere bodily, but it is not integrated as an experience. Through analysis, the patient re-visits the early moments of the trauma, through regressing in the analytic session. In this way there is an opportunity to start integrating the experience for the first time. In going back in order to process the trauma, the patient is then able to move forward and to start life, with the traumas experienced and placed in the past. (*see* REGRESSION: 5, 6)

5   *Psychosomatic illness*

Winnicott considers the unconscious aim of psychosomatic illness to be "to draw the psyche from the mind back to the original intimate association with the soma" ("Mind and Its Relation", p. 254). The theme of psychosomatic illnesses and their meaning in terms of the patient's unconscious motivation is explored by Winnicott in his 1964 paper, "Psycho-Somatic Illness in Its Positive and Negative Aspects", which was presented to the Society for Psychosomatic Research.

This paper analyses the internal dilemma of the psychosomatist and how the mind–body dissociation inside is enacted and externalized, often between different specializations of the medical professions.

Many patients do not split their medical care into two; the split is into many fragments, and as doctors we find ourselves acting in the role of one of these fragments. I have used the term "scatter of responsible agents" to describe this tendency.

(This was first referred to in 1958 in Winnicott's review of Michael Balint's *The Doctor, His Patient and the Illness*.)

> Such patients provide the examples quoted in social casework surveys in which twenty or thirty or more agencies have been found to have been involved in relief of one family's distress. Patients with multiple dissociations also exploit the natural splits in the medical profession. . . .
> ["Psycho-Somatic Illness and Its Positive
> and Negative Aspects", 1964, p. 104]

In order to describe the role of the psychosomatist, Winnicott illustrates with a metaphor the impossibility of psychosomatic illness.

> 4. The psychosomatist prides himself on his capacity to ride two horses, one foot on each of the two saddles, with both reins in his deft hands.
> ["Psycho-Somatic Illness", p. 103]

The bodily symptoms of the psychosomatist do not constitute the illness but are, rather, signifiers of the intrapsychic dissociation.

> 7. The illness in psycho-somatic disorder is not the clinical state expressed in terms of somatic pathology or pathological functioning (colitis, asthma, chronic eczema). It is the persistence of a split in the patient's ego-organization, or of multiple dissociations, that constitutes the true illness.
> ["Psycho-Somatic Illness", p. 103]

These splits in the personality tend to be powerfully entrenched and consequently extremely difficult to treat.

> I have a desire to make it plain that *the forces at work in the patient are tremendously strong*.
> ["Psycho-Somatic Illness", p. 104]

The power of internal splitting is often reflected in the environmental provision as described above, when patients may mobilize scores of medical practitioners. This can achieve no more than to serve as an external representation of the dissociations that exist on the inside. The problem is that as long as the different fragments of the medical profession continue to treat the patient *as if* the problem is only physical, the intrapsychic dissociation responds to the external collusion by becoming more entrenched.

On the other hand, Winnicott makes it clear that it is no use in confronting the patient with what he is doing. This would only serve to amplify his intellectualized defence and thus also keep him in the same place.

> Let us pretend that I have a patient among the readers, a patient with a variety of this disorder that we label psycho-somatic. The patient will probably not mind being quoted, that is not the trouble here. The trouble here is that *it would not be possible for me to give an acceptable account of something that has not yet become acceptable in that patient's internal economy*. Only the continuation of the treatment is of use in the actual case, and in the course of time the patient whose existence I am postulating may come to relieve me of the dilemma that his illness places me in, the dilemma that is the subject of my paper. And one thing I would hate to do would be to seduce the patient to an agreed statement which would involve an abandonment of the psyche–soma and a flight into intellectual collusion.
>
> ["Psycho-Somatic Illness", p. 106]

In other words, the patient with a psychosomatic illness is only too ready to understand something about himself on an intellectual plane. This, after all, is what he has had to do all his life. The alternative is to give the patient time to recover from the dissociation.

> Am I beginning to convey my meaning that *in practice* there does exist a real and insuperable difficulty, the dissociation in the patient, which, as an organized defence, keeps separate the somatic dysfunction and the conflict in the psyche? Given time and favourable circumstances the patient will tend to recover from the dissociation. Integrative forces in the patient tend to make the patient abandon the defence. I must try to make a statement that avoids the dilemma.
>
> It will be evident that I am making a distinction between the true psycho-somatic case and the almost universal clinical problem of functional involvement in emotional processes and mental conflicts. I do not necessarily call my patient

whose dysmenorrhoea is related to anal components in the genital organization a psycho-somatic case, nor the man who must micturate urgently in certain circumstances. This is just life, and living. But my patient who claims that his slipped disc is due to a draught might claim to be labelled psycho-somatic, and so qualify for our attention in this paper.

["Psycho-Somatic Illness", p. 106]

6   A positive force

Winnicott believes in a force that integrates the personality and which, given the right circumstances—a good-enough environment—wins over a defence that, although originally set up to defend the self, now actually drains it.

THE POSITIVE ELEMENT IN THE PSYCHO-SOMATIC DEFENCE

Psycho-somatic illness is the negative of a positive; the positive being the tendency towards integration in several of its meanings and including what I have referred to as personalisation. The positive is the inherited tendency of each individual to achieve a unity of the psyche and the soma, and experiential identity of the spirit or psyche and the totality of physical functioning. A tendency takes the infant and child towards a functioning body on which and out of which there develops a functioning personality, complete with defences against anxiety of all degrees and kinds. . . .

This stage in the integrating process is one that might be called the "I AM" stage. I like this name because it reminds me of the evolution of the idea of monotheism and of the designation of God as the "Great I AM". In terms of childhood play this stage is celebrated (though at a later age than I have in mind now) by the game "I'm the King of the Castle— you're the dirty rascal". It is the meaning of "I" and "I am" that is altered by the psycho-somatic dissociation.

["Psycho-Somatic Illness", p. 112]

In psychosomatic illness, the stage of development between Me and Not-me is arrested. The not-good-enough environment leads to a tendency to psychosomatic disorder, which relates to:

Weak ego (dependent largely on not good-enough mothering) with a feeble establishment of indwelling in personal
development;

and/or

Retreat from I AM and from the world made hostile by the
individual's repudiation of the Not-me, to a special form of
splitting which is in the mind but which is along psycho-
somatic lines.

In this way psycho-somatic illness implies a split in the
individual's personality, with weakness of the linkage between psyche and soma, or a split organised in the mind in
defence against generalised persecution from the repudiated
world. There remains in the individual ill person, however, a
tendency *not* altogether to lose the psychosomatic linkage.

Here then is the *positive value of somatic involvement.*

["Psycho-Somatic Illness", p. 113]

The treatment of the patient with such entrenched dissociations
has to be approached with maximum patience. Winnicott likens
the psychosomatic defence to the antisocial defence, because underneath the defence is hope. The very existence of the split communicates a failure in development, just as the antisocial tendency
communicates deprivation. The hope is that the communication
will be heard and that an opportunity will arise where the integrative forces will win the day.

Our difficult job is to take a unified view of the patient and
of the illness *without seeming to do so in a way that goes ahead
of the patient's ability to achieve integration to a unit.* Often, very
often, we must be contented to let the patient have it, and to
manipulate the symptomatology, in a box-and-cox relation
to our opposite numbers, without attempting to cure the real
illness, the real illness being the patient's personality split
which is organized out of ego weakness and maintained as a
defence against the threat of annihilation at the moment of
integration.

Psychosomatic illness, like the antisocial tendency, has this
hopeful aspect, that the patient is in touch with the possibility
of psychosomatic unity (or personalisation) and dependence,
even though his or her clinical condition actively illustrates
the opposite of this through splitting, through various dis-

sociations, through a persistent attempt to split the medical provision, and through omnipotent self care-taking.

["Psycho-Somatic Illness", p. 114]

A year before his death in 1971, Winnicott emphasized the all-important beginnings of life and mother love as the prerequisite to feeling oneself in one's body:

> Being loved at the beginning means being accepted, and it is a distortion from the child's point of view if the mother-figure has an attitude of: "I love you if you are good, if you are clean, if you smile, if you drink it all up", etc. etc. These sanctions can come later, but at the beginning the child has a blueprint for normality which is largely a matter of the shape and functioning of his or her own body. . . . It is truly at the beginning that the child needs to be accepted as such, and benefits from such acceptance.

["On the Basis for Self in Body", p. 264]

This acceptance, bodily and psychologically, is exactly (unconsciously) what the patient hopes to find within the context of the analytic relationship. It is also that which the analyst hopes to offer through the analytic work within the analytic setting and attitude.

REFERENCES

1949 Mind and Its Relation to the Psyche–Soma   [W6]
1964 Psycho-Somatic Illness and Its Positive and Negative Aspects [W19]
1970 On the Basis for Self in Body   [W19]

Regression

R egression to dependence may occur in the analytic setting as a way of re-living the not-yet-experienced trauma that happened at the time of an early environmental failure. The analytic setting provides the potential for the patient to experience a holding environment, probably for the first time. This holding facilitates the patient to uncover the unconscious hope that an opportunity will arise for the original trauma to be experienced and thus processed. This experience, in turn, will enable the patient, whilst regressed to dependence, to search for and discover the true self. This search within the context of the analytic relationship is part of the healing process.

Withdrawal or the withdrawn state is a type of regression that cannot be processed without the analyst acknowledging and meeting the patient's need to be held.

Regression to dependence, which is relevant to all patient groups, is to be distinguished from the "regressed" patient. The former relates to the patient who, through the course of analysis, regresses to dependence as part of the transference relationship; the latter relates to the patient who has not yet reached maturity of emotional development, probably because of an early environmental failure.

1   A theory of regression

Winnicott's theory of regression came to the fore in the late 1940s and early 1950s. In 1954, he presented his paper, "Metapsychological and Clinical Aspects of Regression within the Psycho-Analytical Set-Up", to the British Psycho-Analytical Society. It is a long, dense paper covering the major aspects of working with patients who regress or are regressed, and it includes recommendations on technique for working psychoanalytically with patients who cannot use psychoanalytic interpretation but need, instead, a literal holding in the management of the sessions.

Simply speaking, regression means a going back to a former stage of development. In analytic work, the patient's regression to dependence is usually associated with re-visiting very early non-verbal experiences, which may often be linked with psychotic mechanisms. This re-visiting occurs within the context of the transference relationship, once a holding environment in the analytic setting has been established and the patient is able to trust the analyst. Within each patient, Winnicott believes, there is an innate force pushing towards health and development.

> For me, the word regression simply means the reverse of progress. This progress itself is the evolution of the individual, psyche–soma, personality, and mind with (eventually) character formation and socialization. Progress starts from a date certainly prior to birth. There is a biological drive behind progress. . . .
>
> It is one of the tenets of psychoanalysis that health implies continuity in regard to this evolutionary progress of the psyche and that health is maturity of emotional development appropriate to the age of the individual, maturity that is to say in regard to this evolutionary process.
>
> ["Metapsychological and Clinical Aspects of Regression within the Psycho-Analytical Set-Up", 1954, pp. 280–281]

This leads Winnicott to the conclusion that in regression

> . . . there cannot be a simple reversal of progress. For this progress to be reversed there has to be in the individual an organization which enables regression to occur"
>
> ["Metapsychological and Clinical Aspects", p. 281]

In other words, the patient has to have an in-built capacity (inner organization) that will enable him to *make use of* being regressed.

Winnicott indicates two aspects of this psychological "organization":

> A failure of adaptation on the part of the environment that
> results in the development of a false self.
> A belief in the possibility of a correction of the original
> failure represented by a latent capacity for regression which
> implies a complex ego organization.
>   ["Metapsychological and Clinical Aspects", p. 281]

The false self develops to defend the core self, and this occurs as a
result of *reactions* to *impingements*.

The elaboration of Winnicott's theory of the true and false self
was to come six years later, in 1960. In 1954, however, when this
paper was presented, Winnicott was in the process of evolving his
true and false self theory. (*see* SELF: 7, 10)

The second sentence contains an important part of Winnicott's
theory of emotional development. He himself had a "belief in" the
individual's capacity, at an unconscious level, to know about the
possibility of finding an opportunity to compensate for the early
disruption. This unconscious drive indicates the existence of a
"complex ego-organization":

> When we speak of regression in psychoanalysis we imply the
> existence of an ego organization and a threat of chaos. There
> is a great deal for study here in the way in which the indi-
> vidual stores up memories and ideas and potentialities. It is
> as if there is an expectation that favourable conditions may
> arise justifying regression and offering a new chance for for-
> ward development, that which was rendered impossible or
> difficult initially by environmental failure.
>   ["Metapsychological and Clinical Aspects", p. 281]

In 1949, in his paper, "Mind and Its Relation to the Psyche–Soma",
Winnicott had referred to the storing up of memories as "cataloguing"—early memories of the minutiae of bodily sensations
occurring before, during, and after birth. (*see* PSYCHE–SOMA: 4)

Memories can, however, be divided into two categories.

The first group consists of memories that are *thinkable*, in as
much as the infant is *not* traumatized (grossly impinged upon) by
the experience. For Winnicott, impingement denotes the impact of

anything external that happens to the infant—birth can in this sense be seen as the first impingement. Impingement in and of itself is not damaging to the baby's development; it is, in fact, a necessary part of healthy development. Traumatic impingement occurs if the infant is not able, for some reason—due to environment or endowment—to process that which has occurred. If the baby is not ready for whatever experience, he is forced to react. Thus it is the *reactions* to impingement that cause a distortion in emotional development. (*see* ENVIRONMENT: 5)

The second group consists of memories that are *unthinkable*; they are gross impingements happening to the infant at a time when he is not ready to process them. It is this group of memories that have to be catalogued (*see* ENVIRONMENT: 7; PSYCHE–SOMA: 4). Both types of memories are, of course, a mixture of unconscious, pre-concious, and cognitive memories.

In his theory of regression, Winnicott makes the point that the unthinkable memories are "frozen"; but, importantly, he believes that along with this freezing is the hope that there will be an opportunity, given a new environmental provision, to carry out the necessary unfreezing. This is what he means when he talks about the experience being experienced for the first time.

The freezing indicates an "ego-organization", because it illustrates that the infant is able to set up a defence against the environment's attack, which is felt to be against the self. The defence can then be seen to be a normal reaction to a not-good-enough environment.

> One has to include in one's theory of the development of a human being the idea that it is normal and healthy for the individual to be able to defend the self against specific environmental failure by a *freezing of the failure situation*. Along with this goes an unconscious assumption (which can become a conscious hope) that opportunity will occur at a later date for a renewed experience in which the failure situation will be able to be unfrozen and re-experienced, with the individual in a regressed state, in an environment that is making adequate adaptation. The theory is here being put forward of regression as part of a healing process, in fact, a normal phenomenon that can properly be studied in the healthy person.
>
> ["Metapsychological and Clinical Aspects", p. 281]

Winnicott sees a relationship between the "freezing of the failure situation" and Freud's "fixation point". This difference, alluded to rather than clarified, is that the fixation point is located at a later stage of emotional development than the "freezing of the failure situation", which occurs between the stages of absolute and relative dependence.

The elaboration and development of the notion of an unconscious force inside each individual, searching for the facilitating environment, is developed in contemporary psychoanalysis—notably in terms of the "destiny drive" in the work of Christopher Bollas (1989a).

Winnicott's thinking on regression came into focus for him particularly while he was working with a patient who, during the course of analysis, needed to return to the trauma of her birth experience. Through Winnicott's experience of working with this patient and allowing her to regress fully, there emerges his original contribution to the meaning of regression in psychoanalytic practice and the necessary adaptation of psychoanalytic technique.

The patient, a woman in her 40s, had already undergone a long analysis, but she came to Winnicott with "the core of her illness unchanged":

> With me it soon became apparent that this patient must make a very severe regression or else give up the struggle. I therefore followed the regressive tendency, letting it take the patient wherever it led; eventually the regression reached the limit of the patient's need, and since then there has been a natural progression with the true self instead of a false self in action. . . .
>
> In the patient's previous analysis there had been incidents in which the patient had thrown herself off the couch in an hysterical way. These episodes had been interpreted along ordinary lines for hysterical phenomena of this kind. In the deeper regression of this new analysis light was thrown on the meaning of these falls. In the course of the two years of analysis with me the patient has repeatedly regressed to an early stage which was certainly prenatal. The birth process had to be relived, and eventually I recognized how this patient's unconscious need to relive the birth process underlay what had previously been an hysterical falling off the couch.
>
> ["Mind and Its Relation", p. 249]

Winnicott does not fail to emphasize that working with patients who become regressed places a huge strain on the analyst.

> The treatment and management of this case has called on everything that I possess as a human being, as a psychoanalyst, and as a paediatrician. I have had to make a personal growth in the course of this treatment which was painful and which I would gladly have avoided. In particular I have had to learn to examine my own technique whenever difficulties arose, and it has always turned out in the dozen or so resistance phases that the cause was in a counter-transference phenomenon which necessitated further self-analysis in the analyst.
>
> ["Metapsychological and Clinical Aspects", p. 280]

One of the major prerequisites of working with the patient who regresses in the analytic setting is for the analyst to know the nature of the work being taken on.

> What we become able to do enables us to co-operate with the patient in following the *process*, that which in each patient has its own pace and which follows its own course; all the important features of this process derive from the patient and not from ourselves as analysts.
>
> ["Metapsychological and Clinical Aspects", p. 278]

Although Winnicott advocated touch for patients who regressed, it should be stressed that the concept of holding is largely metaphorical across his work. The analyst can provide a literal holding without touch. (*see* COMMUNICATION: 3; HATE: 4; HOLDING: 3)

2   Classification

The analyst's following of the patient's process and adapting to the patient's needs parallels, of course, the abilities of the good-enough mother who adapts to her infant's needs. Analysts must, however, be aware of their own limitations and be very careful with their diagnosis and classification.

> Let us also bear in mind that by the legitimate method of careful choice of case we may and usually do avoid meeting aspects of human nature that must take us beyond our technical equipment.

Choice of case implies classification. For my present purpose I group cases according to the technical equipment they
require of the analyst.

["Metapsychological and Clinical Aspects", p. 278]

Winnicott identifies three groups of patients within the context of
the stages of dependence.

The first group has reached maturity and is therefore able to
distinguish between Me and Not-me. The technique for these patients "belongs to psychoanalysis as it developed in the hands of
Freud at the beginning of the century" ("Metapsychological and
Clinical Aspects", p. 279). These patients would have reached the
stage of "towards independence" and are commonly classified as
psychoneurotic.

The second group have reached or achieved the developmental stage in relation to the stage of relative dependence. The
technique required in their case is more or less the same as that for
the first group, but with an emphasis on the analyst's *survival*.
This theme of survival was eventually to lead to Winnicott's
theory of the "use of an object" in 1968. (*see* AGGRESSION: 10)

The third group consists of individuals who had suffered the
consequences of a failure of environmental adaptation at the
very early stages of life, when they were absolutely dependent.
These patients are generally classified as regressed and are usually labelled borderline, schizoid, schizophrenic, and so on:

In the *third* grouping I place all those patients whose analyses
must deal with the early stages of emotional development
before and up to the establishment of the personality as an
entity, before the achievement of space–time unit status. The
personal structure is not yet securely founded. In regard to
this third grouping, the accent is more surely on management,
and sometimes over long periods with these patients ordinary
analytic work has to be in abeyance, management being the
whole thing.

["Metapsychological and Clinical Aspects", p. 279]

By "management", Winnicott is referring here to all the components of holding that in the good-enough environment are taken
for granted.

The issues of classification and assessment were as complex
then as they still are today, and Winnicott points out that the

patient in the clinical illustration in this paper initially appears to be of the first category, but his analytical diagnosis "took into account a very early development of a false self". He concludes therefore that "for treatment to be effectual, there had to be a regression in search of the true self" ("Metapsychological and Clinical Aspects", p. 280).

3   Two kinds of regression

Winnicott posits two kinds of regression:

> Analysts have found it necessary to postulate that more norm-ally there are *good* pregenital situations to which the indi-vidual can return when in difficulties at a later stage. This is a health phenomenon. There has thus arisen the idea of two kinds of regression in respect of instinct development, the one being a going back to an early failure situation and the other to an early success situation.
> . . . In the case of the environmental failure situation what we see is evidence of *personal defences* organized by the indi-vidual and requiring analysis. In the case of the more normal early success situation what we see more obviously is the memory of *dependence,* and therefore we encounter an *environ-mental situation* rather than a personal defence organization. The personal organization is not so obvious because it has remained fluid, and less defensive.
> ["Metapsychological and Clinical Aspects", pp. 282–283]

The latter kind of regression occurs in the patient who has had a good-enough environmental holding, whereas the former occurs through the safety of the setting as the patient re-visits the early environmental failure. Both types of regression take the patient back to the early impingement of the environment.

> I should mention at this point that I am relying on an assump-tion which I have often made before and which is by no means always accepted, namely, that towards the theoretical beginning there is less and less of personal failure, eventually only failure of environmental adaptation.
> We are concerned, therefore, not merely with regression to good and bad points in the instinct experiences of the in-

dividual, but also to good and bad points in the environmental adaptation to ego needs and id needs in the individual's
history.

["Metapsychological and Clinical Aspects", p. 283]

To make sure that his point has been taken in, Winnicott emphasizes several times how the environmental provision influences
the infant's self experience. This relates to his on-going debate
with Melanie Klein, who, he felt, did not pay sufficient attention to
the role of the environment in child development.

Winnicott sees the false-self defence as a component of a
highly organized—by which he means highly defensive and
rigid—ego.

It will be seen that I am considering the idea of regression
within a highly organized ego-defence mechanism, one which
involves the existence of a false self. In the patient referred to
above this false self gradually became a "caretaker self", and
only after some years could the caretaker self become handed
over to the analyst, and the self surrender to the ego.

["Metapsychological and Clinical Aspects", p. 281]

The patient in question is first described in Winnicott's 1949
paper, "Birth Memories, Birth Trauma and Anxiety", then in 1954,
in "Metapsychological and Clinical Aspects of Regression within
the Psychoanalytical Set-up", and once again, briefly, in 1960, in,
"Ego Distortion in Terms of True and False Self". Using the words
of the patient, Winnicott came to see the False Self defence as a
split in the personality that had been set up in reaction to a failing
environment.

If the environment lets the baby down, he is forced to look
after himself; this causes premature ego development, which leads
to the establishment of the false, caretaker self. (*see* SELF: 6)

4   *The sense of feeling real*
         or the sense of futility

Winnicott's theory of the true and false self can be seen to be
germinating during the 1950s, and clearly his work with his patients and their regression to dependence brings him closer to his

formulation of 1960 in "Ego Distortion in Terms of True and False Self".

For Winnicott, especially during the last decade of his life and work, it is the sense of feeling real that makes life worth living. The "highly organized false self system" succeeds in protecting the core self, but at a cost to the sense of feeling real. (*see* EGO: 3)

> The development of a false self is one of *the most successful defence organizations* designed for the protection of the true self's core, and its existence results in the sense of futility. I would like to repeat myself and to say that while the individual's operational centre is in the false self there is a sense of futility, and in practice we find the change to the feeling that life is worth while coming at the moment of shift of the operational centre from the false to the true self, even before full surrender of the self's core to the total ego.
>
> From this one can formulate a fundamental principle of existence: that which proceeds from the true self feels real (later good) whatever its nature, however aggressive; that which happens in the individual as a reaction to environmental impingement feels unreal, futile (later bad) however sensually satisfactory.
>
> ["Metapsychological and Clinical Aspects", p. 292]

Winnicott's axiom for working with patients who had developed a false-self system is that regression to dependence in the analytic setting may help the patient to reach back to the early environmental failure and find the sense of what is true. The search for the true self leads to the sense of feeling real.

At the heart of the sense of feeling real is the good-enough adaptation of the environment to the needs of the patient. Thus the patient is compensated and healed through going back and finding in the analytic setting that which should have been provided earlier but was not available—that is, the facilitating environment, which holds and contains.

The "healing mechanism" inherent in regression is a potential, which can only be realized within a "new and reliable environmental adaptation which can be used by the patient in correction of the original adaptive failure". This environment is absolutely on a par with good-enough child care and that which can be provided "by friendship, by enjoyment of poetry, and cultural

pursuits generally" ("Metapsychological and Clinical Aspects",
pp. 293–294).

The "recovery from regression" takes the patient into the
"ordinary analysis as designed for the management of the depressive position and of the Oedipus Complex in interpersonal relationships" ("Metapsychological and Clinical Aspects", p. 294).

5   "We succeed by failing"

The analyst's failure is a crucial component of this new environment. It has to occur within the transference, in a re-enactment of
early failure situations. The analyst's failure, then, is an enactment, and it too needs to be articulated at the right time.
However, for there to be a healing effect on the patient, it should
only occur *once the analytic frame has been established.*

> What is it that may be enough for some of our patients to get
> well? In the end the patient uses the analyst's failures, often
> quite small ones, perhaps manoeuvred by the patient . . . and
> we have to put up with being in a limited context misunder-
> stood. The operative factor is that the patient now hates the
> analyst for the failure that originally came as an environmen-
> tal factor, outside the infant's area of omnipotent control, but
> that is *now* staged in the transference.
>
> So in the end we succeed by failing—failing the patient's
> way. This is a long distance from the simple theory of cure by
> corrective experience. In this way, regression can be in the
> service of the ego if it is met by the analyst, and turned into a
> new dependence in which the patient brings the bad external
> factor into the area of his or her omnipotent control, and the
> area managed by projection and introjection mechanisms.
>
> ["Dependence in Infant-Care, in Child Care
> and in the Psycho-Analytic Setting", 1963, p. 258]

The crucial point here is the question of whether or not the analyst
is able to recognize the patient's need to regress and is ready to
adapt and meet the need, just as the good-enough mother in her
state of primary maternal preoccupation is able to adapt to her
infant's needs. The analyst needing to succeed through failing in
the transference is like the mother who needs to de-adapt gradually. (*see* DEPENDENCE: 5)

6 *Adaptation not art*

At the time Winnicott was working on issues related to regression, there was general disagreement in the psychoanalytic world as to the value of psychoanalysis to such patients, who were often seen as unanalysable. Although the issue of analysability is still being debated amongst clinicians, much new work has been done with the regressed patient since Winnicott's time.

Winnicott had some criticism coming his way, which he wished to address.

> The idea is sometimes put forward: of course everyone wants to regress; regression is a picnic; we must stop our patients from regression; or Winnicott likes or invites his patients to regress.
>
> ["Metapsychological and Clinical Aspects", p. 290]

He also wished to make clear how extremely painful regression to dependence is for the patient, and that working with somebody going through a regression is *no* picnic.

> There are no reasons why an analyst should *want* a patient to regress, except grossly pathological reasons. If an analyst likes patients to regress, this must eventually interfere with the management of the regressed situation. Further, psychoanalysis which involves clinical regression is very much more difficult all along than that in which no special adaptive environmental provision has to be made. In other words it would be pleasant if we were to be able to take for analysis only those patients whose mothers at the very start and also in the first months had been able to provide good-enough conditions. But this era of psychoanalysis is steadily drawing to a close.
>
> ["Metapsychological and Clinical Aspects", pp. 290–291]

Winnicott is challenging analysts about their practice whilst at the same time making a plea for (a) recognition of the environment's responsibility for the patient's mental health, and (b) adaptation of the analytic environment to suit the needs of the patient who regresses to dependence.

> But the questions arises, what do analysts do when regression (even of minute quantity) turns up?

Some crudely say: Now sit up! Pull your socks up! Come round! Talk!

But this is not psychoanalysis.

Some divide their work into two parts, though unfortunately they do not always fully acknowledge this:

   a. they are strictly analytic (free association in words; interpretation in words; no reassurances)

and also

   b. they act intuitively.

Here comes the idea of psychoanalysis as an *art*.

Some say: unanalysable, and throw up the sponge. A mental hospital takes over.

The idea of psychoanalysis as an art must gradually give way to a study of environmental adaptation relative to patients' regressions. But while the scientific study of environmental adaptation is undeveloped, then I suppose analysts must continue to be artists in their work. An analyst may be a good artist, but (as I have frequently asked): what patient wants to be someone else's poem or picture?

["Metapsychological and Clinical Aspects", p. 291]

7   Reassurance

Reassurance in psychoanalysis was and still is frowned upon; it is not seen as psychoanalytic technique, because the analyst should interpret the patient's unconscious communication. Winnicott addresses his critics again when he explores the meaning of reassurance:

Lastly, let us examine the concept of regression by putting up against it the concept of reassurance. This becomes necessary because of the fact that the adaptive technique that must meet a patient's regression is often classed (wrongly, I am sure) as reassurance. . . .

As we look a little more carefully, however, we see that this is too simple a language. It is not just a question of reassurance and no reassurance.

In fact, the whole matter needs examination. What is a reassurance? What could be more reassuring than to find oneself being well analysed, to be in a reliable setting with a mature person in charge, capable of making penetrating and accurate interpretation, and to find one's personal process respected? It is foolish to deny that reassurance is present in the classical analytic situation.

The whole set-up of psychoanalysis is one big reassurance, especially the reliable objectivity and behaviour of the analyst, and the transference interpretations constructively using instead of wastefully exploiting the moment's passion.

["Metapsychological and Clinical Aspects", p. 292]

This paper again expresses Winnicott's personal passion about the importance of recognizing the patient's needs and distinguishing them from wishes and the notion of gratification. He is strongly pleading for a change in attitude from his fellow analysts:

What would be said of an analyst's *inability* to reassure? If an analyst were suicidal? *A belief in human nature and in the developmental process exists in the analyst* if work is to be done at all, and this is quickly sensed by the patient.

There is no value to be got from describing regression to dependence, with its concomitant environmental adaptation, in terms of reassurance, just as there is a very real point in considering harmful reassurance in terms of counter-transference.

["Metapsychological and Clinical Aspects", pp. 292–293]

By "countertransference", in this context, Winnicott means the analyst's pathological reaction to the strain the regressed patient puts on him. (*see* HATE: 2)

8   A setting that gives confidence

Winnicott recognizes that Freud took the early good-enough environment for granted because it "turns up" in the setting Freud devised. This very setting that evolved for the psycho-neurotic also serves the psychotic or regressed patient very well, because it replicates the holding environment:

Psychotic illness is related to environmental failure at an early stage of the emotional development of the individual. The

sense of futility and unreality belongs to the development of a
false self which develops in protection of the true self.

The setting of analysis reproduces the early and earliest
mothering techniques. It invites regression by reason of its
reliability.

The regression of a patient is an organized return to early
dependence or double dependence. The patient and the setting merge into the original success situation of primary
narcissism.

Progress from primary narcissism starts anew with the true
self able to meet environmental failure situations without
organization of the defences that involve a false self protecting the true self.

To this extent psychotic illness can only be relieved by
specialized environmental provision interlocked with the patient's regression.

Progress from the new position, with the true self surrendered to the total ego, can now be studied in terms of the
complex processes of individual growth.

["Metapsychological and Clinical Aspects", pp. 286–287]

Winnicott uses the term "primary narcissism" to describe the
merging between mother and infant during the time of absolute
dependence—or "double" dependence, as he refers to it in the
1950s. The merging refers to the infant's unawareness of the care
he is receiving. (see DEPENDENCE: 4; MOTHER: 10)

Once the patient has started therapy, a "sequence of events"
arises:

1. The provision of a setting that gives confidence.
2. Regression of the patient to dependence, with due sense of
   the risk involved.
3. The patient feeling a new sense of self, and the self hitherto
   hidden becoming surrendered to the total ego. A new progression of the individual processes which had stopped.
4. An unfreezing of an environmental failure situation.
5. From the new position of ego strength, anger related to the
   early environmental failure, felt in the present and expressed.
6. Return from regression to dependence, in orderly progress
   towards independence.

7. Instinctual needs and wishes becoming realizable with gen-
uine vitality and vigour.
All this repeated again and again.

["Metapsychological and Clinical Aspects", p. 287]

Essentially, Winnicott sees psychotic illness as "a defensive organization designed to protect the true self", caused by very early
environmental failure (mother not able to adapt to infant's needs).
(*see* ENVIRONMENT: 3)

Nine years later, in 1963, Winnicott addresses the question of
the aetiology of psychosis:

> ... do I attribute psychosis mainly to severe traumatic experi-
> ences, partly of deprivations in early infancy? I can well un-
> derstand that this is the impression that I have given, and I
> have changed the way I present my view in the course of the
> past decade. It is necessary, however, to make some correc-
> tions. I have definitely stated that in the aetiology of psychotic
> illness and particularly of schizophrenia ... there has to be
> noted a failure in the total infant-care process. In one paper I
> went so far as to state: "Psychosis is an environmental defi-
> ciency disease". Zetzel uses the term "severe traumatic expe-
> riences", and these words imply bad things happening, things
> that look bad from the observer's point of view. The deficien-
> cies that I am referring to are failures of basic provision. . . .
> The main point is that these failures are unpredictable; they
> cannot be accounted for by the infant in terms of projection,
> because the infant has not yet reached the stage of ego-struc-
> turing that makes this possible, and they result in the *annihila-
> tion* of the individual whose going-on-being is interrupted.

["Dependence in Infant-Care", p. 256]

9   Distinguishing wishes from needs

This part of Winnicott's theory of regression is linked with assessing the patient's ability to symbolize. A patient who is functioning
on a psychotic level finds it more difficult to appreciate a "shared
reality":

> The couch and the pillows are there for the patient's use. They
> will appear in ideas and dreams and then will stand for the

analyst's body, breasts, arms, hands, etc. in an infinite variety
of ways. In so far as the patient is regressed (for a moment or
for an hour or over a long period of time) the couch *is* the
analyst, the pillows *are* breasts, the analyst *is* the mother at a
certain past era. In the extreme it is no longer true to say the
couch stands for the analyst.

It is proper to speak of the patient's *wishes*, the wish (for
instance) to be quiet. With the regressed patient the word
wish is incorrect; instead we use the word *need*. If a regressed
patient *needs* quiet, then without it nothing can be done at all.
If the need is not met the result is not anger, only a reproduction of the environmental failure situation which stopped the
processes of self growth. The individual's capacity to "wish"
has become interfered with, and we witness the reappearance
of the original cause of a sense of futility.

The regressed patient is near to a reliving of dream and
memory situations; an acting out of a dream may be the way
the patient discovers what is urgent, and talking about what
was acted out follows the action but cannot precede it.

["Metapsychological and Clinical Aspects", p. 288]

Winnicott is referring to the patient who cannot yet symbolize in
the analytic setting and can only communicate through enactment.

The "observing ego" is Winnicott's term for the patient's ability to go into a state of regression in the analytic hour and then
come out of it. With the patient whose observing ego is not so
developed, the need to enact is the only way to re-live what needs
to be re-lived.

An important element in this theory is the postulate of the
observing ego. Two patients very similar in their immediate
clinical aspect may be very different in regard to the degree of
organization of the observing ego. At one extreme the observing ego is almost able to identify with the analyst and there
can be recovery from the regression at the end of the analytic
hour. At the other extreme there is very little observing ego,
and the patient is unable to recover from the regression in the
analytic hour, and must be nursed.

Acting out has to be tolerated in this sort of work, and with
the acting out in the analytic hour the analyst will find it

necessary to play a part, although usually in token form. There is nothing more surprising both to the patient and to the analyst than the revelations that occur in these moments of acting out. The actual acting out in the analysis is only the beginning, however, and there must always follow a putting into words of the new bit of understanding.

["Metapsychological and Clinical Aspects", p. 289]

Although the regressed patient is struggling with his ability to symbolize and to distinguish Me from Not-me, the acting out within the analytic setting *is* symbolic; it is the only way the patient is able to communicate something of the past trauma to the analyst. Winnicott emphasizes that whatever acting out occurs in the session, it will be analysable at a later stage of the analysis. He sees a developmental sequence working towards this distinction:

1. A statement of what happened in the acting out.
2. A statement of what was needed of the analyst. From this can be deduced:
3. What went wrong in the original environmental failure situation.
   This produces some relief, but there follows:
4. Anger belonging to the original environmental failure situation. This anger is being felt perhaps for the first time, and the analyst may now have to take part by being used in respect of his failures rather than of his successes. This is disconcerting unless it is understood. The progress has been made through the analyst's very careful attempt at adaptation, and yet it is the failure that at this moment is singled out as important on account of its being a reproduction of the original failure or trauma. In favourable cases there follows at last:

5. A new sense of self in the patient and a sense of the progress that means true growth. It is this last that must be the analyst's reward through his identification with his patient. Not always will a further stage arrive in which the patient is able to understand the strain which the analyst has undergone and is able to say thankyou with real meaning.

["Metapsychological and Clinical Aspects", pp. 289–290]

10 *Regression and withdrawal*

In chapter 8 of *Human Nature* (W18), Winnicott describes withdrawal:

> It is helpful to think of withdrawal as a condition in which the person concerned (child or adult) holds a regressed part of the self and nurses it, at the expense of external relationships.
>
> [*Human Nature*, p. 141]

It is as if the patient were carrying the infant part of the self inside.

> If, at the moment of withdrawal in a psychotherapy where there is opportunity for delicate observation and management, the therapist quickly steps in and holds the baby, then the person hands over the nursing to the therapist and slips over into becoming the infant.
>
> [*Human Nature*, p. 141]

If the patient allows the analyst to "hold the baby", then a regression to dependence has occurred. If the environment (analytic setting) is reliable enough, then the patient can make full use of the regressions to dependence over a period of time.

> Regression has a healing quality, since early experience can be corrected in a regression and there is a true restfulness in the experience and acknowledgement of dependence. Return from regression depends on a regaining of independence, and if this is well managed by the therapist the result is that the person is in a better state than before the episode.
>
> [*Human Nature*, p. 141]

Withdrawal, however, does not have a healing quality and does not benefit the patient. It merely demonstrates that the patient has had to hold the self in the past, and it is, in that sense, a cry for help in the session.

In a paper written in 1954, "Withdrawal and Regression", Winnicott illustrates with clinical data how the analyst must recognize the withdrawn state and subsequently find a way of *holding* the baby in the patient. If the analyst is able to do this, then the patient is able to regress to dependence, and thus the earlier failure situation is corrected.

... if we know about regression in the analytic hour, we can meet it immediately and in this way enable certain patients who are not too ill to make the necessary regression in short phases, perhaps even almost momentarily. I would say that *in the withdrawn state a patient is holding the self* and that if immediately the withdrawn state appears *the analyst can hold the patient*, then what would otherwise have been a withdrawal state becomes a regression. The advantage of a *regression* is that it carries with it the opportunity for correction of inadequate adaptation-to-need in the past history of the patient, that is to say, in the patient's infancy management. By contrast the *withdrawn* state is not profitable and when the patient recovers from a withdrawn state he or she is not changed.

["Withdrawal and Regression", p. 261]

Winnicott makes it clear that there are no dangers inherent in the patient's regression to dependence, other than the inadequacies in the analyst.

It is commonly thought that there is some danger in the regression of a patient during psychoanalysis. The danger does not lie in the regression but in the analyst's unreadiness to meet the regression and the dependence which belongs to it. When an analyst has had experience that makes him confident in his management of regression, then it is probably true to say that the more quickly the analyst accepts the regression and meets it fully the less likely is it that the patient will need to enter into an illness with regressive qualities.

[Withdrawal and Regression, p. 261]

REFERENCES

1949 Mind and Its Relation to the Psyche–Soma   [W6]

1954 Metapsychological and Clinical Aspects of Regression within the Psychoanalytical Set-up   [W6]

1954 Withdrawal and Regression   [W6]

1963 Dependence in Infant-Care, in Child Care and in the Psychoanalytic Setting   [W9]

1988 *Human Nature*   [W18]

Self

Although Winnicott frequently states that there is a difference between the "self" and the "ego", his distinction is not always clear across the whole of his work, because frequently the term "self" is used interchangeably with the terms "ego" and "psyche".

Essentially, for Winnicott, the term "self" is a psychological description of how the individual feels subjectively, and it is the sense of "feeling real" that Winnicott places at the centre of the sense of self.

Developmentally, the "self" starts off as a potential in the new-born infant; given a good-enough environment, it develops into a whole self—that is, a person who is able to distinguish between Me and Not-me.

In the last decade of his life, Winnicott distinguished between the true and false self and emphasized an incommunicado, isolated core self, which for mental health needs to stay protected at all costs.

1   Subjectivity and self

For the reader, Winnicott's precise meaning of the term "self" may often be confusing. Throughout his work, although he often differentiates between the ego and the self (see EGO: 1), it is useful to bear in mind that—although this was never made clear by Winnicott himself—the ego is an aspect of the self that has a particular function: to organize and integrate experience.

Thus the self is made up of all the different aspects of personality that, in Winnicott's language, form the Me, as distinct from the Not-me, of each person. The term "self", therefore, describes a subjective sense of being.

It may be discerned across Winnicott's work that the terms self, ego, and psyche imply different emphases on internal reality and function, and that, as with all the terms he uses, not one can—nor should—be pinned down.

Generally, Winnicott places the self (core or true) at the beginning of life, but when he is referring to a whole self, the birth of the self is located at the stage of concern. (*see* CONCERN: 5; EGO: 2)

2   The self as bubble and kernel

In 1949, in his paper "Birth Memories, Birth Trauma and Anxiety", Winnicott quotes one of his patients, to describe the self:

> I am indebted to a patient for a way of putting this which came from an extremely deep-rooted appreciation of the position of the infant at an early stage. . . . This patient said: "At the beginning the individual is like a bubble. If the pressure from outside actively adapts to the pressure within, then the bubble is the significant thing, that is to say the infant's self. If, however, the environmental pressure is greater or less than the pressure within the bubble, then it is not the bubble that is important but the environment. The bubble adapts to the outside pressure".
>
> ["Birth Memories", pp. 182–183]

Winnicott used this quote to describe the infant's task, during birth, of dealing with the impingement of the environment on the body-self—like the bubble adapting to outside pressure:

Before birth, and especially if there is delay, there can quite easily be repeated experiences for an infant in which, for the time being, the stress is on environment rather than on self, and it is likely that the unborn infant becomes more and more caught up in this sort of intercourse with the environment as the time of birth arrives. Thus, in the natural process *the birth experience is an exaggerated sample of something already known to the infant.* For the time being, during the birth, the infant is a reactor and the important thing is the environment; and then after birth there is a return to a state of affairs in which the important thing is the infant, whatever that means. In health the infant is prepared before birth for some environmental impingement, and already has had the experience of a natural return from reacting to a state of not having to react, which is the only state in which the self can begin to be.

["Birth Memories", p. 183]

In this paper, the self is located even before birth, and it is clear that it cannot begin to "be" if it is in the position of having to *react* to impingements by the environment. (*see* ENVIRONMENT: 5; PSYCHE–SOMA: 4; REGRESSION: 2, 3)

Later, in 1952, in a paper entitled, "Anxiety Associated with Insecurity", Winnicott describes the mother–infant dyad before the beginning of object relationships as an environmental–individual set-up (*see* BEING: 1)—a shell (mother) and kernel (baby)—which metaphorically depicts that the self, and all its parts, begins right inside the mother–infant unit:

The centre of gravity of the being does not start off in the individual. It is in the total set-up. By good-enough child care, technique, holding, and general management the shell becomes gradually taken over and the kernel (which has looked all the time like a baby to us) can begin to be an individual. . . . The human being now developing an entity from the centre can become localized in the baby's body and so can begin to create an external world at the same time as acquiring a limiting membrane and an inside.

["Anxiety Associated with Insecurity", p. 99]

Although self and ego are not mentioned here, the entity, it must be assumed, refers to the potential and developing self or/and ego. (*see* EGO: 1, 2). Ego and self are used interchangeably in the final paragraph of "Primary Maternal Preoccupation" (1956):

Ego here implies a summation of experience. The individual self starts as a summation of resting experience, spontaneous motility, and sensation, return from activity to rest. . . .

["Primary Maternal Preoccupation", p. 305]

The emphasis here, in 1956, is that the beginning of the self is a "summation of experience", which in 1962 is described as the beginning of the ego:

The first question that is asked about that which is labelled the ego is this: is there an ego from the start? The answer is that the start is when the ego starts.

["Ego Integration in Child Development", p. 56]

A footnote added to this reads:

It is well to remember that the beginning is a summation of beginnings.

["Ego Integration", p. 56]

Nevertheless, in the same paper Winnicott writes categorically:

It will be seen that the ego offers itself for study long before the word self has relevance. The word self arrives after the child has begun to use the intellect to look at what others see or feel or hear and what they conceive of when they meet this infant body.

["Primary Maternal Preoccupation", p. 56]

Here it seems that for Winnicott the self does not come into being until the infant begins to separate Me from Not-me—during the stage of concern, as stated above.

3   Primary unintegration

The subject of inner reality and psychic reality is explored by Winnicott in his 1935 paper, "The Manic Defence". By 1945, in "Primitive Emotional Development", the themes of inner reality are elaborated, and Winnicott postulates a state of primary unintegration—sometimes referred to as primary narcissism— which specifically refers to the state of the infant's potential self. So, for Winnicott, the self does not exist until awareness takes place, which emphasizes the "sense" in the existence of "self" (this theme is explored in Winnicott's work on transitional phenomena, playing, and the search for self—*see* PLAYING: 5, 6; SELF: 11; TRANSITIONAL PHENOMENA: 6).

For self-awareness to take place, there are three processes that need to emerge out of the state of primary unintegration. They are:

> . . . integration, personalization, and following these, the appreciation of time and space and other properties of reality—in short realization.
>
> ["Primitive Emotional Development", p. 149]

En passant, Winnicott refers briefly to the problem associated with personalization:

> A problem related to that of personalization is that of the imaginary companions of childhood. These are not simple fantasy constructions. Study of the future of these imaginary companions (in analysis) shows that they are sometimes other selves of a highly primitive type.
>
> ["Primitive Emotional Development", p. 151]

Winnicott does not explore the phenomenon of imaginary companions in this paper, but he states that this sort of use of imagination is a

> . . . very primitive and magical creation [which is] . . . easily used as a defence, as it magically by-passes all the anxieties associated with incorporation, digestion, retention and expulsion.
>
> ["Primitive Emotional Development", p. 151]

This introduces the theme of the nature of defence, which, in this context, suggests that the self is forced to defend itself, if under attack. One useful defence is that of dissociation.

> Out of the problem of unintegration comes another, that of dissociation. Dissociation can usefully be studied in its initial or natural forms. According to my view there grows out of unintegration a series of what are then called dissociations, which arise owing to integration being incomplete or partial.
>
> ["Primitive Emotional Development", p. 151]

From this statement, Winnicott goes on to explain that the infant, right at the start, has not yet been able to appreciate that he remains the same baby whether he is "quiet" or "excited":

> For example, there are quiet and excited states. I think an infant cannot be said to be aware at the start that while feeling this and that in his cot or enjoying the skin stimulations of bathing, he is the same as himself screaming for immediate satisfaction, possessed by an urge to get at and destroy something unless satisfied by milk. This means that he does not know at first that the mother he is building up through his quiet experiences is the same as the power behind the breasts that he has in his mind to destroy.
> ["Primitive Emotional Development", p. 151]

Here are two infants in one and two mothers in one. At the beginning, from the subject's point of view, the emotions involved in the "quiet" and "excited" moods are separate and "dissociated". The work of integration is to bring them together. (*see* AGGRESSION: 6; CONCERN: 3, 4, 5; HATE: 6)

4   *Three selves*

Winnicott refers to the existence of three selves in one personality in only one paper, in 1950, "Aggression in Relation to Emotional Development":

> The personality comprises three parts: a true self, with Me and Not-me clearly established, and with some fusion of the aggressive and erotic elements; a self that is easily seduced along lines of erotic experience, but with the result of a loss of sense of real; a self that is entirely and ruthlessly given over to aggression.
> ["Aggression in Relation to Emotional Development", p. 217]

In this model the true self has already established boundaries—unlike the self that is easily won over and the self "given over to aggression". Later on in the same paper, Winnicott links this ruthless self with the impulsive gesture, in health, that seeks externality (*see* AGGRESSION: 7):

The main conclusion to be made out of these considerations is that confusion exists through our using the term aggression sometimes when we mean spontaneity. The impulsive gesture reaches out and becomes aggressive when opposition is reached. There is reality in this experience, and it very easily fuses into the erotic experiences that await the new-born infant. I am suggesting: *it is this impulsiveness, and the aggression that develops out of it, that makes the infant need an external object,* and not merely a satisfying object.

[*"Aggression in Relation to Emotional Development"*, p. 217]

The content of these two paragraphs illustrates Winnicott's own development at this time (this part of the paper was presented to a private group in 1954), which dispenses with Freud's instinct theory (the impulse now is to seek an object rather than satisfaction), as well as the postulation that creativity comes out of the early "primitive love impulse" rather than the need to repair, as in Klein's theory of the "depressive position".

In other words, whereas Freud believed that the instinct in the human infant strove to be satiated, Winnicott came to see that satisfaction can be a "fobbing-off" if the infant has not felt *his* part in obtaining satisfaction.

In the same year, 1954, in "The Depressive Position in Normal Development", Winnicott explores the meaning of fobbing off.

The baby is fobbed off by the feed itself; instinct tension disappears, and the baby is both satisfied and cheated. It is too easily assumed that a feed is followed by satisfaction and sleep. Often distress follows this fobbing off, especially if physical satisfaction too quickly robs the infant of zest. The infant is then left with: aggression undischarged—because not enough muscle erotism or primitive impulse (or motility), was used in the feeding process; or a sense of "flop"—since a source of zest for life has gone suddenly, and the infant does not know it will return. All this appears clearly in clinical analytic experience, and is at least not contradicted by direct observation of infants.

["Depressive Position", p. 268]

Four years later, in Winnicott's lecture in celebration of Freud's centenary year, he seems to hail the ruthlessness in the creative artist when he says that

> . . . ordinary guilt-ridden people find this bewildering; yet
> they have a sneaking regard for ruthlessness that does in fact
> . . . achieve more than guilt-driven labour.
>
> [" Psychoanalysis and the Sense of Guilt", 1958, p. 27]

Winnicott does not state his thesis clearly, perhaps because this is a lecture in celebration of Freud (and Melanie Klein and her followers are dominating the British Psycho-Analytical Society at this time), but he implies that this ruthlessness is very much part of the creative drive, placed at the beginning of life in love, rather than in the reparation of the depressive position. (*see* AGGRESSION: 7, 8; CREATIVITY: 5)

For the self to develop, however, the aggressive ruthlessness in the infant, which is part and parcel of the "primitive love impulse", has to be met by the external environment, the mother, so as to strengthen the self. Always with the emphasis on the environment, Winnicott finally comes to combine the true self and the ruthless self of 1954 into the true self of 1960.

5 *The quality of care*
   that strengthens the sense of self

Thus the themes of self-defence and dissociation culminate in Winnicott's 1960 paper "Ego Distortion in Terms of True and False Self". Here, Winnicott draws a distinction between true and false self with reference to a spectrum. At one end the false self protects the true self and at the other end the false self does not know about the true self because it is so hidden.

Elaborating on his evolving thoughts on the nature of aggression in relation to instincts and the environment, Winnicott arrives at a clear thesis about the difference between what he calls "ego-needs" and "id-needs". Recall the infant who cannot recognize that he is essentially the same baby whether he is quiet or excited (*see* AGGRESSION: 6; CONCERN: 3)

> It must be emphasised that in referring to the meeting of infant needs I am not referring to the satisfaction of instincts. In the area that I am examining the instincts are not yet clearly defined as internal to the infant. The instincts can be as much

external as can a clap of thunder or a hit. The infant's ego is building up strength and in consequence is getting towards a state in which id-demands will be felt as part of the self, and not as environmental. When this development occurs, then id-satisfaction becomes a very important strengthener of the ego, or of the True Self; but id-excitements can be traumatic when the ego is not yet able to include them, and not yet able to contain the risks involved and the frustrations experienced up to the point when id-satisfaction becomes a fact.

["Ego Distortion", p. 141]

The id-demands—biologically driven instincts—will only become part of the self, integrated into experience, if the mother is able to meet the infant's needs. This meeting of needs consists of receiving as well as giving—responding to the infant's impulsive gesture. (*see* CONCERN: 7)

Always mindful of the parallels between infant care and patient care, Winnicott transposes this notion of ego and id needs:

A patient said to me: "Good management" (ego care) "such as I have experienced during this hour IS a feed" (id satisfaction). He could not have said this the other way round, for if I had fed him he would have complied and this would have played into his False Self defence, or else he would have reacted and rejected my advances, maintaining his integrity by choosing frustration.

["Ego Distortion", p. 141–142]

Good management refers to the holding nature of the analytic frame. This is reminiscent of a paragraph from Winnicott's 1945 paper, "Primitive Emotional Development", where he illustrates the patient's need to use the analyst to collect himself (integrate):

Integration starts right away at the beginning of life, but in our work we can never take it for granted. We have to account for it and watch its fluctuations.

An example of unintegration phenomena is provided by the very common experience of the patient who proceeds to give every detail of the week-end and feels contented at the end if everything has been said, though the analyst feels that no analytic work has been done. Sometimes we must interpret this as the patient's need to be known in all his bits and pieces by one person, the analyst. To be known means to feel integrated at least in the person of the analyst. This is the ordinary stuff of infant life, and an infant who has had no one person to gather his bits together starts with a handicap in his own self-integrating task, and perhaps he cannot succeed, or at any rate cannot maintain integration with confidence.

["Primitive Emotional Development", p. 150]

Winnicott continued to work on this theme in the final decade of his life. He emphasized the holding environment in the consulting room, which would facilitate the patient to arrive at his own interpretation. Like the infant who needs to feel that the satisfactory feed is due to his effort, so, too, the patient needs to feel that the analytic work is part of his effort. (see COMMUNICATION: 6)

6   The false self

It is in his clinical practice that Winnicott came to distinguish between a true and a false self. The false self—called by one patient the "caretaker self"—is the self that Winnicott realizes he has to deal with for the first two or three years of the analytic work with that patient. This case leads him to divide the false-self organization into a spectrum ranging from the pathological to the healthy. In each classification, however, the false self is a structure that is there to *defend* the true self, even—or especially—at the healthy end. The early environment shapes the quality of defence required (see ENVIRONMENT: 1). This theme is further elaborated in Winnicott's 1963 paper, "Communicating and Not Communicating Leading to a Study of Certain Opposites".

7   Split-off intellect

The false-self personality could well deceive the world, says Winnicott when referring to a particularly fine intellect that could become localized in the false self.

When there has taken place this double abnormality, (i) the False Self organized to hide the True Self, and (ii) an attempt on the part of the individual to solve the personal problem by the use of a fine intellect, a clinical picture results which is

peculiar in that it very easily deceives. The world may observe academic success of a high degree, and may find it hard
to believe in the very real distress of the individual concerned,
who feels "phoney" the more he or she is successful. When
such individuals destroy themselves in one way or another,
instead of fulfilling promise, this invariably produces a sense
of shock in those who have developed high hopes of the individual.

["Ego Distortion", p. 144]

In 1965, in a paper he presented to teachers at the Devon Centre
for Further Education, Winnicott locates the aetiology of the split-
off intellect:

If we now take the case of a baby whose mother's failure to
adapt is too rapid, we can find that the baby survives by means
of the mind. The mother exploits the baby's power to think
things out and to collate and to understand. If the baby has a
good mental apparatus this thinking becomes a substitute for
maternal care and adaptation. The baby "mothers" himself by
means of understanding, understanding too much. . . .

This results in the uneasy intelligence of some whose good
brains have become exploited. The intelligence is hiding a
degree of deprivation. In other words, there is always for those
with exploited brains a threat of a breakdown from intelligence and understanding to mental chaos or to disintegration
of the personality.

["New Light on Children's Thinking", p. 156]

8   Symbolic realization

The aetiology of the false self is located in the early mother–infant
relationship, and the mother's part is crucial. Winnicott defines
what he means by good-enough:

The good-enough mother meets the omnipotence of the infant
and to some extent makes sense of it. She does this repeatedly.
A True Self begins to have life, through the strength given to
the infant's weak ego by the mother's implementation of the
infant's omnipotent expressions.

["Ego Distortion", p. 145]

This adaptation on the part of the mother will enable the infant to symbolize. Winnicott stresses that this depends on the infant's gesture *made real* by the mother's response to it, leading on to the infant's ability to use a symbol. (This was elaborated in the last decade of Winnicott's work in all of the papers included in *Playing and Reality*, especially the paper "The Use of an Object and Relating through Identifications). (*see* AGGRESSION: 10; CREATIVITY: 3; PLAYING: 7)

Symbolic Realisation, a book published in 1951 by the French analyst, M. A. Sechehaye, is an account of the analyst's work with a schizophrenic patient over a period of time, detailing the way in which she, the analyst, had to adapt her psychoanalytic technique in order to provide the patient with something she had never received from her early environment. The account presents a journey of how Sechehaye managed to meet the patient's needs and how this "adaptation to needs" contributed to the patient's capacity to begin to make use of symbols. "Symbolic realization" refers to the patient's use of real objects in the sessions, which come to represent and compensate for the early environmental failure. This, in turn, aids the patient to start distinguishing between Me and Not-me.

Winnicott occasionally refers to Sechehaye's work, and his theory of adaptation to need is particularly pertinent in the case of a deprived and disturbed patient. By using the paradigm of the mother in a state of primary maternal preoccupation who is able to adapt to her infant's needs, Winnicott finds a way of recognizing regression to dependence within the analytic session and how the analyst must meet the regression. (*see* REGRESSION: 2, 9, 10)

9   The true self

To balance the concept of the false self, Winnicott suggests the existence of a true self:

> At the earliest stage the True Self is the theoretical position from which comes the spontaneous gesture and the personal idea. The spontaneous gesture is the True Self in action. Only the True Self can be creative and only the True Self can feel

real. Whereas a True Self feels real, the existence of a False
Self results in a feeling unreal or a sense of futility.

["Ego Distortion", p. 148]

Winnicott makes reference to his patient with the "caretaker self"
who came, at the end of her analysis, *to the beginning of her life*
which had so far "contained no true experience. . . . She starts with
fifty years of wasted life, but at last she feels real, and therefore
she now wants to live" ("Ego Distortion", p. 148).

And then Winnicott elaborates his description of the true self,
which seems very similar to, if not the same as, his description,
two years later, of the ego, in "Ego Integration in Child Development" in 1962.

> It is important to note that according to the theory being for-
> mulated here the concept of an individual inner reality of
> objects applies to a stage later than does the concept of what is
> being termed the True Self. The True Self appears as soon as
> there is any mental organization of the individual at all, and it
> means little more than the summation of sensori-motor alive-
> ness.
>
> ["Ego Distortion", p. 149]

Four years later, in 1964, Winnicott addressed an Oxford University group in a talk he entitled "The Concept of the False Self".
Here, he credits the concern for truth to poets and people who feel
intensely.

> Poets, philosophers and seers have always concerned them-
> selves with the idea of a true self, and the betrayal of the self
> has been a typical example of the unacceptable. Shakespeare,
> perhaps to avoid being smug, gathered together a bundle of
> truths and handed them out to us by the mouth of a crashing
> bore called Polonius. In this way we can take the advice:
>
>> This above all: to thine own self be true,
>> And it must follow, as the night the day,
>> Thou canst not then be false to any man.
>
> You could quote to me from almost any poet of standing and
> show that this is a pet theme of people who feel intensely.
> Also, you could point out to me that present-day drama is
> searching for the true core within what is square, sentimental,
> successful or slick.
>
> ["Concept of False Self", pp. 65–66]

10 *Compliance and compromise*

Compliance is always associated with false-self living in Winnicott's language, and it is connected with despair rather than hope (*see* ANTISOCIAL TENDENCY: 2). In his 1963 paper, "Morals and Education", Winnicott states:

> Immorality for the infant is to comply at the expense of the personal way of life. For instance, a child of any age may feel that to eat is wrong, even to the extent of dying for the principle. Compliance brings immediate rewards and adults only too easily mistake compliance for growth.
>
> ["Morals and Education", p. 102]

Nevertheless, the ability to compromise is a sign of health in the appreciation of a shared reality; it is the positive and healthy component of the "normal equivalent of the False Self":

> There is a compliant aspect to the True Self in healthy living, an ability of the infant to comply and not to be exposed. The ability to compromise is an achievement. The equivalent of the False Self in normal development is that which can develop in the child into a social manner, something which is adaptable. In health this social manner represents a compromise. At the same time, in health, the compromise ceases to become allowable when the issues become crucial. When this happens the True Self is able to override the compliant self. Clinically this constitutes a recurring problem of adolescence.
>
> ["Ego Distortion", pp. 149–150]

Winnicott is really referring to what could be seen to be a healthy split in the personality and, as he describes it, a "not-wearing-the-heart-on-the-sleeve" self:

> In one way I am simply saying that each person has a polite or socialized self, and also a personal private self that is not available except in intimacy. This is what is commonly found, and we could call it normal.
>
> If you look around, you can see that *in health* this splitting of the self is an achievement of personal growth; *in illness* the split is a matter of a schism in the mind that can go to any depth; at its deepest it is labelled schizophrenia.
>
> ["Concept of False Self", p. 66]

This is reminiscent of the "persona" (Latin for "mask") in Jung's theory, which is defined by the polite and socialized presentation of the self in society. This makes it similar to the healthy false self of Winnicott's theory, which mediates between the personal private self and the external world at large. However, too much identification with one's persona is seen by Jung as a pathological organization—like the pathological false self of Winnicott's spectrum.

11 Psychotherapy
and the search for self

What is significant about Winnicott's thesis of true and false self is its implication for technique in the analytic relationship. Winnicott encountered many patients who had received long analyses that, he discovered, were tantamount to pseudo-analyses.

> A principle might be enunciated, that in the False Self area of our analytic practice we find we make more headway by recognition of the patient's non-existence than by a long-continued working with the patient on the basis of ego-defence mechanisms. The patient's False Self can collaborate indefinitely with the analyst in the analysis of defences, being so to speak on the analyst's side in the game. This unrewarding work is only cut short profitably when the analyst can point to and specify an absence of some essential feature: "You have no mouth", "You have not started to exist yet", "Physically you are a man, but you do not know from experience anything about masculinity", and so on. These recognitions of important fact, made clear at the right moments, pave the way for communication with the True Self.
>
> ["Ego Distortion", p. 152]

This is characteristic of Winnicott's revolutionary contribution to psychoanalysis, and it is followed by an example from the consulting-room of Winnicott's imaginative use of paradox.

> A patient who had much futile analysis on the basis of a False Self, co-operating vigorously with an analyst who thought this was his whole self, said to me: "The only time I felt hope

was when you told me that you could see no hope, and you
continued with the analysis".

["Ego Distortion", p. 152]

Playing and Reality (W10) is a collection of Winnicott's papers dedicated to the exploration of "transitional phenomena" (*see* TRANS-
ITIONAL PHENOMENA). In Chapter 4, entitled, "Playing and the
Search for Self", Winnicott defines psychotherapy as the search for
the self, meaning the search for the sense of feeling real inside.
The therapeutic area necessarily needs to be, like the good-enough
environment, a facilitating space that is the third area—not inside,
nor outside, but in-between (*see* CREATIVITY: 6; PLAYING: 8):

> ... psychotherapy is done in the overlap of the two play areas,
> that of patient and that of the therapist. If the therapist cannot
> play, then he is not suitable for the work. If the patient cannot
> play, then something needs to be done to enable the patient to
> become able to play, after which psychotherapy may begin.
> The reason why playing is essential is that it is in playing and
> only in playing that the patient is being creative.
> ... I am concerned with the search for self and the restate-
> ment of the fact that certain conditions are necessary if success
> is to be achieved in this search. These conditions are associ-
> ated with what is usually called creativity. It is in playing and
> only in playing that the individual child or adult is able to be
> creative and to use the whole personality, and it is only in
> being creative that the individual discovers the self.
>
> ["Playing: Creative Activity and the Search
> for the Self", 1971, p. 54]

A great work of art or its equivalent does not indicate that the
artist has discovered the self:

> The self is not really to be found in what is made out of
> products of body or mind, however valuable these constructs
> may be in terms of beauty, skill, and impact. .... The finished
> creation never heals the underlying lack of sense of self.
>
> ["Playing: Creative Activity", pp. 54–55]

The "primary unintegration" of Winnicott's 1945 paper, "Primitive Emotional Development", now becomes the "resting state"
and/or "formlessness".

The patient who has not experienced the relaxation of unintegration in his early life with his mother needs to find this experience with his therapist, and this will depend on a sense of trust and reliability in the environment offered:

> The experience is one of a non-purposive state, as one might say a sort of ticking over of the unintegrated personality. I referred to this as formlessness. . . .
>
> Account has to be taken of the reliability or unreliability of the setting in which the individual is operating. We are brought up against a need for a differentiation between purposive activity and the alternative of non-purposive being. . . .
>
> I am trying to refer to the essentials that make relaxation possible. In terms of free association this means that the patient on the couch or the child patient among the toys on the floor must be allowed to communicate a succession of ideas, thoughts, impulses, sensations that are not linked . . . .
>
> ["Playing: Creative Activity", p. 55]

Although Winnicott appears to be celebrating Freud's technique of free association, at the same time he indicates that the linking together of "various components of free association material" is in danger of becoming a defence against the anxiety of *not understanding*. In other words, the analyst who is continually trying to find the links and to "understand" in order to interpret the unconscious will be interrupted in the ability to "be" with the patient and even—or especially—to accept nonsense:

> . . . if one thinks of a patient who is able to rest after work but *not able to achieve the resting state out of which a creative reaching-out can take place*. According to this theory, free association that reveals a coherent theme is already affected by anxiety, and the cohesion of ideas is a defence organization. Perhaps it is to be accepted that there are patients who at times need the therapist to note the nonsense, that is to say, without the need for the patient to organize nonsense. Organized nonsense is already a defence, just as organized chaos is a denial of chaos. The therapist who cannot take this communication becomes engaged in a futile attempt to find some organization in the nonsense, as a result of which the patient leaves the nonsense area because of hopelessness about communicating nonsense.

An opportunity for rest has been missed because of the therapist's need to find sense where nonsense is.

["Playing: Creative Activity", pp. 55–56]

The patient is let down by an environment that does not facilitate
the resting state. Winnicott believes that "creative reaching out"
cannot occur without this allowance of "formlessness", and he
illustrates the meaning he gives to formlessness in his account of
one session with a patient that lasted for three hours. The account
of the session is prefaced by Winnicott's plea to therapists:

> My description amounts to a plea to every therapist to allow
> for the patient's capacity to play, that is, to be creative in the
> . analytic work. The patient's creativity can be only too easily
> stolen by a therapist who knows too much.

["Playing: Creative Activity", p. 57]

Winnicott is specifically suggesting an attitude of mind; he does
not go into whether or not he recommends three-hour sessions.
What he does make clear, however, is that this is what his patient
had requested, and for him to have stipulated a specific period of
time would have been an imposition on her process. His adaptation to her need is to offer an extension of the temporal frame.

The account of this three-hour session illustrates being, formlessness, and playing as part of the journey towards self-discovery.
The search becomes more important (or just as important) as the
discovery.

Winnicott uses the patient's words to summarize what he
wishes to convey:

> She had asked a question, and I said that the answer to the
> question could take us to a long and interesting discussion,
> but it was the *question* that interested me. I said: "You had the
> idea to ask that question".
>
> After this she said the very words that I need in order to
> express my meaning. She said, slowly, with deep feeling:
> "Yes, I see, one could postulate the existence of a ME from the
> question, as from the searching."
>
> She had now made the essential interpretation in that the
> question arose out of what can only be called her creativity,
> creativity that was a coming together after relaxation, which
> is the opposite of integration.

["Playing: Creative Activity", pp. 63–64]

Winnicott's Cartesian conclusion—I question therefore I am—although not specified, involves an *awareness* that comes about through searching and finding the question. This search and discovery, however, *has* to occur within a relationship, and the good-enough relationship is one that will reflect back:

> The searching can come only from desultory formless functioning, or perhaps from rudimentary playing, as if in a neutral zone. It is only here, in this unintegrated state of the personality, that that which we describe as creative can appear. This if reflected back, *but only if reflected back*, becomes part of the organized individual personality, and eventually this in summation makes the individual to be, to be found; and eventually enables himself or herself to postulate the existence of the self.
>
> ["Playing: Creative Activity", p. 64]

A year before his death, Winnicott indicated his personal apprehension about a definition of the self:

> . . . the main thing has to do with the word "self". I did wonder if I could write something out about this word, but of course as soon as I came to do it I found that there is much uncertainty even in my own mind about my own meaning. I found I had written the following:
>
> For me the self, which is not the ego, is the person who is me, who is only me, who has a totality based on the operation of the maturational process. At the same time the self has parts, and in fact is constituted of these parts. These parts agglutinate from a direction interior–exterior in the course of the operation of the maturational process, aided as it must be (maximally at the beginning) by the human environment which holds and handles and in a live way facilitates. The self finds itself naturally placed in the body, but may in certain circumstances become dissociated from the body in the eyes and facial expression of the mother and in the mirror which can come to represent the mother's face. Eventually the self arrives at a significant relationship between the child and the sum of the identifications which (after enough of incorporation and introjection of mental representation) become organised in the shape of an internal psychic living reality. The relationship between the boy or girl with his or her own internal psychic organization becomes modified according to

the expectations that are displayed by the father and mother and those who have become significant in the external life of the individual. It is the self and the life of the self that alone makes sense of action or of living from the point of view of the individual who has grown so far and who is continuing to grow from dependence and immaturity towards independence, and the capacity to identify with mature love objects without loss of individual identity.

["On the Basis for Self in Body", 1970, p. 271]

This description includes just about all the aspects of Winnicott's developmental theory. However, it is striking that although Winnicott clearly states at the start that the self is *not* the ego, he never really explains the difference.

The process that "agglutinates" parts of the self entails the organization of experience. This alludes to a part of the self being the organizer—which must be the ego? Therefore the ego is a part of the self.

Moreover, here the self, which is located in the body, is the same as that referred to by Winnicott as the psyche-indwelling-in-the-soma, to which he also refers as the body-ego related to the process of personalization.

In Bettelheim's book, *Freud and Man's Soul* (1983—a critique of the English translation of Freud's work), he particularly criticizes the translation of *"das Ich"* into the Latin *"ego"* instead of into the English "Me" or "I". Bettelheim believes that the decision to use Latin instead of English must have been due to the wish to medicalize psychoanalysis. For Bettelheim, however, this meant a great cost, not just to the work of Freud, but to the essential intentions behind Freud's original choice of *"das Ich"*.

No word has greater and more intimate connotations than the pronoun "I". It is one of the most frequently used words in spoken language—and, more important, it is the most *personal* word. To mistranslate Ich as "ego" is to transform it into jargon that no longer conveys the personal commitment we make when we say "I" or "me"—not to mention our subconscious memories of the deep emotional experience we had when, in infancy, we discovered ourselves as we learned to say "I". I do not know whether Freud was familiar with Ortega y Gasset's statement that to create a concept is to leave reality behind, but he was certainly aware of its truth and tried to avoid this danger as much as possible. In creating the concept of the Ich, he tied it to reality by using a term that made it practically impossible to leave reality behind. Reading or speaking about the I forces one to look at oneself introspectively. By contrast, an "ego" that uses clear-cut mechanisms, such as displacement and projection, to achieve its purpose in its struggle against the "id" is something that can be studied from the outside, by observing others. With this inappropriate and—as far as our emotional response to it is concerned—misleading translation, an introspective psychology is made into a behavioural one, which observes from the outside.

[Bettelheim, 1983, pp. 53–54]

A close study of Winnicott's use of the word "ego" reveals it to be a specific function of the self. The "Me" is a term Winnicott came to use precisely for the same reason as Freud used *"das Ich"*—that is, to accentuate the subjective and internal experience. In fact, the whole of Winnicott's work can be seen to be dedicated to the evocation of subjectivity. It is therefore deeply ironic that in his description of the self at the very end of his life, Winnicott still insists that the ego is not the self. One possible explanation to this puzzle is that it was a response to the political tensions within the British Psycho-Analytical Society, where an allegiance to Freud had to be demonstrated, as well as the fact that Winnicott's first analyst was James Strachey, the translator of Freud's work.

REFERENCES

1945 Primitive Emotional Development   [W6]

1949 Birth Memories, Birth Trauma, and Anxiety   [W6]

1950 Aggression in Relation to Emotional Development   [W6]

1952 Anxiety Associated with Insecurity   [W6]

1954 The Depressive Position in Normal Development   [W6]

1956 Primary Maternal Preoccupation   [W6]

1958 Psychoanalysis and the Sense of Guilt   [W9]

1960 Ego Distortion in Terms of True and False Self   [W9]

1962 Ego Integration in Child Development   [W9]

1963 Morals and Education   [W9]
1964 The Concept of the False Self   [W14]
1965 New Light on Children's Thinking   [W19]
1970 On the Basis for Self in Body   [W19]
1971 Playing: Creative Activity and the Search for the Self   [W10]

Spatula Game

T   he Spatula Game consists of observing the way an infant aged
         between 5 and 13 months responds to a shiny spatula placed
         on the edge of a table and within easy reach. The infant has to
be in what Winnicott describes as a "set situation".

Winnicott says that for the majority of infants a sequence of
three stages can be observed in terms of what the baby does with
the spatula. Deviation from these stages indicates that something is
wrong. Thus, the Spatula Game is used by Winnicott as a diagnostic
tool.

1   The set situation

Winnicott qualified as a psychoanalyst in 1935, and as a child
analyst in 1936. After his qualification as an analyst, he continued
to run a clinic at Paddington Green Children's Hospital, where
thousands of consultations were carried out.

The Spatula Game is described in greatest detail in Winnicott's
1941 paper, "The Observation of Infants in a Set Situation", but

already in his 1936 paper, "Appetite and Emotional Disorder", the Spatula Game is being used by Winnicott as a means of assessing the infant's inner world.

It is worth mentioning that in the 1930s various sizes of spatulas were available, depending on the age of the person for whom they were to be used. They were shiny silver metal objects and set at a right angle.

In a section in "Appetite and Emotional Disorder", entitled, "The Hospital Out Patient Clinic", Winnicott describes the clinic at Paddington Green, wishing "to convey an impression of the morning's pageantry", as if it were a royal court, or perhaps a church or even a theatre.

> First I want to give an account of what a baby does as he sits on his mother's lap with the corner of the table between them and me.
>
> A child of one year behaves in the following way. He sees the spatula and soon puts his hand to it, but he probably withdraws interest once or twice, before actually taking it, all the while looking at my face and at his mother's to gauge our attitudes. Sooner or later he takes it and mouths it. He now enjoys possession of it and at the same time he kicks and shows eager bodily activity. He is not yet ready to have it taken away from him. Soon he drops the spatula on the floor; at first this may seem like a chance happening, but as it is restored to him he eventually repeats the mistake, and at last he throws it down and obviously intends that it shall drop. He looks at it, and often the noise of its contact with the floor becomes a new source of joy for him. He will like to throw it down repeatedly if I give him the chance. He now wants to get down to be with it on the floor.
>
> ["Appetite and Emotional Disorder", pp. 45–46]

Here, then, are the three stages associated with normality: (a) seeing and reaching out for the spatula and then withdrawing interest as the adult's attitude is gauged; (b) taking it and mouthing it; (c) dropping it.

> It is, on the whole, true to say that deviations from this mean of behaviour indicate deviations from normal emotional development, and often it is possible to correlate such deviations with the rest of the clinical picture. There are of

course, age differences. Children of over one year tend to short-circuit the incorporation process (mouthing the spatula) and to become more and more interested in what can be done with the spatula in play.

["Appetite and Emotional Disorder", p. 46]

Using two cases, Winnicott is able to illustrate both the healthy and the pathological use of the spatula. There are two striking elements to these descriptions. First, Winnicott demonstrates a faith and trust in the mother's ability to predict her baby's behaviour *and* know whether something is wrong. Second, the mothers and infants—who are waiting to consult Winnicott—are at some distance from the area of consultation in the same large room, and they somehow come to be included in the set situation as an audience. Their response is determined by the protagonist—the baby with the spatula.

A mother brings her extremely healthy-looking baby for me to see as a routine measure, three months after the first consultation. The baby, Philip, is now eleven months old, and today he pays me his fourth visit. His difficult phase is past and he is now quite well physically and emotionally.

No spatula is placed out, so he takes the bowl, but his mother prevents this. The point is that he reaches for something immediately, remembering past visits.

I place a spatula for him, and as he takes it his mother says: "He'll make more noise this time than last", and she is right. Mothers often tell me correctly what the baby will do, showing, if any should doubt it, that our picture gained in the out-patient department is not unrelated to life. Of course the spatula goes to the mouth and soon he uses it for banging the table or the bowl. So to the bowl with many bangs. All the time he is looking at me, and I cannot fail to see that I am involved. In some way he is expressing his attitude to me. Other mothers and babies are sitting in the room behind the mother some yards away, and the mood of the whole room is determined by the baby's mood. A mother over the way says: "He's the village blacksmith". He is pleased at such success and adds to his play an element of showing off. So he puts the spatula towards my mouth in a very sweet way, and is pleased that I play the game and pretend to eat it, not really getting in contact with it; he understands perfectly if I only show him I am playing his game. He offers it also to his mother, and then with a magnanimous gesture turns round and gives it magically to the audience over the way. So he returns to the bowl and the bangs go on.

After a while he communicates in his own way with one of the babies the other side of the room, choosing him from about eight grown-ups and children there. Everyone is now in hilarious mood, the clinic is going very well.

["Appetite and Emotional Disorder", p. 46]

Clearly Winnicott is also enjoying himself, whilst at the same time being acutely aware of the significance of what is taking place in terms of the mother–infant relationship and the communication of the infant's internal world.

His mother now lets him down and he takes the spatula on the floor, playing with it and gradually edging over towards the other small person with whom he has just communicated by noises.

You notice how he is interested not only in his own mouth, but also in mine and in his mother's, and I think he feels he has fed all the people in the room. This he has done with the spatula, but he could not have done so if he had not just felt he had incorporated it, in the way I have described.

This is what is sometimes called "possessing a good internalized breast" or just "having confidence in a relationship with the good breast, based on experience."

The point I wish to make here is this: when in physical fact the baby takes the spatula to himself and plays with it and drops it, at the same time, physically, he incorporates it, possesses it, and gets rid of the idea of it.

What he does with the spatula (or with anything else) between the taking and the dropping is a film-strip of the little bit of his inner world that is related to me and his mother at that time, and from this can be guessed a good deal about his inner world experiences at other times and in relation to other people and things.

["Appetite and Emotional Disorder", pp. 46–47]

And here, in 1936, Winnicott introduces the notion of play and the different qualities of play relevant to the individual's inner world.

In classification of a series of cases one can use a scale: at the
normal end of the scale there is play, which is simple and
enjoyable dramatization of inner world life; at the abnormal
end of the scale there is play which contains a denial of
the inner world, the play being in that case always compulsive, excited, anxiety-driven, and more sense-exploiting than
happy.

["Appetite and Emotional Disorder", p. 47]

The next case contrasts sharply with the first, although there are
common features such as the mother's ability to predict the baby's
action as well as her knowledge that something is wrong, and the
baby's ability to determine the atmosphere of the clinic.

The next boy, David, is eighteen months old, and his behaviour has a special characteristic.

His mother brings him over and sits him on her lap by the
table and he soon goes for the spatula I place within his reach.
His mother knows what he will do, for this is part of what is
wrong with him. She says: "He'll throw it on the floor". He
takes the spatula and quickly throws it on the floor. He re-
peats this with everything available. The first stage of timid
approach and the second of mouthing and of live play are
both absent. This is a symptom with which we are all familiar,
but it is pathological in degree in this case, and the mother is
right in bringing him because of it. She lets him follow the
object by getting down and he takes it up, drops it, and smiles
in an artificial attempt at reassurance, meanwhile screwing
himself into a position in which his forearms are pressed into
his groins. While he does this he looks hopefully round, but
the other parents in the room are anxious to distract their
children from the sight which to them means something to do
with masturbation. The little boy finds himself up in his own
peculiar fashion and smiling in a way that indicates a desper-
ate attempt to deny misery and a sense of rejection. Note the
way in which this child creates an abnormal environment for
himself.

["Appetite and Emotional Disorder", p. 47]

Of course, this "abnormal environment" that the child creates is a
communication to Winnicott that the early environment had failed
him. But at this time in 1936 Winnicott had not yet made his
discovery, that "there's no such thing as a baby". That was to

come six years later in 1942 (*see* ENVIRONMENT: 3, 4). Therefore, at this time Winnicott emphasizes the demonstration of the infant's inner world, without the concern with the environment that he starts to elaborate some years later.

By 1941, Winnicott had considerably extended his earlier observations, and the importance of the environment had begun to come to the fore; and by the 1950s, the set situation and all its components are referred to as the "holding environment". (*see* HOLDING: 2)

2   The three stages

In 1941, Winnicott had been working in his clinic at the Paddington Green Children's Hospital for nearly twenty years. In addition, he had been qualified as a psychoanalyst for six years. The paper that explores the details and meanings of the Spatula Game, "The Observation of Infants in a Set Situation", also anticipates all that he is to develop during the course of the subsequent twenty years: playing, creativity, transitional phenomena, and the use of an object.

> Here we have in front of us the baby, attracted by a very attractive object, and I will now describe what, in my opinion, is a normal sequence of events. I hold that any variation from this, which I call normal, is significant.
>
> Stage 1.   The baby puts his hand to the spatula, but at this moment discovers unexpectedly that the situation must be given thought. He is in a fix. Either with his hand resting on the spatula and his body quite still he looks at me and his mother with big eyes, and watches and waits, or, in certain cases, he withdraws interest completely and buries his face in the front of his mother's blouse. It is usually possible to manage the situation so that active reassurance is not given, and it is very interesting to watch the gradual and spontaneous return of the child's interest in the spatula.
>
> Stage 2.   All the time, in the period of hesitation (as I call it), the baby holds his body still (but not rigid). Gradually he becomes brave enough to let his feelings develop, and then the picture changes quite quickly. The moment at which this first phase changes into the second is evident, for the

child's acceptance of the reality of desire for the spatula is
heralded by a change in the inside of the mouth, which
becomes flabby, while the tongue looks thick and soft, and
saliva flows copiously. Before long he puts the spatula into
his mouth and is chewing it with his gums, or seems to be
copying father smoking a pipe. The change in the baby's
behaviour is a striking feature. Instead of expectancy and
stillness there now develops self-confidence, and there is
free bodily movement, the latter related to manipulation of
the spatula.

I have frequently made the experiment of trying to get the
spatula to the infant's mouth during the stage of hesitation.
Whether the hesitation corresponds to my normal or differs
from it in degree or quality, I find that it is impossible during
this stage to get the spatula to the child's mouth apart from
the exercise of brutal strength. In certain cases where the inhibition is acute any effort on my part that results in the spatula
being moved towards the child produces screaming, mental
distress, or actual colic.

["Observation of Infants", pp. 53–54]

This is reminiscent of Winnicott's 1963 paper, "Morals and Education". In this paper he posits an innate morality in the infant
emanating from the true self. Therefore, moral values can only be
understood and appreciated by the child if he has had the experience of a facilitating environment, where he has been allowed to
develop his sense of self. For the infant who has not had this good-
enough start, the antisocial tendency may be a feature. The cure of
this tendency cannot be through teaching moral values by force.
In other words, the object cannot be imposed upon the infant; it
has to be created by the infant, for it to have any meaning at all.
(*see* CONCERN: 9; CREATIVITY: 2; DEPENDENCE: 6)

This second stage is linked with the baby's sense of control—
his feeling of omnipotence, which Winnicott considers so crucial
for the infant to develop normally. This "area of omnipotence" is
the baby's illusion that he is God and in full control of his environment.

The baby now seems to feel that the spatula is in his possession, perhaps in his power, certainly available for the
purposes of self-expression. He bangs with it on the table or
on a metal bowl which is nearby on the table, making as

much noise as he can; or else he holds it to my mouth and to his mother's mouth, very pleased if we *pretend* to be fed by it. He definitely wishes us to *play* at being fed, and is upset if we should be so stupid as to take the thing into our mouths and spoil the game as a game.

At this point, I might mention that I have never seen any evidence of a baby being disappointed that the spatula is, in fact, neither food nor a container of food.

["Observation of Infants", p. 54]

Here, then, is a demonstration that the infant is able to use his imagination and play, which is the positive outcome of the illusion related to the internal world. The third stage is linked with repudiation of the object, and in this sense the spatula can be seen to represent a transitional object. (*see* TRANSITIONAL PHENOMENA: 4)

Stage 3. There is a third stage. In the third stage the baby first of all drops the spatula as if by mistake. If it is restored he is pleased, plays with it again, and drops it once more, but this time less by mistake. On its being restored again, he drops it on purpose, and thoroughly enjoys aggressively getting rid of it, and is especially pleased when it makes a ringing sound on contact with the floor.

The end of this third phase comes when the baby either wishes to get down on the floor with the spatula, where he starts mouthing it and playing with it again, or else when he is bored with it and reaches out to any other objects that lie at hand.

["Observation of Infants", p. 54]

These are the stages of the Spatula Game which normally occur in an infant of between 5 and 13 months of age. Winnicott comments that the set situation—with him observing the infant with the spatula whilst on his mother's lap—can be useful and therapeutic. He describes in some detail a baby who suffered from fits and another who suffered from asthma. In both cases Winnicott details that through the consultant's ability to hold the set situation, the infant is enabled, sometimes for the first time, to process the internal difficulty. In each case the problem is linked with the moment of hesitation.

It is worth noting that in 1936 Winnicott referred to the moment of hesitation as the "period of suspicion". "Hesitation", as a word, has a more positive connotation, implying health, normality, and, above all, value. Nevertheless, suspicion can also be healthy.

3   The period of hesitation and the role of fantasy

The period of hesitation, although normal, indicates anxiety. The baby hesitates, not because of an expectation of disapproval from the parents—although this may have something to do with it—but mostly in his struggle with working out the reality of the situation (the set situation) and his own personal inner world of impulses, feelings, memories, and so on:

> ... whether it is or is not the mother's attitude that is deter-mining the baby's behaviour, I suggest that the hesitation means that the infant *expects* to produce an angry and perhaps revengeful mother by his indulgence. In order that a baby shall feel threatened, even by a truly and obviously angry mother, he must have in his mind the notion of an angry mother. . . .
>
> If the mother has been really angry and if the child has real reason to expect her to be angry in the consultation when he grabs the spatula, we are led to the infant's apprehensive fan-tasies, just as in the ordinary case where the child hesitates in spite of the fact that the mother is quite tolerant of such behav-iour and even expects it. The "something" which the anxiety is about is in the infant's mind, an idea of potential evil or strict-ness, and into the novel situation anything that is in the infant's mind may be projected. When there has been no experience of prohibition, the hesitation implies conflict, or the existence in the baby's mind of a *fantasy* corresponding to the other baby's *memory* of his really strict mother. In either case, as a conse-quence, he has first to curb his interest and desire, and he only becomes able to find his desire again in so far as his testing of the environment affords satisfactory results. I supply the set-ting for such a test.
>
> ["Observation of Infants", p. 60]

Winnicott does not really explain why the infant who does not have a strict mother is still anxious. Could it have do with the unconscious communication of hatred from mother to infant, which is explored by Winnicott in 1947? (*see* HATE: 6)

4   *The spatula as breast or penis*

Winnicott points out that the spatula can represent either breast or penis, the symbols of mother and father, because by the time an infant is 5 or 6 months old, he is able to differentiate between Me and Not-me, which means that people are perceived as whole objects. However, the set situation of infant sitting on mother's lap opposite a stranger (who is also a man) is a replica of the oedipal triangle; here the infant is put in the position of having to negotiate his relationship to two people at the same time.

> In so far as the baby is normal, one of the main problems before him is the management of two people at once. In this set situation I seem sometimes to be the witness of the first success in this direction. At other times I see reflected in the infant's behaviour the successes and failures he is having in his attempts to become able to have a relation to two people at once at home. Sometimes I witness the onset of a phase of difficulties over this, as well as a spontaneous recovery.
>
> ["Observation of Infants", p. 66]

Herein lies the crucial nature of the set situation, in terms of relating not just to two people but to mother and father. Winnicott is not ignoring the oedipal issues, but he chooses to emphasize the parents' tolerance of the infant and the influence this will have on his developing sense of self in relation to his desires.

> It is as if the two parents allow the infant gratification of desires about which he has conflicting feelings, tolerating his expression of his feelings about themselves. In my presence he cannot always make use of my consideration of his interests, or he can only gradually become able to do so.
>
> The experience of daring to want and to take the spatula and to make it his own without in fact altering the stability of the immediate environment acts as a kind of object-lesson which has therapeutic value for the infant. At the age which we are considering and all through childhood such an experience is not merely temporarily reassuring: the cumulative effect of happy experiences and of a stable and friendly atmosphere round a child is to build up his confidence in people in the external world, and his general feeling of security.
>
> ["Observation of Infants", p. 66]

5   Permission from the environment

The good environment, for Winnicott, is one that allows the infant to run through the whole course of an experience with as little interruption as possible. This is represented by the parents who can see what the infant is doing and allow him to take his time and achieve the task in his own time. This is the facilitating environment, which is also applicable to the psychoanalytic environment.

> WHOLE EXPERIENCES
>
> What there is of therapeutics in this work lies, I think, in the fact that the *full course of an experience is allowed*. From this one can draw some conclusions about one of the things that go to make a good environment for the infant. In the intuitive management of an infant a mother naturally allows the full course of the various experiences, keeping this up until the infant is old enough to understand her point of view. She hates to break into such experiences as feeding or sleeping or defecating. In my observations I artificially give the baby the right to complete an experience which is of particular value to him as an object-lesson.
>
> ["Observation of Infants", p. 67]

"Object-lesson" here implies increasing the infant's capacity to use objects (*see* AGGRESSION: 5). There is a sequence of a beginning, a middle, and an end to experiences controlled by the subject. In that sense, psychoanalysis is also an object-lesson:

> In psychoanalysis proper there is something similar to this. The analyst lets the patient set the pace and he does the next best thing to letting the patient decide when to come and go, in that he fixes the time and the length of the session, and sticks to the time that he has fixed. Psychoanalysis differs from this work with infants in that the analyst is always groping, seeking his way among the mass of material offered and trying to find out what, at the moment, is the shape and form of the thing which he has to offer to the patient, that which he calls the interpretation. Sometimes the analyst will find it of value to look behind all the multitude of details and to see how far the analysis he is conducting could be thought of in the same terms as those in which one can think of the rela-

tively simple set situation which I have described. Each interpretation is a glittering object which excites the patient's
greed.

["Observation of Infants", p. 67]

Thus the emphasis here, and in Winnicott's attitude to psychoanalysis in general, is that the interpretation is not as significant as
the way in which it is first offered by the analyst and subsequently
used by the patient.

Towards the end of his life, the greatest pleasure Winnicott
experienced in the consulting-room was when his patients arrived
at their *own* interpretations.

> . . . it is only in recent years that I have become able to wait
> and wait for the natural evolution of the transference arising
> out of the patient's growing trust in the psychoanalytic tech-
> nique and setting, and to avoid breaking up this natural
> process by making interpretations. It will be noticed that I am
> talking about the making of interpretations and not about in-
> terpretations as such. It appals me to think how much deep
> change I have prevented or delayed in patients . . . by my
> personal need to interpret. If only we can wait, the patient
> arrives at understanding creatively and with immense joy,
> and I now enjoy this joy more than I used to enjoy the sense of
> having been clever. I think I interpret mainly to let the patient
> know the limits of my understanding. The principle is that it
> is the patient and only the patient who has the answers.
>
> ["The Use of an Object and Relating
> through Identifications", 1968, pp. 86–87]

6 Hesitation, resistance, and illusion

Winnicott's theory of "the period of hesitation" in the patient towards his analyst's "glittering objects" (shiny spatulas?) changes
Freud's concept of resistance. Instead of working against the
analysis, as Freud considered it, resistance is *part and parcel* of the
normal occurrence in the analytic relationship. The analyst who is
able to wait and allow the patient to take his time is like the
mother who is able to allow her infant to process things in his own
time and thus go through a "whole experience".

Winnicott's development of the necessity of hesitation leads him to say, in his 1963 paper, "Communicating and Not Communicating Leading to a Study of Certain Opposites", that each individual has the right *not* to communicate. Thus, whereas Freud recommended that the patient should say everything that came into his head (free association), Winnicott, by 1963, advocates that each patient has the right to keep things to himself—to be private and "incommunicado". (*see* BEING: 2; COMMUNICATION: 5, 11)

The mutuality between mother and infant can be seen in the way the infant uses the spatula/object. The *use* of the object, therefore, comes about through the infant and mother "living an experience together".

In 1945, four years after "Observation of Infants in a Set Situation", Winnicott wrote "Primitive Emotional Development". In this paper he brings together his twenty years working as a paediatrician and his ten years working as a psychoanalyst with adults and children, and he both uses the past and anticipates the future in terms of his own development of psychoanalytic theory. The use of words such as "personalization", "realization", "illusion", and "disillusion" indicates his personal discoveries, whilst altering Freudian and Kleinian terminology.

Six years later, in 1951, in his paper "Transitional Objects and Transitional Phenomena", Winnicott's ideas, rooted in his observations of the Spatula Game, culminate in his contributions concerning transitional phenomena.

As a subsequent development of the Spatula Game, Winnicott devised the Squiggle Game for older children. All the foundation stones for his therapeutic consultations with the use of the Squiggle Game are set down in the 1930s in the clinics at Paddington Green.

REFERENCES

1936 Appetite and Emotional Disorder   [W6]
1941 Observation of Infants in a Set Situation   [W6]
1945 Primitive Emotional Development   [W6]
1968 The Use of an Object and Relating through Identifications [W10]

Squiggle Game

W innicott initiated the Squiggle Game in first assessment interviews with children. He started off by drawing a squiggle on a piece of paper; he then asked the child to add to it. Over the course of the initial interview, Winnicott and the child took it in turns to draw something in response to the other's squiggle. In this way, the squiggles sometimes turned into pictures. For each interview, there were usually about thirty drawings produced.

For Winnicott, the Squiggle Game was not only a tool for diagnosis, but also what he called a "psychotherapeutic consultation".

1   A therapeutic diagnostic tool

The "Squiggle Game" was invented by Winnicott, emerging from his own interest in drawing, combined with an ability to find an appropriate way of communicating with a young child by inviting him to play.

Just as the Spatula Game originated from Winnicott's diagnostic clinics for mothers and babies, so the Squiggle Game emerged from his child psychiatry practice. The posthumously published paper simply entitled "The Squiggle Game" is an amalgamation of two papers, one published in 1964 and the other in 1968, at a time when Winnicott was in his late 60s and early 70s and nearing the end of his life.

The main features of the Squiggle Game are that:

- It is a diagnostic tool but also psychotherapeutic for the child in a good-enough environment.
- It is based on the child's (and family's) hope and trust that help is to be found.
- It is initiated and held, but must never be dominated by, the consultant—equality is crucial.
- The technique is straightforward; the aim is to facilitate play and the element of surprise.
- The results of the interaction on paper can be likened to dreams, as representations of the unconscious.

Winnicott came to call his use of the Squiggle Game a "psychotherapeutic consultation", to distinguish it from psychoanalysis or psychotherapy and to indicate that the first consultation, in and of itself, can be therapeutic.

> In my child psychiatry practice I have found that a special place has to be given for a first interview. Gradually I have developed a technique for fully exploiting first interview material. To distinguish this work from psychotherapy and from psychoanalysis I use the term "psychotherapeutic consultation". It is a diagnostic interview, based on the theory that no diagnosis can be made in psychiatry except over the test of therapy.
>
> ["Squiggle Game", p. 299]

By "test of therapy" Winnicott means that he is assessing, throughout the game, how the child can make *use* of the situation offered, just as he assessed the baby in relation to the spatula and the patient to the analytic setting. (*see* SPATULA GAME: 1)

Winnicott points out that the child needs to be in an environment where use can be made of the consultation:

> There is a category of case in which this kind of psychotherapeutic interview is to be avoided. I would not say that with very ill children it is not possible to do useful work. What I would say is that if the child goes away from the therapeutic consultation *and returns to an abnormal family or social situation* then there is not environmental provision of the kind that is needed and that I take for granted. I rely on an "average expectable environment" to meet and to make use of the changes that have taken place in the boy or girl in the interview, changes which indicate a loosening of the knot in the developmental process.
>
> [*Therapeutic Consultations in Child Psychiatry*, 1971, p. 5]

2   A belief in

Winnicott had faith in the individual's unconscious belief in finding help. He found it in all the individuals and families he consulted over the years, who had suffered deprivation and psychosomatic illnesses. Symptoms were seen by him as a sign of hope in patients that their communication would be heard. Psychotherapy and management could provide an opportunity for re-living the past deprivation in order to integrate the experience. (*see* ANTISOCIAL TENDENCY: 4, 5; PSYCHE–SOMA: 4, 5, 6)

> The basis for this specialized work is the theory that a patient—child or adult—will bring to the first interview a certain amount of capacity to *believe* in getting help and to trust the one who offers help. What is needed from the helper is a strictly professional setting in which the patient is free to explore the exceptional opportunity that the consultation provides for communication. The patient's communication with the psychiatrist will have reference to the specific emotional tendencies which have a current form and which have roots that go back into the past or deep into the structure of the patient's personality and of his personal inner reality.
>
> ["Squiggle Game", p. 299]

3   "Let's play"

As, in the Spatula Game, the "set situation" is crucial, so in the Squiggle Game the framework offered by the consultant is crucial as a foundation from which to move freely. This will depend on the consultant's ability to *hold* the child, metaphorically and emotionally.

> In this work the consultant or specialist does not need to be clever so much as to be able to provide a natural and freely moving human relationship within the professional setting while the patient gradually *surprises* himself by the production of ideas and feelings that have not been previously integrated into the total personality. Perhaps the main work done is of the nature of integration, made possible by the reliance on the human but professional relationship—a form of "holding".
>
> ["Squiggle Game", p. 299]

The consultant's role is to hold the situation of the assessment consultation, *as well as* engaging in playing the game. This means that the consultation consists of two human beings relating to each other, equal in their human condition, rather than an expert who "knows" and a patient who "doesn't know".

> The fact that the consultant freely plays his own part in the exchange of drawings certainly has a great importance for the success of the technique; such a procedure does not make the patient feel inferior in any way as, for instance, a patient feels when being examined by a doctor in respect of physical health, or, often, when being given a psychological test (especially a personality test).
>
> ["Squiggle Game", p. 301]

In fact, Winnicott was quite reluctant to write about the Squiggle Game, lest it should be turned by some into a psychological test:

> . . . I have hesitated to describe this technique, which I have used a great deal over a number of years, not only because it is a natural game that any two people might play, but also, if I begin to describe what I do, then someone will be likely to begin to rewrite what I describe as if it were a set technique with rules and regulations. Then the whole value of the procedure would be lost. If I describe what I do there is a very

real danger that others will take it and form it into something that corresponds to a Thematic Apperception Test. The difference between this and a T.A.T. is firstly that it is not a test, and secondly that the consultant contributes from his own ingenuity almost as much as the child does. Naturally, the consultant's contribution drops out, because it is the child, not the consultant, who is communicating distress.

["Squiggle Game", p. 301]

4 The technique

Winnicott describes the simplicity of the technique:

At a suitable moment after the arrival of the patient, usually after asking the parent to go to the waiting-room, I say to the child: "Let's play something. I know what I would like to play and I'll show you." I have a table between the child and myself, with paper and two pencils. First I take some of the paper and tear the sheets in half, giving the impression that what we are doing is not frantically important, and then I begin to explain. I say: "This game that I like playing has no rules. I just take my pencil and go like that . . .", and I probably screw up my eyes and do a squiggle blind. I go on with my explanation and say: "You show me if that looks like anything to you or if you can make it into anything, and afterwards you do the same for me and I will see if I can make something of yours".

This is all there is by way of technique, and it has to be emphasised that I am absolutely flexible even at this very early stage, so that if the child wishes to draw or to talk or to play with toys or to make music or to romp, I feel free to fit in with the child's wishes. Often a boy will want to play what he calls a "points game"; that is to say, something that can be won or lost. Nevertheless, in a high proportion of first-interview cases the child fits in sufficiently long with my wishes and with what I like playing for some progress to be made. Soon the rewards begin to come in, so that the game continues. Often in an hour we have done twenty to thirty drawings together, and gradually the significance of these composite drawings has become deeper and deeper, and is felt by the child to be part of communication of significance.

["Squiggle Game", pp. 301–302]

In order to carry out the technique, however, Winnicott points out that it is vital to have in mind—or, rather, in your bones—the theory of emotional development.

> The only companion that I have in exploring the unknown territory of the new case is the theory that I carry around with me and that has become part of me and that I do not even have to think about in a deliberate way. This is the theory of the emotional development of the individual which includes for me the total history of the individual child's relationship to the child's specific environment. It cannot be avoided that changes in this theoretical basis for my work do occur in the course of time and on account of experience. One could compare my position with that of a 'cellist who first slogs away at *technique* and then actually becomes able to play *music*, taking the technique for granted. I am aware of doing this work more easily and with more success than I was able to do it thirty years ago and my wish is to communicate with those who are still slogging away at technique, at the same time giving them the hope that will one day come from playing music.
>
> [*Therapeutic Consultations*, p. 6]

5   A dream screen

Winnicott's analysis of how the squiggles relate to each other can be seen to be parallel to a conversation in the analytic setting in the first meeting:

> It is interesting to note, regarding the squiggles themselves, that
>
> 1. I am better at them than the children are, and the children are usually better than I am at drawing.
> 2. They contain an impulsive movement.
> 3. They are mad, unless done by a sane person. For this reason some children find them frightening.
> 4. They are incontinent, except that they accept limitations, so some children feel them to be naughty. This is allied to the subject of form and content. The size and shape of the paper is a factor.
> 5. There is an integration in each squiggle that comes from the

integration that is part of me; this is not, I believe, a typi-
cally obsessional integration, which would contain the
element of denial of chaos.

6. Often the result of a squiggle is satisfactory in itself. It is then
   like a "found object", for instance a stone or piece of old
   wood that a sculptor may find and set up as a kind of
   expression, without needing work. This appeals to lazy boys
   and girls, and throws light on the meaning of laziness. Any
   work done spoils what starts off as an idealised object. It
   may be felt by an artist that the paper or the canvas is too
   beautiful, it must not be spoiled. Potentially, it *is* a master-
   piece. In psychoanalytic theory we have the concept of the
   dream screen, a place into or onto which a dream might be
   dreamed.

["Squiggle Game", pp. 302–303]

By "dream screen", Winnicott is referring to the unconscious
nature of the squiggles, akin to a pencil drawing of a dream, repli-
cating aspects of the early mother–infant relationship.

Occasionally, Winnicott would show the squiggles to the parents; this also had a therapeutic implication:

There is also a practical significance of the squiggle or drawing material in that there can be a gain from taking the
parents into one's confidence and letting them know what
their child was like in the special circumstances of the therapeutic consultation. This is more real for them than if I report
what the child said. They recognise the types of drawing that
adorn the nursery wall or that the child brings home from
school, but often they are amazed when they see the drawings
in sequence, drawings which display personality qualities
and perceptive abilities which may not have been evident in
the home setting.

[*Therapeutic Consultations*, pp. 3–4]

However, Winnicott adds a caveat:

. . . naturally it is not always good to give parents this insight
(that can be so useful). Parents might perhaps abuse the confidence that the therapist has placed in them, and so undo the
work that depends on a kind of intimacy between child and
therapist.

[*Therapeutic Consultations*, p. 4]

Clearly, Winnicott found that the Squiggle Game suited his purpose for the first—although usually not more than the first—
therapeutic interview. It was very much part of his character and
the way in which he enjoyed playing; other consultants will need
to find their own style, which may or may not involve squiggles.

> The principle is that psychotherapy is done in an overlap of
> the area of play of the child and the area of play of the adult
> or therapist. The Squiggle Game is one example of the way in
> which such an interplay may be facilitated.
>
> ["Squiggle Game", p. 317]

(Detailed accounts of how Winnicott used the Squiggle Game can
be found in *Therapeutic Consultations in Child Psychiatry* [W11].)

REFERENCES

1968   The Squiggle Game   [W19]
1971   *Therapeutic Consultations in Child Psychiatry*   [W11]

Transitional phenomena

T he concept of transitional phenomena refers to a dimension of living that belongs neither to internal nor to external reality; rather, it is the place that both connects and separates inner and outer. Winnicott uses many terms to refer to this dimension—the third area, the intermediate area, the potential space, a resting place, and the location of cultural experience.

Developmentally, transitional phenomena occur from the beginning, even before birth, in relation to the mother–infant dyad. Here is located culture, being, and creativity.

As the infant begins to separate Me from Not-me, going from absolute dependence into the stage of relative dependence, he makes use of the transitional object. This necessary developmental journey leads to the use of illusion, the use of symbols, and the use of an object.

Transitional phenomena are inextricably linked with playing and creativity.

1   *A triple statement on human nature*

Before 1951, when Winnicott presented his seminal paper, "Transitional Objects and Transitional Phenomena", there was no accounting for the space between inside and outside in the psychoanalytic literature. Freud's concept of the developmental sequence of the pleasure principle moving on to the reality principle had contributed to an understanding of the transition the human infant has to go through, without focusing on the transitional process itself. Melanie Klein's focus on the inner world and the infant's phantasies did not seem to take sufficient account of the impact of the outer world on his perception, in Winnicott's opinion. Much work had also been done on the point in human development when the infant emerged from his own subjective state and began to become more objective and able to think symbolically. After more than thirty years of working with mothers and infants, and nearly twenty years of working as a psychoanalyst, Winnicott found himself positing an intermediate area: an area that is not completely subjective, nor completely objective.

> It is generally acknowledged that a statement of human nature is inadequate when given in terms of interpersonal relationships, even when the imaginative elaboration of function, the whole of fantasy both conscious and unconscious, including the repressed unconscious, is allowed for. There is another way of describing persons that comes out of the researches of the past two decades, that suggests that of every individual who has reached to the stage of being a unit (with a limiting membrane and an outside and an inside) it can be said that there is an *inner reality* to that individual, an inner world which can be rich or poor and can be at peace or in a state of war.
>
> My claim is that if there is a need for this double statement, there is need for a triple one; there is the third part of the life of a human being, a part that we cannot ignore, an intermediate area of *experiencing*, to which inner reality and external life both contribute. It is an area which is not challenged, because no claim is made on its behalf except that it shall exist as a resting-place for the individual engaged in the perpetual human task of keeping inner and outer reality separate yet inter-related.
>
> ["Transitional Objects", p. 230]

Winnicott came to this realization of the third area from seeing a link between the newborn infant's use of fist, fingers, and thumbs and the older (anything from 3 to 12 months) infant's use of teddy, doll, or soft toy, sometimes in addition to thumb or finger sucking.

> There is a wide variation to be found in a sequence of events which starts with the new-born infant's fist-in-mouth activities, and that leads eventually on to an attachment to a teddy, a doll or soft toy, or to a hard toy.
>
> It is clear that something is important here other than oral excitement and satisfaction, although this may be the basis of everything else. Many other important things can be studied, and they include:
>
> The nature of the object.
>
> The infant's capacity to recognize the object as Not-me.
>
> The place of the object—outside, inside, at the border.
>
> The infant's capacity to create, think up, devise, originate, produce an object.
>
> The initiation of an affectionate type of object relationship.
>
> ["Transitional Objects", pp. 229–230]

2   The truly Not-me object is a possession

The external object that the infant or child adopts is his first possession. In other words, from the observer's point of view, it is a symbol of the journey the infant is making from the experience of his mother's adaptation to his needs during the time of absolute dependence, to relative dependence, where he begins to see his mother as not himself and realizes that he must now start to stand on his own two feet so to speak (see DEPENDENCE: 1, 6). Thus although the external object represents all the components of mothering, it also signifies the infant's ability to *create* what he needs. This is how the transitional object is the infant's first possession: it truly belongs to him, because he has created it. (see CREATIVITY: 2; DEPENDENCE: 6)

Each individual infant finds his own unique way of creating the first possession:

In the case of some infants the thumb is placed in the mouth while fingers are made to caress the face by pronation and supination movements of the forearm. The mouth is then active in relation to the thumb, but not in relation to the fingers. The fingers caressing the upper lip, or some other part, may be or may become more important than the thumb engaging the mouth. Moreover this caressing activity may be found alone, without the more direct thumb–mouth union.

In common experience one of the following occurs, complicating an auto-erotic experience such as thumb-sucking:

1. with the other hand the baby takes an external object, say a part of a sheet or blanket, into the mouth along with the fingers; or
2. somehow or other the bit of cloth is held and sucked, or not actually sucked. The objects used naturally include napkins and (later) handkerchiefs, and this depends on what is readily and reliably available; or
3. the baby starts from early months to pluck wool and to collect it and to use it for the caressing part of the activity. Less commonly, the wool is swallowed, even causing trouble; or
4. mouthing, accompanied by sounds of "mum–mum", babbling, anal noises, the first musical notes and so on.

["Transitional Objects", pp. 231–232]

The transitional object need not be a real object; it may be

. . . a word or tune, or a mannerism, which becomes vitally important to the infant for use at the time of going to sleep, and is a defence against anxiety, especially anxiety of the depressive type.

["Transitional Objects", p. 232]

Mothers and fathers intuitively appreciate the importance of these objects to their child.

The parents get to know its value and carry it round when travelling. The mother lets it get dirty and even smelly, knowing that by washing it she introduces a break in continuity in the infant's experience, a break that may destroy the meaning and value of the object to the infant.

["Transitional Objects", p. 232]

The parents seem to know that for the infant the transitional object is absolutely a part of himself, like a mouth or breast:

> ... parents respect this object even more than they do the teddies and dolls and toys that quickly follow. The baby who loses the transitional object at the same time loses both mouth and breast, both hand and mother's skin, both creativity and objective perception. The object is one of the bridges that make contact possible between the individual psyche and external reality.
>
> ["Group Influences and the Maladjusted Child", 1955, p. 149]

Winnicott observes that apart from object choice, there is no difference in the way boys and girls use the transitional object:

> Gradually in the life of an infant teddies and dolls and hard toys are acquired. Boys to some extent tend to go over to use hard objects, whereas girls tend to proceed right ahead to the acquisition of a family. It is important to note, however, that *there is no noticeable difference between boy and girl in their use of the original Not-me possession,* which I am calling the transitional object.
>
> ["Transitional Objects", p. 232]

The transitional object is usually named by the child as he acquires the use of sound, and it usually has a word used by the adult partly incorporated in it. For instance, "baa" may be the name, and the "b" may have come from the adult's use of the word "baby" or "bear". Although language acquisition is relevant here, Winnicott's emphasis is on the infant's creation of a personal word.

There are many other aspects to the transitional object, all part of what Winnicott describes as "special qualities in the relationship". He lists seven qualities:

1. The infant assumes rights over the object, and we agree to this assumption. Nevertheless some abrogation of omnipotence is a feature from the start.
2. The object is affectionately cuddled as well as excitedly loved and mutilated.

["Transitional Objects", p. 233]

Winnicott uses the word "affection" a great deal in relation to the infant's use of the transitional object. "Affectionately cuddled as well as excitedly loved" refers to the infant's quiet and excited states in relation to his mother. At this stage of development, the infant is having to struggle inside with his experience of the object–mother, whom he excitedly loves, and his environment–mother, who is the mother of the quiet times. The transitional object can be seen as being used by the infant, through enactment, to relate to these two mothers and bring the two together (*see* AGGRESSION: 6, 9; CONCERN: 3; DEPENDENCE: 6, 7). This applies to Points 3 and 4.

3. It must never change, unless changed by the infant.
4. It must survive instinctual loving, and also hating, and, if it be a feature, pure aggression.
5. Yet it must seem to the infant to give warmth, or to move, or to have texture, or to do something that seems to show it has vitality or reality of its own.
6. It comes from without from our point of view, but not so from the point of view of the baby. Neither does it come from within; it is not an hallucination.
7. Its fate is to be gradually allowed to be decathected, so that in the course of years it becomes not so much forgotten as relegated to limbo. By this I mean that in health the transitional object does not "go inside" nor does the feeling about it necessarily undergo repression. It is not forgotten and it is not mourned. It loses meaning, and this is because the transitional phenomena have become diffused, have become spread out over the whole intermediate territory between "inner psychic reality" and "the external world as perceived by two persons in common", that is to say, over the whole cultural field.

[*"Transitional Objects"*, p. 233]

This last item makes the transitional object a unique object not just for the child in his developmental journey, but also for the development of psychoanalytic theory. Hitherto in psychoanalysis objects were either internalized or lost. For the first time, here is an object that is neither internalized nor lost but, rather, "relegated to limbo". But why?

Once the transition from object-relating to object-usage has taken place, the transitional object, in and of itself, is no longer needed by the infant, because its task, so to speak, is over. By now the small child is able to distinguish between Me and Not-me *and* live in the third area, keeping inside and outside apart and yet inter-related. This is the "diffusion" and "spreading out" into, as Winnicott describes it, "the whole cultural field". Fifteen years later, on the occasion of the celebration of the completion of Strachey's translation of the complete works of Freud, Winnicott introduced the theme of the location of culture, which in 1967 became a paper—"The Location of Cultural Experience". (*see* CREATIVITY: 3; PLAYING: 1, 2)

The infant's use of the transitional object and the parent's ability to allow for this play are building on the foundations already set down in the early mother–infant relationship. (*see* BEING: 1, 3; CREATIVITY: 1; PLAYING: 2)

3   Transitional objects and the journey to symbolism

The transitional object is a symbol, from the observer's point of view, of an aspect of the infant's experience of his environment. However, this does not mean that the infant using a transitional object has reached the capacity to use symbols; rather, he is *on his way* to using symbols. Thus the transitional object indicates a transitional stage of development, from object-relating to use of an object. (*see* AGGRESSION: 10)

> It is true that the piece of blanket (or whatever it is) is symbolical of some part-object, such as the breast. Nevertheless the point of it is not its symbolic value so much as its actuality. Its not being the breast (or the mother) is as important as the fact that it stands for the breast (or mother).
>
> When symbolism is employed the infant is already clearly distinguishing between fantasy and fact, between inner objects and external objects, between primary creativity and perception. But the term transitional object, according to my suggestion, gives room for the process of becoming able to accept difference and similarity. I think there is use for a term for the root of symbolism in time, a term that describes the infant's journey from the purely subjective to objectivity; and it seems to me that the transitional object (piece of blanket,

etc.) is what we see of this journey of progress towards experiencing.

> ["Transitional Objects", pp. 233–234]

Symbolism, for Winnicott, is variable, depending on the infant's
stage of development.

> It seems that symbolism can only be properly studied in the
> process of the growth of an individual, and that it has at
> the very best a variable meaning. For instance, if we consider
> the wafer of the Blessed Sacrament, which is symbolic of the
> body of Christ, I think I am right in saying that for the Roman
> Catholic community it *is* the body, and for the Protestant com-
> munity it is a *substitute*, a reminder, and is essentially not, in
> fact, actually the body itself. Yet in both cases it is a symbol.
>
> A schizoid patient asked me, after Christmas, had I enjoyed
> eating her at the feast. And then, *had I really eaten her or only in
> fantasy*. I knew that she could not be satisfied with either alter-
> native. Her split needed the double answer.
>
> ["Transitional Objects", p. 234]

The "double answer", we may assume, is that Winnicott eats her
in fantasy and reality, in a parallel with the belief in transubstan-
tiation in the Roman Catholic Church.

4   The function of the transitional object

At first the infant needs to believe that he is responsible for
creating the breast. He is hungry, he cries, the breast is offered just
at the right time, and he obtains what he needs. All this leads him
to believe that he has created the breast. This is the necessary
illusion (*see* MOTHER: 4). Once the illusion has been established, the
mother's function, during the time of the infant's relative dependence, is to *disillusion* him. The infant starts to perceive objectively,
instead of apperceiving subjectively (*see* DEPENDENCE: 6). But—and
this is crucial to Winnicott's theory—if the infant has not had
enough experience of this illusion, he will not be able to perceive
objectively, and the journey involved in working out the difference between Me and Not-me will be distorted.

> From birth . . . the human being is concerned with the prob-
> lem of the relationship between what is objectively perceived

and what is subjectively conceived of, and in the solution of this problem there is no health for the human being who has not been started off well enough by the mother. *The intermediate area to which I am referring is the area that is allowed to the infant between primary creativity and objective perception based on reality-testing.* The transitional phenomena represent the early stages of the use of illusion, without which there is no meaning for the human being in the idea of a relationship with an object that is perceived by others as external to that being.

["Transitional Objects", p. 239]

Winnicott illustrates his point with two diagrams. The first shows how object-presenting by the mother in a state of primary maternal preoccupation leads to the infant's illusion that he has created what he needs, and the second demonstrates how the area of illusion is transformed into a shape—the transitional object.

In Fig. 20 a shape is given to the area of illusion, to illustrate what I consider to be the main function of the transitional object and of transitional phenomena. The

 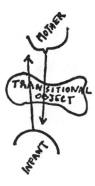

FIGURE *19*   FIGURE *20*

transitional object and the transitional phenomena start each human being off with what will always be important for them, i.e.: a neutral area of experience which will not be challenged. *Of the transitional object it can be said that it is a matter of agreement between us and the baby that we will never ask the question "Did you conceive of this or was it presented to you from without?" The important point is that no decision on this point is expected. The question is not to be formulated.*

["Transitional Objects", pp. 239–240]

In another paper, "The Deprived Child and How He Can Be Compensated for Loss of Family Life" (1950), written a year prior to the paper on transitional phenomena, Winnicott explains a little further why the question must not be formulated:

> . . . one difficulty every child experiences is to relate subjective reality to shared reality which can be objectively perceived. From waking to sleeping the child jumps from a perceived world to a self-created world. In between there is a need for all kinds of transitional phenomena—neutral territory. I would describe this precious object by saying that there is a tacit understanding that no one will claim that this real thing is a part of the world, or that it is created by the infant. It is understood that both these things are true: the infant created it and the world supplied it. This is the continuation forward of the initial task which the ordinary mother enables her infant to undertake, when by a most delicate active adaptation she offers herself, perhaps her breast, a thousand times at the moment that the baby is ready to create something like the breast that she offers.
>
> ["Deprived Child", pp. 143–144]

"From waking to sleeping" clearly illustrates the quality of the two different worlds—"inner" belonging to sleeping and dreaming, the unconscious and "subjective reality"; "outer" belonging to the environment and a "shared reality", which is perceived more consciously as Not-me. The transitional object can then be seen to be used by the child to bridge these two states, which accounts for children's need of the transitional object particularly at the time of going to sleep. By this time, the small child is already living in the intermediate area, although, as Winnicott points out, none of us are ever clear of the struggle of the inter-relationship between inside and outside.

> It is assumed here that the task of reality-acceptance is never completed, that no human being is free from the strain of relating inner and outer reality, and that relief from this strain is provided by an intermediate area of experience which is not challenged (arts, religion, etc.) This intermediate area is in direct continuity with the play area of the small child who is "lost" in play.
>
> ["Transitional Objects", p. 241]

The themes related to transitional phenomena play a large part in Winnicott's writings, and the chapters in his book, *Playing and Reality*, are all associated with the different aspects of transitional phenomena.

5   Cultural experience

In one chapter Winnicott examines "The Place Where We Live" (1971):

> I wish to examine the place, using the word in an abstract sense, where we most of the time are when we are experiencing life.
>
> ["Place Where We Live", p. 104]

Here Winnicott extends the early mother–infant relationship into adult life and living. He looks at two extremes—that of behaviour and that of the inner life.

> When considering the lives of human beings there are those who like to think superficially in terms of behaviour, and in terms of conditioned reflexes and conditioning; this leads to what is called behaviour therapy. But most of us get tired of restricting ourselves to behaviour or to the observable extrovert life of persons who, whether they like it or not, are motivated from the unconscious. By contrast, there are those who place emphasis on the "inner" life, who think that the effects of economics and even of starvation itself have but little importance as compared with mystical experience. . . .
>
> I am attempting to get in between these two extremes. If we look at our lives we shall probably find that we spend most of our time neither in behaviour nor in contemplation, but somewhere else. I ask: where? And I try to suggest an answer.
>
> ["Place Where We Live", pp. 104–105]

The psychoanalytic literature, Winnicott points out, does not give an answer to the question of where we all live in our day-to-day lives.

> What, for instance, are we doing when we are listening to a Beethoven symphony or making a pilgrimage to a picture gallery or reading Troilus and Cressida in bed, or playing tennis? What is a child doing when sitting on the floor play-

ing with toys under the aegis of the mother? What is a group of teenagers doing participating in a pop session?

It is not only: what are we doing? The question also needs to be posed: where are we (if anywhere at all)? We have used the concepts of inner and outer, and we want a third concept. Where are we when we are doing what in fact we do a great deal of our time, namely, enjoying ourselves?

["Place Where We Live", pp. 105–106]

Winnicott's answer is that we are living, in health, in the intermediate zone, the third area, the transitional space. And, depending into which culture we are born, our enjoyment will be pursued in different ways—reading, playing football, dancing. The primary culture, however, is the early mother–infant relationship. (*see* CREATIVITY: 3)

It is in the pursuit of these cultural activities that our self-experiencing is enhanced and developed. All these activities contribute to the quality of life.

... playing and cultural experience are things that we do value in a special way; these link the past, the present, and the future; *they take up time and space.* They demand and get our concentrated deliberate attention, deliberate but without too much of the deliberateness of trying.

["Place Where We Live", p. 109]

Marion Milner has written a great deal about the third area of experience throughout the whole of her work and her ideas were developed in parallel to Winnicott's. *On Not Being Able to Paint* (1950) is probably her major contribution to the themes of transitional phenomena.

6   Friendship and groups

The ego-relatedness of the mother–infant relationship, where being, creativity, unintegration, and cultural experiences are located, is seen by Winnicott as "the stuff out of which friendship is made" ("The Capacity to Be Alone", 1958, p. 33). It is from the original enjoyment of the relationship with mother and the environment (father, siblings, etc.) that the ability to play and make friends is made possible.

Just as some adults make friends and enemies easily at work whereas others may sit in a boarding-house for years and do no more than wonder why no one seems to want them, so do children make friends and enemies during play, while they do not easily make friends apart from play. Play provides an organization for the initiation of emotional relationships, and so enables social contacts to develop.

["Why Children Play", 1942, pp. 144–145]

The ability to make friends and maintain friendships is based on the capacity to be alone (*see* ALONE: 1, 2). Indeed a description of friendship, based on Winnicott's thesis, entails the capacity to hold the friend in mind whilst also recognizing separateness. Following cultural pursuits within the relationships of friendship is making use of the transitional space between individuals. (*see* PLAYING: 7)

Moving on from this, Winnicott speculates that the experience of transitional phenomena that are highly satisfactory could be thought of in terms of ecstasy or "ego orgasm". He asks:

... only whether there can be a value in thinking of ecstasy as an ego orgasm. In the normal person a highly satisfactory experience such as may be obtained at a concert or at the theatre or in a friendship may deserve a term such as ego orgasm, which draws attention to the climax and the importance of the climax.

["Capacity to Be Alone", p. 35]

The expression "ego orgasm" is not referred to specifically again by Winnicott to describe the sense of joy, happiness, and all those aspects involved in creative living. In 1960, Lacan refers to something of the same phenomenon as *"jouissance"*, which later on in 1989 is taken up by Bollas in *Forces of Destiny*:

Jouissance is the subject's inalienable right to ecstasy, a virtually legal imperative to pursue desire.

[Bollas, 1989a, pp. 19–20]

The pursuit of happiness takes place in the transitional space, where satisfaction may or may not be fulfilled. If desire comes from the true self, there is more chance of a fulfilling outcome, in as much as it will "feel real".

Winnicott sees cultural pursuits as taking place in the third area through playing:

> . . . it is play that is universal, and that belongs to health, play-ing facilitates growth and therefore health; playing leads into group relationships; playing can be a form of communication in psychotherapy; and, lastly, psychoanalysis has been devel-oped as a highly specialized form of playing in the service of communication with oneself and others.
>
> The natural thing is playing, and the highly sophisticated twentieth century phenomenon is psychoanalysis.
>
> ["Playing: A Theoretical Statement", 1971, p. 41]

7   The potential space and separation

The infant needs a good start by being merged with his mother. This experience, if all goes well, leads the infant to rely and trust in his mother, by internalizing the good experience of being inside her, born to her, and living with her. As he develops and comes out of the stage of absolute dependence, he needs to repudiate her as Not-me in order to separate out and understand the difference between inside and outside. As this happens, the mother must start to de-adapt—that is, remember her own self-needs—and thus disillusion the infant.

> From a state of being merged in with the mother the baby is at a stage of separating out the mother from the self, and the mother is lowering the degree of adaptation to the baby's needs (both because of her recovery from a high degree of identification with her baby and because of her perception of the baby's new need, the need for her to be a separate phe-nomenon).
>
> ["Place Where We Live", p. 107]

Winnicott likens this period to the time in psychotherapy when the patient, having experienced trust and reliability, needs to separate and achieve autonomy.

> Like the baby with the mother, the patient cannot become autonomous except in conjunction with the therapist's readi-ness to let go. . . .
>
> ["Place Where We Live", p. 107]

Winnicott poses the paradox that there is no such thing as separation, only the threat of separation. This is based on the same paradox that the capacity to be alone is based on the experience of being alone in the presence of another. In that sense, in unconscious fantasy, no one is ever truly alone, unless the continuity of being has been severed.

> It could be said that with human beings there can be no separation, only a threat of separation; and the threat is maximally or minimally traumatic according to the experience of the first separatings.
>
> How, one may ask, does separation of subject and object, of baby and mother, seem in fact to happen, and to happen with profit to all concerned, and in the vast majority of cases? And this in spite of the impossibility of separation? (The paradox must be tolerated).
>
> ["Place Where We Live", p. 108]

Through the mother's empathy with her infant and the therapist's empathy with the patient, the infant/patient is able to internalize and feel safe in his move from dependence to autonomy. Only through this reliability and trust does a potential space start to occur. Winnicott posits the paradox that at the point of the infant separating from mother he is at the same time filling up the potential space through playing and cultural experience.

> The baby's confidence in the mother's reliability, and therefore in that of other people and things, makes possible a separating-out of the not-me from the me. At the same time, however, it can be said that separation is avoided by the filling in of the potential space with creative playing, with the use of symbols, and with all that eventually adds up to a cultural life.
>
> ["Place Where We Live", p. 109]

The "avoidance" to which Winnicott is referring here is another way of describing the inner phenomenon of relating to subjective objects. Autonomy, therefore, implies the continuation of the experienced union *in fantasy*. The use of the transitional object can be seen to be the enactment of both repudiation and internalization of the baby's first object.

This concept of Winnicott's that there is never separation, only the threat of separation, is not one he explores in any great detail, but it is central to the concept of transitional phenomena because the transitional space both separates and brings together. It is a paradox that must be tolerated and not resolved.

> The transitional object and the transitional phenomena start each human being off with what will always be important for them, i.e. a neutral area of experience which will not be challenged. *Of the transitional object it can be said that it is a matter of agreement between us and the baby that we will never ask the question: "Did you conceive of this or was it presented to you from without?" The important point is that no decision on this point is expected. The question is not to be formulated.*
>
> ["Transitional Objects", pp. 239–240]

The paradox can be resolved through "flight to split-off intellectual functioning", but at the cost of losing its value.

> This paradox, once accepted and tolerated, has value for every human individual who is not only alive and living in this world but is also capable of being infinitely enriched by exploitation of the cultural link with the past and with the future.
>
> [*Playing and Reality*, 1971, p. xii]

REFERENCES

1942 Why Children Play   [W7]
1950 The Deprived Child and How He Can Be Compensated for a Loss of Family Life   [W8]
1951 Transitional Objects and Transitional Phenomena   [W6]
1955 Group Influences and the Maladjusted Child   [W8]
1958 The Capacity to Be Alone   [W9]
1971 The Place Where We Live   [W10]
1971 *Playing and Reality*   [W10]
1971 Playing: A Theoretical Statement   [W10]

REFERENCES:
SECONDARY SOURCES

Axline, V. M. (1947). *Play Therapy: The Inner Dynamics of Childhood.* Boston, MA: Houghton Mifflin.

Bettelheim, B. (1983). *Freud and Man's Soul.* London: Chatto & Windus.

Bollas, C. (1989a). *Forces of Destiny.* London: Free Association Books.

Bollas, C. (1989b). The Psychoanalyst's Celebration of the Analysand. In: *Forces of Destiny.* London: Free Association Books.

Casement, P. (1982). Some Pressures on the Analyst for Physical Contact during the Reliving of an Early Trauma. In: G. Kohon (Ed.), *The British School of Psychoanalysis: The Independent Tradition.* London: Free Association Books, 1986.

Davis, M., & Wallbridge, D. (1981). *Boundary and Space: An Introduction to the Work of D.W. Winnicott.* New York: Brunner-Mazel. [Revised edition London: Karnac Books, 1991.]

Fairbairn, W. R. D. (1952). *Psycho-Analytic Studies of the Personality.* London: Tavistock.

Freud, S. (1915c). Instincts and Their Vicissitudes. *S.E. 18.*

Freud, S. (1916d). Crime Due to Sense of Guilt. Some Character Types Met with in Psycho-Analytic Work (Chapter 3). Criminals from a Sense of Guilt. *S.E.14.*

Freud, S. (1920g). Beyond the Pleasure Principle. *S.E. 14.*

Goldman, D. (1993). *In Search of the Real*. New York: Jason Aronson.

Heimann, P. (1950). On Countertransference. In: *About Children and Children-no-longer: Collected Papers 1942–1980*. London: Tavistock, 1989.

Kahr, B. (1996). *D. W. Winnicott: A Biographical Portrait*. London: Karnac Books.

Khan, M. M. R. (1975). Introduction. In: D. W. Winnicott, *Through Paediatrics to Psycho-Analysis*. London: Hogarth Press & the Institute of Psycho-Analysis. [Reprinted London: Karnac Books, 1992].

King, P., & Steiner, R. (1992). *The Freud–Klein Controversies 1941–45*. London: Routledge.

Klein, M. (1957). Envy and Gratitude. In: *The Writings of Melanie Klein, Vol. 3*. London: Hogarth Press, 1975. [Reprinted London: Karnac Books, 1993.]

Lacan, J. (1960). The Subversion of the Subject and the Dialectic of Desire in the Freudian Unconscious. In: *Écrits: A Selection* (pp. 292–325). London: Tavistock.

Milner, M. (1950). *On Not Being Able to Paint*. London: Heinemann.

Niblett, W. R. (Ed.) (1963). *Moral Education in a Changing Society*. London: Faber.

Pedder, J. R. (1976). Attachment and New Beginning: Some Links between the Work of Michael Balint and John Bowlby. International Review of Psycho-Analysis, 3: 491–497. Also in: G. Kohon (Ed.), *The British School of Psychoanalysis: The Independent Tradition*. London: Free Association Books, 1986.

Pedder, J. (1992). Psychoanalytic Views of Aggression: Some Theoretical Problems. *British Journal of Medical Psychology, 65*, 95–106.

Phillips, A. (1988). *Winnicott*. Cambridge, MA: Harvard University Press.

Sechehaye, M. A. (1951). *Symbolic Realisation*. New York: International Universities Press.

Stern, D. (1985). *The Interpersonal World of the Infant*. New York: Basic Books.

Winnicott, Clare (1984). Introduction. In: D. W. Winnicott, *Deprivation and Delinquency* (ed. C. Winnicott, R. Shepherd, & M. Davis). London: Tavistock; New York: Methuen.

BIBLIOGRAPHY

Compiled by Harry Karnac

List of volumes

W1 *Clinical Notes on Disorders of Childhood.* London: Heinemann, 1931.

W2 *Getting to Know Your Baby.* London: Heinemann, 1945.

W3 *The Ordinary Devoted Mother and Her Baby.* Privately published, 1949.

W4 *The Child and the Family.* London: Tavistock, 1957.

W5 *The Child and the Outside World.* London: Tavistock, 1957.

W6 *Collected Papers: Through Paediatrics to Psycho-Analysis.* London: Tavistock, 1958. New York: Basic Books, 1958. [Reprinted as *Through Paediatrics to Psycho-Analysis.* London: Hogarth Press & the Institute of Psycho-Analysis, 1975; reprinted London: Karnac Books, 1992].

W7 *The Child, the Family and the Outside World.* London: Penguin, 1964. Reading, MA: Addison-Wesley, 1987.

W8 *The Family and Individual Development.* London: Tavistock, 1965.

W9 *The Maturational Processes and the Facilitating Environment: Studies in the Theory of Emotional Development.* London: Hogarth Press & The Institute of Psycho-Analysis, 1965. New York: International Universities Press, 1965. [Reprinted London: Karnac Books, 1990.]

W10 *Playing and Reality.* London: Tavistock, 1971. New York: Methuen, 1982.

W11 *Therapeutic Consultations in Child Psychiatry.* London: Hogarth Press
     & The Institute of Psycho-Analysis, 1971. New York: Basic Books,
     1971.

W12 *The Piggle: An Account of the Psychoanalytic Treatment of a Little Girl*
     (ed. Ishak Ramzy). London: Hogarth Press & The Institute of
     Psycho-Analysis, 1977. New York: International Universities Press,
     1977.

W13 *Deprivation and Delinquency* (ed. C. Winnicott, R. Shepherd, & M.
     Davis). London: Tavistock, 1984. New York: Methuen, 1984.

W14 *Home Is Where We Start From* (ed. C. Winnicott, R. Shepherd, & M.
     Davis). London: Penguin, 1986. New York: W. W. Norton, 1986.

W15 *Holding and Interpretation: Fragment of an Analysis.* London: Hogarth
     Press & The Institute of Psycho-Analysis, 1986. New York: Grove
     Press, 1986. [Reprinted London: Karnac Books, 1989.]

W16 *Babies & Their Mothers* (ed. C. Winnicott, R. Shepherd, & M. Davis).
     London: Free Association Books, 1987. Reading, MA: Addison-
     Wesley, 1987.

W17 *The Spontaneous Gesture* (selected letters, ed. F. R. Rodman).
     Cambridge, MA: Harvard University Press, 1987.

W18 *Human Nature.* London: Free Association Books, 1988. New York:
     Schocken Books, 1988.

W19 *Psycho-Analytic Explorations* (ed. C. Winnicott, R. Shepherd, & M.
     Davis). London: Karnac Books, 1989. Cambridge, MA: Harvard
     University Press, 1989.

W20 *Talking to Parents* (ed. C. Winnicott, C. Bollas, M. Davis, & R.
     Shepherd). Reading, MA: Addison-Wesley, 1993.

W21 *Thinking about Children* (ed. R. Shepherd, J. Johns, & H. Taylor
     Robinson). London: Karnac Books, 1996. Reading, MA: Addison-
     Wesley, 1996.

Alphabetical list

*** Indicates that the entry does not appear in volumes W1 to W21.

Aims of Psycho-Analytical Treatment (The)   1962   W9:166–170
American Correspondent (An): Letter to [Jan. 14th]   1969   W17:183–185
Antisocial Tendency (The)   1956   W6:306–315
Antisocial Tendency (The)   1956   W13:120–131
Anti-Social Tendency Illustrated by a Case (The)   1962
   A Criança Portuguesa Vol. 21
   Also appears as Case VII in: W11:110–126
Anxiety   1931   W1:122–128
Anxiety Associated with Insecurity   1952   W6:97–100
Appetite and Emotional Disorder [read before the Medical
   Section, British Psychological Society]   1936   W6:33–51
Art versus Illness by A. Hill [review]   1949   W19:555–557
   Brit. J. Med. Psychol. 22
Arthritis Associated with Emotional Disturbance   1931   W1:81–86
Association for Child Psychology and Psychiatry Observed as
   a Group Phenomenon (The) [President's address,
   A.C.P.P.]   1967   W21:235–254
Asthma: Attitude & Milieu by Aaron Lask [review]   1966   ***
   New Society 17/11
Autism [paper prepared for the Society for Autistic Children]   1966   W21:197–217
Babies as Persons (Further Thoughts on)   1947   W5:134–140
   New Era in Home & School 28/10:199 under title "Babies are
   Persons"
Babies as Persons (Further Thoughts on)   1964   W7:85–92
Baby as a Going Concern (The) [B.B.C. radio broadcast]   1949   W3:7–11
Baby as a Going Concern (The)   1949   W4:13–17
Baby as a Going Concern (The)   1964   W7:25–29
Baby as a Person (The) [B.B.C. radio broadcast]   1949   W3:22–26
Baby as a Person (The)   1949   W4:33–37
Baby as a Person (The)   1964   W7:75–79
Balint, Enid: Letter to [March 22nd]   1956   W17:97–98
Balint, Michael: Letter to [Feb. 5th]   1960   W17:127–129
Basis for Self in Body (On the)   1970   W19:261–283
   Nouvelle Revue de Psychanalyse [1971]
   International Journal of Child Psychotherapy [1972]
Bearing of Emotional Development on Feeding Problems (The)
   [Symposium on Environmental Health in Infancy at the
   Royal Society of Medicine]   1967   W21:39–41
Becoming Deprived as a Fact: A Psychotherapeutic
   Consultation   1966
   J. Child Psychother. 1
   Appears as Case XVII in: W11:315–331
Beginning of the Individual (The)   1966   W16:51–58
Beginnings of a Formulation of an Appreciation and Criticism
   of Klein's Envy Statement (The)   1962   W19:447–457
Behaviour Therapy [letter]   1969   W19:558–560
   Child Care News [June 1969]
Berlin Walls   1969   W14:221–227
Beveridge, Lord: Letter to [Oct. 15th]   1946   W17:8
Bick, Esther: Letter to [June 11th]   1953   W17:50–52
Bion, Wilfred R.: Letter to [Oct. 7th]   1955   W17:89–93
Bion, Wilfred R.: Letter to [Nov. 17th]   1960   W17:131
Bion, Wilfred R.: Letter to [Nov. 16th]   1961   W17:133
Bion, Wilfred R.: Letter to [Oct. 5th]   1967   W17:169–170

Childhood and Society by E. H. Erikson, 1965 (Review of)   1965   W19:493–494
   New Society [Sept.]
Childhood Schizophrenia by William Goldfarb, 1961 [review]   1963   W21:193–194
   Brit. J. Psychiatric Social Work 7
Children and Their Mothers   1940   W13:14–21
   New Era in Home & School 21
Children in Distress by Alec Clegg & Barbara Megson [review]   1968   ***
   New Society 7/11
Children in the War   1940   W5:69–74
   New Era in Home & School 21/9:229
Children in the War   1940   W13:25–30
Children Learning   1968   W14:142–149
   In *The Family & God*, Christian Teamwork Inst. of Education
Children's Hostels in War and Peace   1948   W5:117–121
   Brit. J. Med. Psychol. 21/3:175
Children's Hostels in War and Peace   1948   W13:73–77
Child's Needs and the Rôle of the Mother in the Early Stages
   (The)   1953   W5:13–23
   [An excerpt] published in series *Problems in Education*
Classification: Is There a Psycho-Analytic Contribution to
   Psychiatric Classification? [postscript dated 1964]   1959   W9:124–139
Clinical Approach to Family Problems (A): The Family [lecture
   at London School of Economics]   1959   W21:54–56
Clinical Example of Symptomatology Following the Birth of a
   Sibling (A)   1931ca W21:97–101
Clinical Illustration of "The Use of an Object"   1968   W19:235–238
Clinical Regression Compared with That of Defence
   Organisation (The Concept of)   1967   W19:193–199
   In *Psychotherapy in the Designed Therapeutic Milieu* ed.
   Eldred & Vanderpol [1968]
Clinical Study of the Effect of a Failure of the Average
   Expectable Environment on a Child's Mental
   Functioning (A)   1965
   IJP 46:81
   Appears also as Case IV in: W11:64–88
Clinical Varieties of Transference   1955   W6:295–299
   IJP 37 [1956]:386
Close-Up of Mother Feeding Baby [B.B.C. radio broadcast]   1949   W3:27–31
Close-Up of Mother Feeding Baby   1949   W4:38–42
Close-Up of Mother Feeding Baby   1964   W7:45–49
Colleague (A): Letter to [Sept. 4th]   1967   W17:165
Collection of children's books reviewed under the title "Small
   Things for Small People" (A)   1967   ***
   New Society 7/12
Collinson, J. D.: Letter to [March 10th]   1969   W17:186–188
Comments on My Paper "The Use of an Object"   1968   W19:238–240
Communicating and Not Communicating Leading to a Study
   of Certain Opposites   1963   W9:179–192
Communication between Infant and Mother, and Mother and
   Infant, Compared and Contrasted   1968   W16:89–103
   In *What Is Psychoanalysis?* [Inst. PsA. Winter Lectures]
Concept of the False Self (The)   1964   W14:65–70
Confidant (A): Letter to [April 15th]   1966   W17:155

Disease of the Nervous System   1931   W1:129–142
Dissociation Revealed in a Therapeutic Consultation   1965   W13:256–282
   In *Crime, Law and Corrections* ed. R. Slovenko [1966]
   Also published as Case XIII in: W11:220–238
Disturbed Children ed. Robert J. N. Tod (Foreword to)   1968   ***
   Longmans' Papers on Residential Work Vol. 2
Do Progressive Schools Give Too Much Freedom to the Child?   1965   W13:209–219
   In *Who Are the Progressives Now?* ed. M. Ash [1969]
Doctor (The), His Patient and the Illness by M. Balint, 1957
      (Review of)   1958   W19:438–442
   IJP 39
Dowling, R. S. W.: Letter to [Dec. 8th]   1967   W17:174–175
Dreaming, Fantasying, and Living: A Case-History Describing
      a Primary Dissociation   1971   W10:26–37
D.W.W. on D.W.W.   1967   W19:569–582
D.W.W.'s Dream Related to Reviewing Jung   1963   W19:228–230
Early Disillusion   1939   W19:21–23
Educational Diagnosis   1946   W5:29–34
   National Froebel Foundation Bulletin 41:3
Educational Diagnosis   1964   W7:205–210
Effect of Loss on the Young (The) [talk written for the Cruse
      Club]   1968   W21:46–47
Effect of Psychosis on Family Life (The)   1960   W8:61–68
Effect of Psychotic Parents on the Emotional Development of
      the Child (The)   1959   W8:69–78
   Brit. J. Psychiatric Social Work 6/1 [1961]
Ego Distortion in Terms of True and False Self   1960   W9:140–152
Ego Integration in Child Development   1962   W9:56–63
End of the Digestive Process (The) [B.B.C. radio broadcast]   1949   W3:17–21
End of the Digestive Process (The)   1949   W4:28–32
End of the Digestive Process (The)   1964   W7:40–44
Environmental Health in Infancy   1967   W16:59–68
   Portions published in *Maternal & Child Care*
Environmental Needs; The Early Stages; Total Dependence
      and Essential Independence [talk given at The Institute
      of Education, Univ. of London]   1948   W21:29–36
Envy and Gratitude by M. Klein, 1957 (Review of)   1959   W19:443–446
   Case Conference [Jan.]
Envy and Jealousy (Contribution to a Symposium on)   1969   W19:462–464
Ernest Jones: Obituary & Funeral Address   1958   W19:393–407
   IJP 39
Evacuated Child (The) [B.B.C. radio broadcast]   1945   W5:83–87
Evacuated Child (The)   1945   W13:39–43
Evacuation of Small Children [letter: with J. Bowlby & E.
      Miller]   1939   W13:13–14
   Brit. Med. J.
Excitement in the Aetiology of Coronary Thrombosis   1957   W19:34–38
Ezriel, H.: Letter to [June 20th]   1952   W17:31–32
Failure of Expectable Environment on Child's Mental
      Functioning   1965
   IJP 46:81.
      Appears also as Case IV in: W11:64–88
Family Affected by Depressive Illness in One or Both Parents
      (The)   1958   W8:50–60

Guntrip, Harry: Letter to [Aug. 13th]   1954   W17:77–79
Hallucination and Dehallucination   1957   W19:39–42
Hate in the Countertransference   1947   W6:194–203
   IJP 30 [1949]:69
Hazlehurst, R. S.: Letter to [Sept. 1st]   1949   W17:17
Haemoptysis: Case for Diagnosis   1931   ***
   Proceedings of the Royal Society of Medicine 24:855–856
Health Education through Broadcasting   1957   W20:1–6
   Mother and Child 28
Healthy Individual (The Concept of a)   1967   W14:22–38
   In *Towards Community Health* ed. J. D. Sutherland [1971]
Heart (The), with Special Reference to Rheumatic Carditis   1931   W1:42–57
Henderson, Sir David K.: Letter to [May 10th]   1954   W17:63–65
Henderson, Sir David K.: Letter to [May 20th]   1954   W17:68–71
History-Taking   1931   W1:7–21
Hobgoblins and Good Habits   1967   ***
   Parents 22:9
Hodge, S. H.: Letter to [Sept. 1st]   1949   W17:17–19
Hoffer, Willi: Letter to [April 4th]   1952   W17:29–30
Holding and Interpretation: Fragment of an Analysis   1986   W15:1–202
   An earlier version published in *Tactics and Techniques in*
     Psychoanalytic Therapy ed. P. L. Giovacchini [1972]
Home Again [B.B.C. radio broadcast]   1945   W5:93–97
Home Again   1945   W13:49–53
Hospital Care Supplementing Intensive Psychotherapy in
   Adolescence   1963   W9:242–248
How a Baby Begins to Feel Sorry and to Make Amends   1967   ***
   Parents 22:7
How to Survive Parenthood by Edna J. LeShan [review]   1967   ***
   New Society 26/10
Human Aggression by Anthony Storr [review]   1968   ***
   New Statesman 5/7
Human Nature   1988   W18:1–189
Human Relations   1969   ***
   Physiotherapy 55
Ideas and Definitions [probably early 1950s]   n.d.   W19:43–44
Importance of the Setting in Meeting Regression in Psycho-
   Analysis (The)   1964   W19:96–102
Impulse to Steal (The)   1949   W5:176–180
Indications for Child Analysis & Other Papers by A. Freud
   (Review of)   1969   W19:511–512
   New Society [Aug. 1969]
Individuation   1970   W19:284–288
Infant Feeding [B.B.C. radio broadcast]   1945   W2:12–16
   New Era in Home & School 26/1:9
Infant Feeding   1945   W4:18–22
Infant Feeding   1964   W7:30–34
Infant Feeding and Emotional Development   1968   ***
   Maternal & Child Care 4
Infantile Autism by B. Rimland [review]   1966   W21:195–196
   Brit. Med. J. 10/9
Influencing and Being Influenced (On)   1941   W5:24–28
   New Era in Home & School 22/6:118

Masturbation	1931	W1:183–190
Maternal Care and Mental Health by John Bowlby, 1951		
(Review of)	1953	W19:423–426
Brit. J. Med. Psychol. 26		
McKeith, Ronald: Letter to [Jan. 31st]	1963	W17:138–139
Meaning of Mother Love (The)	1967	***
Parents 22:6		
Meltzer, Donald: Letter to [May 21st]	1959	W17:124–125
Meltzer, Donald: Letter to [Oct. 25th]	1966	W17:157–161
Memories, Dreams, Reflections by C. G. Jung, 1963 (Review of)	1964	W19:482–492
IJP 45		
Mental Defect	1931	W1:152–156
Mental Hygiene of the Pre-school Child [talk given to the		
Nursery School Association]	1936	W21:59–76
Mentally Ill in Your Caseload (The)	1963	W9:217–229
In *New Thinking for Changing Needs,* Association of Social		
Workers		
Metapsychological and Clinical Aspects of Regression within		
the Psycho-Analytical Set-Up	1954	W6:278–294
IJP 36:16		
Micturition Disturbances	1931	W1:172–182
Mind and Its Relation to the Psyche–Soma	1949	W6:243–254
Brit. J. Med. Psychol. 27 [1954]		
Mirror-rôle of Mother and Family in Child Development	1971	W10:111–118
In *The Predicament of the Family* ed. P. Lomas [1967]		
Money-Kyrle, Roger: Letter to [Nov. 27th]	1952	W17:38–43
Money-Kyrle, Roger: Letter to [Sept. 23rd]	1954	W17:79–80
Money-Kyrle, Roger: Letter to [Feb. 10th]	1955	W17:84–85
Money-Kyrle, Roger: Letter to [March 17th]	1955	W17:85
Moral Paradox of Peace and War (The) by J. C. Flugel [review]	1941	***
New Era in Home and School 22:183		
Morals and Education	1963	W9:93–105
In *Moral Education in a Changing Society* ed. W. R. Niblett,		
under the title "The Young Child at Home and at		
School"		
Mother–Foetus Relationship (A Note on the) [probably mid-		
1960s]	n.d.	W19:161–162
Mother–Infant Experience of Mutuality (The)	1969	W19:251–260
Mother's Contribution to Society (The) [published as		
Postscript]	1957	W4:141–144
Mother's Contribution to Society (The)	1957	W14:123–127
Mother's Madness Appearing in the Clinical Material as an		
Ego-Alien Factor	1969	W19:375–382
In *Tactics & Techniques in Psychoanalytic Therapy* ed. P.		
Giovacchini [1972]		
Mother, Teacher, and the Child's Needs	1964	W7:189–198
In *Parenthood: Its Psychology & Psychopathology* ed.		
Anthony & Benedek [1970]		
Nagera, Humberto: Letter to [Feb. 15th]	1965	W17:147–148
Needs of the Under-Fives in a Changing Society	1954	W5:3–13
Nursery Journal 44/396:15		
Needs of the Under-Fives	1964	W7:179–188
New Light on Children's Thinking	1965	W19:152–157
Nelson, Gillian: Letter to [Oct. 6th]	1967	W17:170–171

Neonate and His Mother (The)	1964	***
Acta Paediatrica Latina Vol. 17		
Newborn and His Mother (The)	1964	W16:35–49
Acta Pediatrica Latina Vol. 17 under title "The Neonate & His Mother"		
New Society: Letter to [March 23rd]	1964	W17:140–142
Niffle (The)	n.d.	W21:104–109
Non-Human Environment in Normal Development and in Schizophrenia (The) by H. F. Searles, 1960 (Review of)	1963	W19:478–481
IJP 44		
Non-Pharmacological Treatment of Psychosis in Childhood (The)	1968	***
Concilium Paedopsychiatricum [Proc. 3rd Eur. Cong. Pedopsychiat.]		
Normality and Anxiety (A Note on)	1931	W1:98–121
Normality and Anxiety (A Note on)	1931	W6:3–21
Nose and Throat (The)	1931	W1:38–41
Note of Contribution to Symposium on Child Analysis and Paediatrics	1968	***
IJP 49:279		
Notes Made on a Train, Part 2	1965	W19:231–233
Notes on a Little Boy	1938	W21:102–103
New Era in Home & School 19		
Notes on the Time Factor in Treatment [preparation for lecture to West Sussex County Council Children's Dept.]	1961	W21:231–234
Nothing at the Centre	1959	W19:49–52
Now They Are Five [B.B.C. radio broadcast, June]	1962	W20:111–120
Originally published under title "The Five-Year Old" in W8 [*q. v.*]		
Observation of Infants in a Set Situation (The)	1941	W6:52–69
IJP 22:229		
Observer (The): Letter to [Oct. 12th]	1964	W17:142–144
Observer (The): Letter to [Nov. 5th]	1964	W17:146
Obsessional Neurosis and "Frankie" (Comment on)	1965	W19:158–160
Ocular Psychoneuroses of Childhood	1944	W6:85–90
Transactions of the Ophthalmological Society 64		
On Not Being Able to Paint by Marion Milner (Critical Notice of) [originally written under the name of Joanna Field, 1950]	1951	W19:390–392
On the Concept of the Superego [paper by J. Sandler, *PSC* 15] (Comments on)	1960	W19:465–473
On Transference	1956	***
IJP 37:386		
Only Child (The) [B.B.C. radio broadcast]	1945	W4:107–111
Only Child (The)	1964	W7:131–136
Ordinary Devoted Mother (The)	1966	W16:3–14
Ordinary Devoted Mother and Her Baby (The) [Intro.] [B.B.C. radio broadcast]	1949	W3:3–6
Out of the Mouths of Adolescents [review of E. M. & M. Eppel: *Adolescents and Morality*]	1966	W21:48–49
New Society [Sept.]		
Paediatrics and Childhood Neurosis	1956	W6:316–321
Paediatrics and Psychiatry	1948	W6:157–173
Brit. J. Med. Psychol. 21		

Papular Urticaria and the Dynamics of Skin Sensation   1934   W21:157–169
    Brit. J. Children's Diseases 31:5–16
Parent–Infant Relationship (The Theory of the)   1960   W9:37–55
    IJP 41:585
Parent–Infant Relationship (Further Remarks on the Theory of
    the)   1961   W19:73–75
    IJP 43 [1962]:238
Parfitt, D. N.: Letter to [Dec. 22nd]   1966   W17:162–163
Patient (A): Letter to [Dec. 13th]   1966   W17:162
Payne, Sylvia: Letter to [Oct. 7th]   1953   W17:52–53
Payne, Sylvia: Letter to [May 26th]   1966   W17:157
Peller, Lili E.: Letter to [April 15th]   1966   W17:156–157
Persecution That Wasn't (The) [review of *A Home from a Home*
    by S. Stewart]   1967   W13:200–201
    New Society [May]
Perversions and Pregenital Fantasy   1963   W19:79–80
Physical and Emotional Disturbances in an Adolescent Girl   1968   W19:369–374
Physical Examination   1931   W1:22–31
Physical Therapy of Mental Disorder   1947   W19:534–541
    Brit. Med. J. [May 1947]
Physiotherapy and Human Relations   1969   W19:561–568
    Physiotherapy [June 1969]
    In *A Survey of Child Psychiatry* ed. R. G. Gordon [pp. 28–44]
Piggle (The): An Account of the Psychoanalytic Treatment of a
    Little Girl   1977   W12:1–201
Pill and the Moon (The)   1969   W14:195–209
Pitfalls in Adoption   1954   W5:45–51
    Medical Press 232/6031
Pitfalls in Adoption   1954   W21:128–135
Place of the Monarchy (The)   1970   W14:260–268
Place Where We Live (The)   1971   W10:104–110
Play in the Analytic Situation   1954   W19:28–29
Play Therapy by V. Axline, 1947 (A Commentary on)
    [transcript from tape recording: unfinished & unedited
    by D.W.W.; probably mid-1960s]   n.d.   W19:495–498
Play (Notes on)   n.d.   W19:59–63
Playing and Culture   1968   W19:203–206
Playing: A Theoretical Statement   1971   W10:38–52
Playing: Creative Activity and the Search for the Self   1971   W10:53–64
Point in Technique (A)   n.d.   W19:26–27
Playing: Its Theoretical Status in the Clinical Situation   1968   ***
    IJP 49:591
Prefrontal Leucotomy [letter]   1943   W19:542–543
    The Lancet [April]
Prefrontal Leucotomy [letter]   1956   W19:553–554
    Brit. Med. J. [Jan. 1956]
Pre-Systolic Murmur, Possibly Not Due to Mitral Stenosis   1931   ***
    Proceedings of the Royal Society of Medicine 24:1354
Price of Disregarding Psychoanalytic Research (The)   1965   W14:172–182
    *The Price of Mental Health: Report of N. A. M. H. Annual
    Conference*
Primary Introduction to External Reality: The Early Stages   1948   W21:21–28
    [talk given at the London School of Economics]

Reparation in Respect of Mother's Organized Defence against
    Depression [revised August 1954]   1948   W6:91–96
Residential Care as Therapy   1970   W13:220–228
Residential Management as Treatment for Difficult Children
    [with Claire Britton]   1947   W5:98–116
    Human Relations 1/1:87
Residential Management as Treatment for Difficult Children
    [with Claire Britton]   1947   W13:54–72
Return of the Evacuated Child (The) [B.B.C. radio broadcast] 1945   W5:88–92
Return of the Evacuated Child (The)   1945   W13:44–48
Rheumatic Clinic (The)   1931   W1:64–68
Rheumatic Fever   1931   W1:58–63
Ries, Hannah: Letter to [Nov. 27th]   1953   W17:54–55
Riviere, Joan: Letter to [Feb. 3rd]   1956   W17:94–97
Riviere, Joan: Letter to [June 13th]   1958   W17:118–119
Rodman, F. Robert: Letter to [Jan. 10th]   1969   W17:180–182
Rodrigue, Emilio: Letter to [March 17th]   1955   W17:86–87
Roots of Aggression   1964   W7:232–239
Roots of Aggression   1968   W19:458–461
Rosenfeld, Herbert: Letter to [Jan. 22nd]   1953   W17:43–46
Rosenfeld, Herbert: Letter to [Oct. 16th]   1958   W17:120
Rosenfeld, Herbert: Letter to [March 17th]   1966   W17:153–154
Rycroft, Charles E.: Letter to [April 21st]   1955   W17:87
Sargant, William W.: Letter to [June 24th]   1969   W17:192–194
Saying "No" [three B.B.C. radio broadcasts, Jan./Feb.]   1960   W20:21–39
Schizophrénie Infantile en Termes d'Echec d'Adaptation (La) 1968   ***
    Recherches (Special Issue: Enfance alienée) II
Scott, P. D.: Letter to [May 11th]   1950   W17:22–23
Scott, W. Clifford M.: Letter to [March 19th]   1953   W17:48–50
Scott, W. Clifford M.: Letter to [Jan. 27th]   1954   W17:56–57
Scott, W. Clifford M.: Letter to [Feb. 26th]   1954   W17:57–58
Scott, W. Clifford M.: Letter to [April 13th]   1954   W17:60–63
Security [B.B.C. radio broadcasts, April]   1960   W20:87–93
    Also published under title "Security (On)"   1960   W8:30–33
Segal, Hanna: Letter to [Feb. 21st]   1952   W17:25–27
Segal, Hanna: Letter to [Jan. 22nd]   1953   W17:47
Segal, Hanna: Letter to [Oct. 6th]   1955   W17:89
Sex Education in Schools   1949   W5:40–44
    Medical Press 222/5761
    Also in *The Case against Pornography* ed. David Holbrook
    [1972]
Sex Education in Schools   1964   W7:216–220
Shared Fate by H. David Kirk [review]   1965   ***
    New Society [Sept. 9]
Sharpe, Ella: Letter to [Nov. 13th]   1946   W17:10
Shock Therapy [letter]   1944   W19:523–525
    Brit. Med. J. [Dec.]
Shock Treatment of Mental Disorder [letter]   1943   W19:522–523
    Brit. Med. J. [Dec.]
Short Communication on Enuresis   1930   W21:170–175
    St. Bartholomew's Hospital Journal 37
Shyness and Nervous Disorders in Children   1938   W5:35–39
    New Era in Home & School 19/7:189
Shyness and Nervous Disorders in Children   1964   W7:211–215

Sleep Refusal in Children   1968   W21:42–45
    Medical News Magazine (Paediatrics) [July]
Smirnoff, Victor: Letter to [Nov. 19th]   1958   W17:120–124
Some Psychological Aspects of Juvenile Delinquency   1946   W5:181–187
    New Era in Home & School 27/10:295 & *Delinquency Research*
    24/5
Some Psychological Aspects of Juvenile Delinquency   1946   W13:113–119
Some Thoughts on the Meaning of the Word "Democracy"   1950   W8:155–169
    Human Relations 3/2
Some Thoughts on the Meaning of the Word "Democracy"   1950   W14:239–259
Speech Disorders   1931   W1:191–200
Spence, Marjorie: Letter to [Nov. 23rd]   1967   W17:172–173
Spence, Marjorie: Letter to [Nov. 27th]   1967   W17:173–174
Split-Off Male and Female Elements to Be Found in Men and
      Women (The)   1966   W19:169–183
    Clinical Material [1959–1963]   W19:183–188
    Answers to Comments [1968–1969]   W19:189–192
Split-off Male and Female Elements (On the) [Editors' Note]   1989   W19:168
Spock, Benjamin: Letter to [April 9th]   1962   W17:133–138
Squiggle Game (The) [an amalgamation of two papers: one
      unpublished,written in 1964, the other published 1968]   1968   W19:299–317
    Voices: The Art & Science of Psychotherapy 4/1
    Also appears as Case III in: W11:42–63
Stealing and Telling Lies   1949   W4:117–120
Stealing and Telling Lies   1964   W7:161–166
Stierlin, Helm: Letter to [July 31st]   1969   W17:195–196
Stone, L. Joseph: Letter to [June 18th]   1968   W17:177–178
Stone, Marjorie: Letter to [Feb. 14th]   1949   W17:14 15
Storr, Charles Anthony: Letter to [Sept. 30th]   1965   W17:151
Strachey, James: Letter to [May 1st]   1951   W17:24
Strachey (James): Obituary   1969   W19:506–510
    IJP 50 [1969]
String: A Technique of Communication   1960   W9:153–157
    Journal of Child Psychology & Psychiatry 4:85
Struggling through the Doldrums   1963   W13:145–155
    New Society [April]
Study of Three Pairs of Identical Twins (A) by D. Burlingham
      (Review of)   1953   W19:408–412
    New Era in Home & School [March]
Successful Step-parent (The) by Helen Thomson [review]   1967   ***
    New Society 13/4
Sum, I Am   1968   W14:55–64
    Mathematics Teaching [March 1984]
Support for Normal Parents [B.B.C. radio broadcast; published
      as "Postscript"]   1945   W2:25–27
    New Era in Home & School 26/1:16
Support for Normal Parents   1945   W4:137–140
Support for Normal Parents   1964   W7:173–176
Susan Isaacs by D. E. M. Gardner (Foreword to)   1969   W19:387–389
Susan Isaacs: Obituary   1948   W19:385–387
    Nature [Dec.]
Symptom Tolerance in Paediatrics: A Case History   1953   W6:101–117
    Proceedings of the Royal Society of Medicine 46/8

Szasz, Thomas: Letter to [Nov. 19th]	1959	W17:126–127
Teacher, the Parent, and the Doctor (The) [read before the Ideals in Education Conference]	1936	W21:77–93
Temperature and the Importance of Charts (A Note on)	1931	W1:32–37
Their Standards and Yours [B.B.C. radio broadcast] *New Era in Home & School* 26/1:13	1945	W2:21–24
Their Standards and Yours	1945	W4:87–91
Their Standards and Yours	1964	W7:119–123
Theme of the Mother's Unconscious as Discovered in Psycho-Analytic Practice (Development of the)	1969	W19:247–250
Theoretical Statement of the Field of Child Psychiatry *Modern Trends in Paediatrics* [Second Series]	1958	W8:97–105
Therapy in Child Care: Collected Papers by B. Docker-Drysdale (Foreword to) Longmans' Papers on Residential Work Vol. 3	1968	***
Thinking and Symbol-Formation [probably 1968]	n.d.	W19:213–216
Thinking and the Unconscious *The Liberal Magazine* [March]	1945	W14:169–171
This Feminism	1964	W14:183–194
Thorner, Hans: Letter to [March 17th]	1966	W17:154
Times (The): Letter to [Nov. 6th]	1946	W17:9
Times (The): Letter to [Aug. 10th]	1949	W17:15–16
Times (The): Letter to [probably May]	1950	W17:21
Times (The): Letter to [July 21st]	1954	W17:76–77
Times (The): Letter to [Nov. 1st]	1954	W17:82–83
Times (The): Letter to [March 3rd]	1966	W17:152–153
Tizard, J. P. M.: Letter to [Oct. 23rd]	1956	W17:103–107
Tod, Robert: Letter to [Nov. 6th]	1969	W17:196–197
Torrie, Margaret: Letter to [Sept. 4th]	1967	W17:166–167
Torrie, Margaret: Letter to [Sept. 5th]	1967	W17:167–169
Towards an Objective Study of Human Nature *New Era in Home & School* 26/8:179 under title "Talking about Psychology" *New Era in Home & School* 33/3 [1952]:55 under title "What Is Psycho-Analysis?"	1945	W5:125–133
Towards an Objective Study of Human Nature	1945	W21:3–12
Training for Child Psychiatry: The Paediatric Department of Psychology In *St. Mary's Hospital Gazette* [Sept.] under title "The Paediatric Department of Psychology"	1961	W21:227–230
Training for Child Psychiatry *Journal of Child Psychology & Psychiatry* 4:85	1963	W9:193–202
Transitional Objects and Transitional Phenomena *IJP* 34 [1953]:89	1951	W6:229–242
Transitional Objects and Transitional Phenomena	1953	W10:1–25
Trauma in Relation to the Development of the Individual within the Family (The Concept of)	1965	W19:130–148
Treatment of Mental Disease by Induction of Fits	1943	W19:516–521
Tribute on the Occasion of W. Hoffer's 70th Birthday (A) *Psyche* [in German]	1967	W19:499–505
Twins [B.B.C. radio broadcast]	1945	W4:112–116
Twins	1964	W7:137–142
Two Adopted Children *Case Conference* [Dec.]	1953	W5:52–65

Why Do Babies Cry?   1945   W4:43–52
Why Do Babies Cry?   1964   W7:58–68
Widow's Child (The) by Margaret Torrie (Foreword to)   1964   ***
Wilkinson, Agnes: Letter to [June 9th]   1969   W17:192
Winnicott, Violet: Letter to [Nov. 15th]   1919   W17:1–4
Wisdom, John O.: Letter to [Oct. 26th]   1964   W17:144–146
Withdrawal and Regression   1954   W6:255–261
   Revue Française de Psychanalyse XIX/1–2 [1955]
   Psyche Heft X [1956–1957]
Withdrawal and Regression (Notes on)   1965   W19:149–151
World in Small Doses (The) [B.B.C. radio broadcast]   1949   W3:32–37
World in Small Doses (The)   1949   W4:53–58
World in Small Doses (The)   1964   W7:69–74
Yes, But How Do We Know It's True? [talk given at the
   London School of Economics]   1950   W21:13–18
Young Children and Other People   1949   W4:92–99
   Young Children 1/3:36
Young Children and Other People   1964   W7:103–110
Your Child Is a Person by Chess, Thomas, Birch [review]   1966   ***
   Medical News [Oct.]
Youth Will Not Sleep   1964   W13:156–158
   New Society [May 1964]

Chronological list

*** Indicates that the entry does not appear in volumes W1 to W21.

1936 Contribution to a Discussion on Enuresis   W21:151–156
        Proceedings of the Royal Society of Medicine 29
1936 Appetite and Emotional Disorder [read before the Medical
        Section, British Psychological Society]   W6:33–51
1936 The Teacher, the Parent, and the Doctor [read before the Ideals
        in Education Conference]   W21:77–93
1938 Shyness and Nervous Disorders in Children   W5:35–39
        New Era in Home & School 19/7:189
1938 Chamberlain, Mrs. Neville: Letter to [Nov. 10th]   W17:4
1938 *Child Psychiatry* by Leo Kanner, 1937 [review]   W21:191–193
        IJP 19
1938 Notes on a Little Boy   W21:102–103
        New Era in Home & School 19
1939 Early Disillusion   W19:21–23
1939 Evacuation of Small Children [letter: with J. Bowlby & E.
        Miller]   W13:13–14
        Brit. Med. J.
1939 The Deprived Mother [B.B.C. radio broadcast]   W5:75–82
        New Era in Home & School 221/3 [1940]:64
1939 The Deprived Mother   W13:31–38
1939 Aggression   W5:167–175
1939 The Psychology of Juvenile Rheumatism   ***
        In *A Survey of Child Psychiatry* ed. R. G. Gordon [pp. 28–44]
1940 Friedlander, Kate: Letter to [Jan. 8th]   W17:5–6
1940 Children and Their Mothers   W13:14–21
        New Era in Home & School 21
1940 Children in the War   W5:69–74
        New Era in Home & School 21/9:229
1940 Children in the War   W13:25–30
1940 Discussion of War Aims   W14:210–220
1941 On Influencing and Being Influenced   W5:24–28
        New Era in Home & School 22/6:118
1941 Review of *The Cambridge Education Survey*, ed. S. Isaacs   W13:22–24
        New Era in Home & School 22
1941 The Observation of Infants in a Set Situation   W6:52–69
        IJP 22:229
1941 *The Moral Paradox of Peace and War*, by J. C. Flugel [review]   ***
        New Era in Home and School 22:183
1942 Child Department Consultations   W6:70–84
        IJP 23:139
1942 Why Children Play   W5:149–152
        New Era in Home & School 23/1:12
1943 Prefrontal Leucotomy [letter]   W19:542–543
        The Lancet [April 1943]
1943 Shock Treatment of Mental Disorder [letter]   W19:522–523
        Brit. Med. J. [Dec.]
1943 Treatment of Mental Disease by Induction of Fits   W19:516–521
1943 Delinquency Research   ***
        New Era in Home and School 24:65–67
1944 Correspondence with a Magistrate   W13:163–167
        New Era in Home & School [Jan. 1944]
1944 Introduction to a Symposium on the Psycho-Analytic
        Contribution to the Theory of Shock Therapy   W19:525–528

1946 Some Psychological Aspects of Juvenile Delinquency   W5:181–187
         New Era in Home & School 27/10:295 & *Delinquency Research*
         24/5
1946 Some Psychological Aspects of Juvenile Delinquency   W13:113–119
1946 What Do We Mean by a Normal Child?   W4:100–106
         New Era in Home & School 27/3:61
1947 Further Thoughts on Babies as Persons   W5:134–140
         New Era in Home & School 28/10:199 under title "Babies are
         Persons"
1947 Hate in the Countertransference   W6:194–203
         IJP 30 [1949]:69
1947 Physical Therapy of Mental Disorder   W19:534–541
         Brit. Med. J. [May 1947]
1947 Residential Management as Treatment for Difficult Children
         [with Claire Britton]   W5:98–116
         Human Relations 1/1:87
1947 Residential Management as Treatment for Difficult Children W13:54–72
1947 The Child and Sex   W5:153–166
1948 Freud, Anna: Letter to [July 6th]   W17:10–12
1948 Children's Hostels in War and Peace   W5:117–121
         Brit. J. Med. Psychol. 21/3:175
1948 Children's Hostels in War and Peace   W13:73–77
1948 Paediatrics and Psychiatry   W6:157–173
         Brit. J. Med. Psychol. 21
1948 Reparation in Respect of Mother's Organized Defence against
         Depression [revised Aug. 1954]   W6:91–96
1948 Susan Isaacs: Obituary   W19:385–387
         Nature [Dec.]
1948 Primary Introduction to External Reality: The Early Stages [talk
         given at the London School of Economics]   W21:21–28
1948 Environmental Needs; The Early Stages; Total Dependence and
         Essential Independence [talk given at The Institute of
         Education, Univ. of London]   W21:29–36
1949 Federn, Paul: Letter to [Jan. 3rd]   W17:12
1949 *British Medical Journal*: Letter to [Jan. 6th]   W17:13–14
1949 Stone, Marjorie: Letter to [Feb. 14th]   W17:14–15
1949 *The Times*: Letter to [Aug. 10th]   W17:15–16
1949 Hazlehurst, R. S.: Letter to [Sept. 1st]   W17:17
1949 Hodge, S. H.: Letter to [Sept. 1st]   W17:17–19
1949 A Man Looks at Motherhood [B.B.C. radio broadcast]   W4:3–6
1949 Birth Memories, Birth Trauma, and Anxiety [rewritten, in part,
         1954]   W6:174–193
1949 Close-Up of Mother Feeding Baby [B.B.C. radio broadcast]   W3:27–31
1949 Close-Up of Mother Feeding Baby   W4:38–42
1949 Leucotomy   W19:543–547
         Brit. Medical Students' Journal 3
1949 Mind and Its Relation to the Psyche-Soma   W6:243–254
         Brit. J. Med. Psychol. 27 [1954]
1949 *Art versus Illness* by A. Hill [review]   W19:555–557
         Brit. J. Med. Psychol. 22
1949 Sex Education in Schools   W5:40–44
         Medical Press 222/5761
         Also in *The Case against Pornography* ed. D. Holbrook [1972]

1952 Money-Kyrle, Roger: Letter to [Nov. 27th]   W17:38–43
1952 Anxiety Associated with Insecurity   W6:97–100
1952 Psychoses and Child Care   W6:219–228
        Brit. J. Med. Psychol. 26 [1953]
1953 Rosenfeld, Herbert: Letter to [Jan. 22nd]   W17:43–46
1953 Segal, Hanna: Letter to [Jan. 22nd]   W17:47
1953 Scott, W. Clifford M.: Letter to [March 19th]   W17:48–50
1953 Bick, Esther: Letter to [June 11th]   W17:50–52
1953 Payne, Sylvia: Letter to [Oct. 7th]   W17:52–53
1953 Rapaport, David: Letter to [Oct. 9th]   W17:53–54
1953 Ries, Hannah: Letter to [Nov. 27th]   W17:54–55
1953 Discussion on *Grief and Mourning in Infancy* by J. Bowlby   W19:426–432
        PSC 15 [1960]
1953 Review of *A Study of Three Pairs of Identical Twins* by D.
        Burlingham   W19:408–412
          New Era in Home & School [March]
1953 Review of *Maternal Care and Mental Health* by John Bowlby,
        1951   W19:423–426
          Brit. J. Med. Psychol. 26
1953 Review of *Psychoanalytic Studies of the Personality* by W. R. D.
        Fairbairn, 1952 [written with M. Masud R. Khan]   W19:413–422
        IJP 34
1953 Symptom Tolerance in Paediatrics: A Case History   W6:101–117
        Proceedings of the Royal Society of Medicine 46/8
1953 The Child's Needs and the Rôle of the Mother in the Early
        Stages   W5:13–23
        [An excerpt] published in series *Problems in Education*
1953 Transitional Objects and Transitional Phenomena   W10:1–25
        IJP 34:89
1953 Two Adopted Children   W5:52–65
        Case Conference [Dec.]
1953 Two Adopted Children   W21:113–127
1954 Scott, W. Clifford M.: Letter to [Jan. 27th]   W17:56–57
1954 Scott, W. Clifford M.: Letter to [Feb. 26th]   W17:57–58
1954 Freud, Anna: Letter to [March 18th]   W17:58
1954 Joseph, Betty: Letter to [April 13th]   W17:59–60
1954 Scott, W. Clifford M.: Letter to [April 13th]   W17:60–63
1954 Henderson, Sir David K.: Letter to [May 10th]   W17:63–65
1954 Bowlby, John: Letter to [May 11th]   W17:65–66
1954 Frank, Klara: Letter to [May 20th]   W17:67–68
1954 Henderson, Sir David K.: Letter to [May 20th]   W17:68–71
1954 Freud, Anna, and Klein, Melanie: Letter to [June 3rd]   W17:71–74
1954 Fordham, Michael: Letter to [June 11th]   W17:74–75
1954 Guntrip, Harry: Letter to [July 20th]   W17:75–76
1954 *The Times*: Letter to [July 21st]   W17:76–77
1954 Guntrip, Harry: Letter to [Aug. 13th]   W17:77–79
1954 Money-Kyrle, Roger: Letter to [Sept. 23rd]   W17:79–80
1954 Chaplin, D.: Letter to [Oct. 18th]   W17:80–82
1954 *The Times*: Letter to [Nov. 1st]   W17:82–83
1954 Character Types: The Foolhardy and the Cautious [comments
        on paper by Michael Balint]   W19:433–437
1954 Metapsychological and Clinical Aspects of Regression within
        the Psycho-Analytical Set-Up   W6:278–294
        IJP 36:16

1957 Klein, Melanie: Letter to [March 7th]   W17:114–115
1957 James, Martin: Letter to [April 17th]   W17:115–116
1957 Bonnard, Augusta: Letter to [Oct. 1st]   W17:116–117
1957 Bonnard, Augusta: Letter to [Nov. 7th]   W17:117
1957 Advising Parents   W8:114–120
1957 Excitement in the Aetiology of Coronary Thrombosis   W19:34–38
1957 Hallucination and Dehallucination   W19:39–42
1957 Integrative and Disruptive Factors in Family Life   W8:40–49
         Canadian Medical Association Journal [1961]
1957 On the Contribution of Direct Child Observation to Psycho-
         Analysis   W9:109–114
         First published in Revue française de Psychanalyse 22:205 [in
         French]
1957 The Contribution of Psycho-Analysis to Midwifery   W8:106–113
         Nursing Times [May 1957]
1957 The Contribution of Psycho-Analysis to Midwifery   W16:69–81
1957 The Mother's Contribution to Society [published as Postscript] W4:141–144
1957 The Mother's Contribution to Society   W14:123–127
1957 Health Education through Broadcasting   W20:1–6
         Mother and Child 28
1958 Riviere, Joan: Letter to [June 13th]   W17:118–119
1958 Laing, R. D.: Letter to [July 18th]   W17:119
1958 Rosenfeld, Herbert: Letter to [Oct. 16th]   W17:120
1958 Smirnoff, Victor: Letter to [Nov. 19th]   W17:120–124
1958 Child Analysis in the Latency Period   W9:115–123
         A Criança Portuguesa 17:219
1958 Ernest Jones: Obituary & Funeral Address   W19:393–407
         IJP 39
1958 Psychogenesis of a Beating Fantasy   W19:45–48
1958 Psycho-Analysis and the Sense of Guilt   W9:15–28
         In Psycho-Analysis & Contemporary Thought ed. J. D.
         Sutherland
1958 Review of The Doctor, His Patient and the Illness by M. Balint,
         1957   W19:438–442
         IJP 39
1958 The Capacity to Be Alone   W9:29–36
         IJP 39:416
1958 The Family Affected by Depressive Illness in One or Both
         Parents   W8:50–60
1958 The First Year of Life: Modern Views on the Emotional
         Development   W8:3–14
         Medical Press [March]
1958 The Psychology of Separation   W13:132–135
1958 Theoretical Statement of the Field of Child Psychiatry   W8:97–105
         Modern Trends in Paediatrics [Second Series]
1959 Meltzer, Donald: Letter to [May 21st]   W17:124–125
1959 Jaques, Elliot: Letter to [Oct. 13th]   W17:125–126
1959 Szasz, Thomas: Letter to [Nov. 19th]   W17:126–127
1959 Casework with Mentally Ill Children   W8:121–131
1959 Classification: Is There a Psycho-Analytic Contribution to
         Psychiatric Classification? [postscript dated 1964]   W9:124–139
1959 Nothing at the Centre   W19:49–52
1959 Review of Envy and Gratitude by M. Klein, 1957   W19:443–446
         Case Conference [Jan.]

1962 Spock, Benjamin: Letter to [April 9th]   W17:133–138
1962 A Personal View of the Kleinian Contribution   W9:171–178
1962 Ego Integration in Child Development   W9:56–63
1962 Providing for the Child in Health and in Crisis   W9:64–72
1962 Review of *Letters of Sigmund Freud 1873–1939*, 1961   W19:474–477
      Brit. J. Psychology 53
1962 The Aims of Psycho-Analytical Treatment   W9:166–170
1962 The Beginnings of a Formulation of an Appreciation and
      Criticism of Klein's Envy Statement   W19:447–457
1962 Now They Are Five [B.B.C. radio broadcast, June]   W20:111–120
      Originally published under the title "The Five-Year Old" in
      W8 [*q. v.*]   W8:34–39
1962 The Development of a Child's Sense of Right and Wrong
      [B.B.C. radio broadcast, June]   W20:105–110
1962 The Anti-Social Tendency Illustrated by a Case
      A Criança Portuguesa Vol. 21
      Also appears as Case VII in: W11:110–126
1962 A Child Psychiatry Interview
      St. Mary's Hospital Gazette [Jan./Feb.]
      Appears as Case VI in: W11:105–109
1963 McKeith, Ronald: Letter to [Jan. 31st]   W17:138–139
1963 Raison, Timothy: Letter to [April 9th]   W17:139–140
1963 A Note on a Case Involving Envy   W19:76–78
1963 Communicating and Not Communicating Leading to a Study
      of Certain Opposites   W9:179–192
1963 Dependence in Infant-Care, in Child-Care, and in the Psycho-
      Analytic Setting   W9:249–259
      IJP 44:339
1963 D.W.W.'s Dream Related to Reviewing Jung   W19:228–230
1963 From Dependence towards Independence in the Development
      of the Individual   W9:83–92
1963 Hospital Care Supplementing Intensive Psychotherapy in
      Adolescence   W9:242–248
1963 Morals and Education   W9:93–105
      In *Moral Education in a Changing Society* ed. W. R. Niblett,
      under the title "The Young Child at Home and at School"
1963 Perversions and Pregenital Fantasy   W19:79–80
1963 Psychiatric Disorder in Terms of Infantile Maturational
      Processes   W9:230–241
1963 Psychotherapy of Character Disorders   W13:241–255
1963 Psychotherapy of Character Disorders   W9:203–216
1963 Review of *The Non-Human Environment in Normal Development
      and in Schizophrenia* by H. F. Searles, 1960   W19:478–481
      IJP 44
1963 Struggling through the Doldrums   W13:145–155
      New Society [April]
1963 The Development of the Capacity for Concern   W9:73–82
      Bulletin of the Menninger Clinic 2:167
1963 The Development of the Capacity for Concern   W13:100–105
1963 The Mentally Ill in Your Caseload   W9:217–229
      In *New Thinking for Changing Needs*, Association of Social
      Workers
1963 The Value of Depression   W14:71–79
      Brit. J. Psychiatric Social Work 7/3 [1964]:123–127

1964	Visiting Children in Hospital	W7:221–226
1964	Weaning	W7:80–84
1964	What about Father?	W7:113–118
1964	What Do We Mean by a Normal Child?	W7:124–130
1964	Where the Food Goes	W7:35–39
1964	Why Children Play	W7:143–146
1964	Why Do Babies Cry?	W7:58–68
1964	Young Children and Other People	W7:103–110
1964	Youth Will Not Sleep	W13:156–158
	New Society [May 1964]	
1964	Foreword to *The Widow's Child* by Margaret Torrie	***
1964	The Neonate and His Mother	***
	Acta Paediatrica Latina Vol. 17	
1965	Nagera, Humberto: Letter to [Feb. 15th]	W17:147–148
1965	Fordham, Michael: Letter to [June 24th]	W17:148–150
1965	Fordham, Michael: Letter to [July 15th]	W17:150–151
1965	Storr, Charles Anthony: Letter to [Sept. 30th]	W17:151
1965	A Child Psychiatry Case Illustrating Delayed Reaction to Loss	W19:341–368
	In *Drives, Affects, Behavior* Vol. 2 ed. M. Schur	
1965	Comment on Obsessional Neurosis and "Frankie"	W19:158–160
1965	Dissociation Revealed in a Therapeutic Consultation	W13:256–282
	In *Crime, Law and Corrections* ed. R. Slovenko [1966]	
	Also published as Case XIII in:	W11:220–238
1965	Do Progressive Schools Give Too Much Freedom to the Child?	W13:209–219
	In *Who Are the Progressives Now?* ed. M. Ash [1969]	
1965	New Light on Children's Thinking	W19:152–157
1965	Notes Made on a Train, Part 2	W19:231–233
1965	Notes on Withdrawal and Regression	W19:149–151
1965	Review of *Childhood and Society* by E. H. Erikson, 1965	W19:493–494
	New Society [Sept.]	
1965	The Concept of Trauma in Relation to the Development of the Individual within the Family	W19:130–148
1965	The Price of Disregarding Psychoanalytic Research	W14:172–182
	The Price of Mental Health: Report of N.A.M.H. Annual Conference	
1965	The Psychology of Madness: A Contribution from Psycho-Analysis	W19:119–129
1965	The Value of the Therapeutic Consultation	W19:318–324
	In *Foundations of Child Psychiatry* ed. E. Miller	
1965	*Shared Fate* by H. David Kirk [review]	***
	New Society [Sept. 9]	
1965	Child Therapy: A Case of Anti-Social Behaviour	
	In *Perspectives on Child Psychiatry* ed. J. Howells	
	Appears also as Case XV in:	W11:270–295
1965	A Clinical Study of the Effect of a Failure of the Average Expectable Environment on a Child's Mental Functioning	
	IJP 46:81	
	Appears also as Case IV in:	W11:64–88
1966	*The Times*: Letter to [March 3rd]	W17:152–153
1966	Rosenfeld, Herbert: Letter to [March 17th]	W17:153–154
1966	Thorner, Hans: Letter to [March 17th]	W17:154
1966	A Confidant: Letter to [April 15th]	W17:155
1966	Peller, Lili E.: Letter to [April 15th]	W17:156–157

1967 A Colleague: Letter to [Sept. 4th]   W17:165
1967 Torrie, Margaret: Letter to [Sept. 4th]   W17:166–167
1967 Torrie, Margaret: Letter to [Sept. 5th]   W17:167–169
1967 Bion, Wilfred R.: Letter to [Oct. 5th]   W17:169–170
1967 Nelson, Gillian: Letter to [Oct. 6th]   W17:170–171
1967 Dahlberg, Charles Clay: Letter to [Oct. 24th]   W17:171–172
1967 Spence, Marjorie: Letter to [Nov. 23rd]   W17:172–173
1967 Spence, Marjorie: Letter to [Nov. 27th]   W17:173–174
1967 Dowling, R. S. W.: Letter to [Dec. 8th]   W17:174–175
1967 A Tribute on the Occasion of W. Hoffer's 70th Birthday   W19:499–505
         Psyche [in German]
1967 Addendum to "The Location of Cultural Experience"   W19:200–202
         IJP 48:368
         (The Location of Cultural Experience)   W10:95–103
1967 Delinquency as a Sign of Hope   W14:90–100
         Prison Service Journal 7/27 [1968]
1967 D.W.W. on D.W.W.   W19:569–582
1967 Environmental Health in Infancy   W16:59–68
         Portions published in *Maternal & Child Care*
1967 The Concept of a Healthy Individual   W14:22–38
         In *Towards Community Health* ed. J. D. Sutherland [1971]
1967 The Concept of Clinical Regression Compared with That of
         Defence Organisation   W19:193–199
         In *Psychotherapy in the Designed Therapeutic Milieu* ed.
         Eldred & Vanderpol [1968]
1967 The Persecution That Wasn't: Review of *A Home from a Home*
         by S. Stewart   W13:200–201
         New Society [May]
1967 A Collection of children's books reviewed under the title
         "Small Things for Small People"   ***
         New Society 7/12
1967 *Eine Kinderbeobachtung* [A Child Observation]   ***
         Psyche 21
1967 Hobgoblins and Good Habits   ***
         Parents 22:9
1967 How a Baby Begins to Feel Sorry and to Make Amends   ***
         Parents 22:7
1967 *How to Survive Parenthood* by Edna J. LeShan [review]   ***
         New Society 26/10
1967 The Meaning of Mother Love   ***
         Parents 22:6
1967 *The Successful Step-parent* by Helen Thomson [review]   ***
         New Society 13/4
1967 The Bearing of Emotional Development on Feeding Problems
         [Symposium on Environmental Health in Infancy at the Royal
         Society of Medicine]   W21:39–41
1967 The Aetiology of Infantile Schizophrenia in Terms of Adaptive
         Failure [paper prepared for a study day on Psychosis in
         Infancy, Paris]   W21:218–223
1967 The Association for Child Psychology and Psychiatry Observed
         as a Group Phenomenon [President's address, A.C.P.P.]   W21:235–254
1968 Gough, Donald: Letter to [March 6th]   W17:176
1968 Stone, L. Joseph: Letter to [June 18th]   W17:177–178

1968 The Effect of Loss on the Young [talk written for the Cruse
       Club]   W21:46–47
1968 A Link between Paediatrics and Child Psychology: Clinical
       Observations [Catherine Chisholm Memorial Lecture,
       Manchester]   W21:255–276
1969 Rodman, F. Robert: Letter to [Jan. 10th]   W17:180–182
1969 An American Correspondent: Letter to [Jan. 14th]   W17:183–185
1969 Freud, Anna: Letter to [Jan. 20th]   W17:185
1969 Collinson, J. D.: Letter to [March 10th]   W17:186–188
1969 Conran, M. B.: Letter to [May 8th]   W17:188–191
1969 Wilkinson, Agnes: Letter to [June 9th]   W17:192
1969 Sargant, William W.: Letter to [June 24th]   W17:192–194
1969 Stierlin, Helm: Letter to [July 31st]   W17:195–196
1969 Tod, Robert: Letter to [Nov. 6th]   W17:196–197
1969 Additional Note on Psycho-Somatic Disorder   W19:115–118
1969 Behaviour Therapy [letter]   W19:558–560
         Child Care News [June]
1969 Berlin Walls   W14:221–227
1969 Contribution to a Symposium on Envy and Jealousy   W19:462–464
1969 Development of the Theme of the Mother's Unconscious as
       Discovered in Psycho-Analytic Practice   W19:247–250
1969 Foreword to Susan Isaacs by D. E. M. Gardner   W19:387–389
1969 Freedom   W14:228–238
         Nouvelle Revue de Psychanalyse 30 [1984] [in French]
1969 James Strachey: Obituary   W19:506–510
         IJP 50 [1969]
1969 Mother's Madness Appearing in the Clinical Material as an
       Ego-Alien Factor   W19:375–382
         In Tactics & Techniques in Psychoanalytic Therapy ed. P.
           Giovacchini [1972]
1969 Physiotherapy and Human Relations   W19:561–568
         Physiotherapy [June 1969]
1969 Review of Indications for Child Analysis & Other Papers by A.
       Freud   W19:511–512
         New Society [Aug. 1969]
1969 The Mother–Infant Experience of Mutuality   W19:251–260
         In Parenthood: Its Psychology & Psychopathology ed. Anthony
           & Benedek [1970]
1969 The Pill and the Moon   W14:195–209
1969 The Use of an Object in the Context of Moses and Monotheism   W19:240–246
1969 The Building up of Trust   W20:121–134
1969 Adolescent Process and the Need for Personal Confrontation   ***
         Pediatrics 44:5 part 1
1969 Eine Verbindung zwischen Kinderheilkunde und
       Kinderpsychologie, klinische Betrachtungen [translation of: "A
       Link between Paediatrics and Child Psychology"]   ***
         Dynam. Psychiat. 2
1969 First Interview with Child May Start Resumption of Maturation ***
         Frontiers of Clinical Psychiatry 6
1969 Human Relations   ***
         Physiotherapy 55
1969 Verso una teoria sulla psicoterapia: il suo rapporto col gioco
       [translation of "Towards a Theory of Psychotherapy: The Link

1989 On "The Use of an Object" [Editors' Note]   W19:217–218
n.d. Knowing and Not-Knowing: A Clinical Example   W19:24–25
n.d. The Niffle   W21:104–109
n.d. Notes on Play   W19:59–63
n.d. A Point in Technique   W19:26–27
n.d. The Delinquent and Habitual Offender [probably early 1940s] W21:51–53
n.d. Ideas and Definitions [probably early 1950s]   W19:43–44
n.d. Absence and Presence of a Sense of Guilt Illustrated in Two
      Patients [probably 1966]   W19:163–167
n.d. A Commentary on Play Therapy by V. Axline, 1947 [transcript
      from tape recording, unfinished & unedited by D.W.W.;
      probably mid-1960s]   W19:495–498
n.d. A Note on the Mother–Foetus Relationship [probably mid-
      1960s]   W19:161–162
n.d. Thinking and Symbol-Formation [probably 1968]   W19:213–216

INDEX